JOURNAL OF RECOGNITION

U.S. ARMY-NAVY JOURNAL OF
RECOGNITION

INTRODUCTION BY NORMAN FRIEDMAN

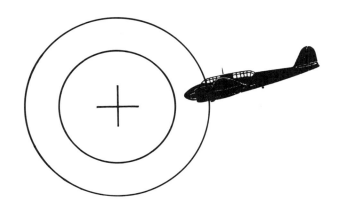

NAVAL INSTITUTE PRESS
ANNAPOLIS, MARYLAND

SEPTEMBER 1943–FEBRUARY 1944, NUMBERS 1–6

Introduction © 1990
by the United States Naval Institute
Annapolis, Maryland
All rights reserved.

ISSN 1052-4444
ISBN 0-87021-775-5

Printed in the United States of America
on acid-free paper☺
9 8 7 6 5 4 3 2
First printing

CONTENTS

INTRODUCTION

The twenty-four issues of the World War II *Recognition Journal* are a graphic record of the evolution of wartime ships, aircraft, and armored vehicles, as the United States and our allies, particularly Britain, then understood that evolution. Although the *Journal* carried only the lowest possible classification (so that it could be widely distributed), it mirrored contemporary ideas and contemporary understanding to an extent that is now unavailable almost anywhere else. It also carried some of the clearest wartime photographs, arranged particularly well by the staff of *Life* magazine (from which the *Journal* took its layout).

The *Journal* was a very American approach to a basic military problem. There were no (or very few) experts available, so every man had to be educated. That was not a universal approach. Britain, for example, is very much a country of ship and airplane enthusiasts. During World War II many British warships carried recognition specialists, men who really liked airplanes or ships and could be relied upon to know them at very long distances, for example, by the way the airplanes sat as they flew.

During the early part of the war there were some attempts to teach recognition. There were aircraft and ship silhouettes, printed either as sheets to be posted or in books, and there were models, some of them assembled by schoolchildren. There were special classes and special flash cards. Silhouettes were even painted inside splinter shields (a practice still common in the Soviet Navy). But these were essentially static approaches; something with more urgency and vitality was needed, something similar to the contemporary news magazines. It arrived in September 1943 in the form of the *Army-Navy Journal of Recognition*, and it lasted, as the *Recognition Journal* (from May 1944) through August 1945. The *Recognition Journal* was a Navy Bureau of Aeronautics initiative, for clearly, proper recognition was most important among the air forces, since improperly identified aircraft were vulnerable to both ground and air fire.

Repeated articles in these reprinted pages of the *Recognition Journal* tell much the same story of disaster due to wrong identification, and make another important point: most soldiers, sailors, and airmen do not find it inherently fascinating to learn to recognize particular tanks, ships, and airplanes. The people must be motivated. The editors of the *Journal* tried two approaches. One was the horror story, often illustrated by dramatic drawings, for example, of American PT boats firing on American bombers. The other was to provide news (or history) so well illustrated that readers would be inclined to notice the illustrations. The captions pointed out tricks that would make recognition easier. The problem of making recognition training interesting is unlikely ever to disappear, but it is difficult to appreciate in peacetime.

The *Recognition Journal* incorporated early examples of an aspect of recognition now so common that many will have forgotten that it dates back only to World War II: the creation and use of code names, or reporting names, for foreign equipment. It is useless to be taught the shape of something that has no name.

Apparently, it was relatively easy to obtain the nomenclature of new German airplanes and tanks, and the names were in the roman alphabet. Thus, we think of the standard German fighters by their German names: Me 109, FW 190. Japanese nomenclature presented a more severe challenge. Often it was altogether unknown, and even the system for designating aircraft was not understood at first. The solution was a series of reporting names, Western names easy to remember. For example, the standard Imperial Japanese Navy bomber was Betty, not G4M (the Japanese term).

After the war the Soviets, like the Japanese, succeeded in concealing the designations of their aircraft and missiles and the names of their ships. U.S. forces initially assigned Type numbers to aircraft (many of which turned out not to exist), but after 1954 a NATO Air Standards Coordinating Committee took over, assigning the now-familiar names, such as Bear and Badger (rather than Tu-20 and Tu-16). Ships were assigned reporting names; Kara, for example, is a NATO rather than a Soviet designation. The reporting names of ships so often sound Russian that a casual reader may be surprised at their origin. Submarines, however, have generally been assigned letters of the NATO phonetic alphabet. Missiles were assigned dummy designations (such as SS-N-2 for a very familiar antiship missile) and reporting nicknames (Styx, in this case); only much later (and in only a few cases) did the Soviet designations surface. Similar NATO practices apply to Soviet electronic equipment, although in these cases the reporting nicknames are often released slowly.

Because it was designed to interest its military readers, the *Recognition Journal* had to be much more than a simple repetition of the visual aspects of equipment. It became a sort of technical news magazine, carrying numerous articles on past and current trends. In this sense the set of journals is still valuable as an introduction to the much more detailed literature on the technology of World War II ships, aircraft, and armored vehicles. That introductory nature is an important part of its current charm. Postwar recognition journals showed much less interest in technological trends, the official German military magazine *Soldat und Technik* being an important exception, a magazine that has combined technology with recognition.

The *Journal* gives a clear idea of just how well and how quickly Allied intelligence gained information about new Axis weapons. Despite the low level of classification, new information had to be disseminated almost immediately, since otherwise men in the field would form a false impression of what they were seeing. For example, in the Battle of Britain many RAF pilots reported seeing the new German He 113 fighter, an airplane well publicized at the outbreak of war, and prominently represented in the British aeronautical magazines they read. Unfortunately, none was present; the He 113 never went into series production. Timely publication of newly gained intelligence would have prevented this and other instances of false identification. On the other hand, it would have enabled bomber crews, for instance, during mission debriefings, to report the presence or absence of the new German rocket fighters.

Similarly, new Allied equipment had to be described, at least as soon as it was operational, and sometimes rather earlier. The 1945 issues give notice of British aircraft prototypes not yet ready for production; perhaps their inclusion reflected British propaganda efforts. In any case, there was always fear that Allied craft even barely resembling Axis types would be attacked in error, and the *Journal* sought to minimize that possibility. For example, descriptions of the new British radial-engined Tempest fighter stressed its superficial similarity to the German FW 190.

Sometimes there was disinformation. A 1945 chart of the Royal Navy carries a note to the effect that the new *Lion* class is missing, implying that ships are either complete or well along in construction. In fact, they were never built. In one case, there seems to have been a security problem. A page of the January 1944 issue, on Japanese efforts to teach aircraft recognition, was razored out of the magazine; the deletion may have reflected fears that the Japanese would know just what materials U.S. troops had captured, presumably in the Aleutians and at Tarawa.

Since airborne observers also needed an appropriate understanding of whatever they saw, the *Journal* ran an article on ships' wakes, and it often showed how troop formations on land could be read. Some of these lessons are still quite meaningful.

The concept of the news magazine, so important in the United States before World War II, led to the creation of several specialized wartime equivalents, only one of which was the *Recognition Journal*. Another, reprinted in 1979, the Army Air Forces' classified (Confidential) *Impact*, used to spread important information about new air tactics and weapons, with extensive accounts of the success (i.e., the impact) of air power. Presumably, it was part of the wartime drive toward an independent air force. *Impact* was roughly contemporary with the *Recognition Journal* and seems to have shared much the same layout and typography.

Postwar, the recognition problem no longer seemed so urgent, and there was no immediate successor to the *Journal*. Handbooks for the identification of different ships, aircraft, and land vehicles survived, but they were not packaged as news magazines, and they often evolved into technical handbooks of foreign materiel, classified at the Secret or higher level. Later, the British supplied a successor to the wartime magazine in the form of their *Joint Services Recognition Journal*, which is still widely distributed but carries a "For Official Use Only" classification. The Dutch produced their own recognition magazine, *Herkenning*. *Soldat und Technik* regularly carries recognition quizzes. In the 1960s and 1970s the United States published a classified journal specifically for photo interpreters, but nothing similar to the *Recognition Journal*.

The recognition problem that prompted the U.S. government to issue the *Journal* did not end in 1945, however. In peacetime, recognition becomes an important aspect of intelligence. What is that ship? What kind of radar is it carrying? What weapons? Is it worth photographing at very close range? Errors are clearly not as devastating as during war, but they can still be costly, particularly if they are errors of omission that obscure important new developments. Recognition issues merge with photo interpretation to yield intelligence.

Much more than interesting history, the *Journal* emphasizes a lesson, often repeated but much less often taken to heart: unless our own forces can recognize their own and the enemy's equipment, fatal mistakes will be made, and made often. During World War II identification was mostly visual, not electronic. The suggestion that up to a quarter of all Allied aircraft lost during the war fell victim to friendly fire reveals the critical importance of recognition training. Such training is still vital, for recent suggestions, from war games simulating a NATO–Warsaw Pact war, are that approximately 40 percent of all NATO aircraft would be shot down by friendly forces during the first week or so of hostilities. The other side might do even worse.

A reader might protest that recognition is now almost always electronic (i.e., by IFF [identification friend or foe]), but that is not so. U.S. Navy F-14 fighters carry television cameras peering through telescopes so that the pilots can see distant targets to decide whether they are hostile. These telescopes were installed because during the Vietnam War pilots sometimes had to fly almost alongside prospective targets to be sure that they were enemy aircraft. These awkward tactics were a reaction to a series of accidents in which American pilots shot down American airplanes thought to be enemy. Numerous accounts of the air war in Vietnam tell of pilots who were about to open fire on an airplane positively identified, thanks to electronic information, as belonging to the enemy when at the last minute they saw that the "target" was a U.S. airplane, off course or unknown to the controllers. The potential victim lived only because the pilots were able to recognize what they saw with their eyes. A more recent example of the need for telescopes occurred when American F-14 pilots used television viewers to spot two fighters armed with air-to-air missiles off the Libyan coast. Recognizing the airplanes as Soviet-built and thus as probably Libyan, and determining that they were actively hostile, the F-14s attacked.

The F-14 telescopes use some very sophisticated technology: they are gyrostabilized, and the faint images they capture are electronically enhanced for easier recognition. There was no World War II equivalent. Similarly, there was no World War II technique to cut through fog or other weather (apart from radar, which could not give a recognizable image), nor could any World War II device capture a fleeting image for immediate recognition (as a modern video camera can). Even so, the importance of visual recognition prompted major World War II efforts in areas such as camouflage. Special recognition signs, such as the D-Day invasion stripes, were used to aid in the recognition of friendly aircraft (it is somewhat bizarre to see an airplane, carefully camouflaged, but painted with invasion stripes to make it more recognizable).

The current situation is, of course, very much complicated by the arms trade, which may put the same airplane on both sides of a war. For example, Pakistan buys Soviet-designed aircraft from China, whereas Pakistan's sometime enemy, India, has bought much the same airplanes from the Soviet Union itself. In this particular case, the Indian aircraft are of a later generation than the Pakistani, but family resemblances may greatly complicate the task of the observer. So many countries have bought Western airplanes that no observer, knowing what sort of airplane he or she is seeing, can be absolutely certain who owns or operates it. Even so, recognition of the type can make an enormous difference.

The lesson seems to be that, whatever its deficiencies, the human eye is by far the best means of recognition—when it is appropriately educated. For example, some of the most sophisticated modern identification systems are really means of providing a pilot or sailor with a radar-generated image of a distant object, an image that he or she must then identify, largely by eye. When the observer's eye is not educated, disaster looms. Sometimes the result is attack on a friendly airplane (a problem that led to the awkward Vietnam-era fighter tactics requiring visual identification). However, the result can be much worse. For example, for years the U.S. Army in Europe has sought a means of quickly determining the axis of a major attack. One much-touted solution has been the computer fusion of data from numerous forward observers, who would send messages like "fifty T-55 tanks moving along Highway 5, bound west." What happens when, in the heat of battle, a lot of those observers mistake Western for Soviet tanks, or armored personnel carriers for tanks? The product of carefully analyzed but grossly wrong data is unlikely to be terribly accurate, yet it is to be used to call down air strikes and long-range missile fire. The problem becomes quite complex if the enemy employs decoying tactics; presumably, better-educated observers would have a better chance of distinguishing between a real and a dummy tank. Even if they cannot distinguish, they may help by reporting which type they think they are seeing. A clever analyst may detect the fraud by noting that the type apparently seen cannot correspond with other known intelligence data.

Many veterans took home copies of the *Recognition Journal*, and many of their children (among them the present writer) saw their first clear and uncensored pictures of military hardware in those magazines. Unfortunately, wartime paper was flimsy, so few copies have survived intact, to be prized by collectors and enthusiasts (some of whom undoubtedly greatly regret roughly handling those valuable copies when they were still children). Reprinting these journals will allow the lessons underlying the magazine to find a wider audience among historians and modern military people. It seems particularly appropriate that these magazines, which summarized the technology of World War II so well, are being reproduced fifty years later.

The present reprint project was proposed to the Naval Institute by Paul Silverstone, and he in turn was inspired and assisted in this project by Arnold Gouldner, who has some of the few surviving copies in his possession.

This first volume of the *Recognition Journal* covers the six issues of the magazine published between September 1943 and February 1944. These first six issues were written as World War II neared its half-way point, both chronologically and strategically. The Allies invaded Italy in September 1943, knocking the weakest of their enemies out of the war and into cobelligerency (note that Italian aircraft have been crossed out of a list of important recognition topics). In the Central Pacific, the great offensive was about to begin with the assault on Tarawa.

By the fall of 1943, the U.S. Navy had just completed its recovery from the early disasters, the attack on Pearl Harbor and the loss of so many cruisers and carriers in the South Pacific. An article highlights the revival of the old battleships, and elsewhere we see the extemporized light fleet and auxiliary carriers that helped fill the gap until new *Essex*-class fleet carriers entered service. We also see one of the most important fruits of wartime mobilization, the mass of new specialized amphibious shipping, mainly the LSTs.

At this time, too, the Battle of the Atlantic had just passed its peak. We see it from several different points of view. In the air, we see how pilots were taught to recognize a ship by its wake and to identify surfaced submarines under various conditions. On the surface, we see the small ships that actually fought the U-boats, a mixture of extemporized escorts and newly built specialist ships. We also see the fruits of the big merchant shipbuilding programs, in this case from both world wars. These ships are contrasted with the prewar-designed quality Maritime Commission types, built

with government funds to revive the U.S. merchant fleet and to provide the navy with the wartime auxiliaries it so badly needed but could not hope to buy.

Modern readers must wonder where the mass of merchant shipping will come from in any future conflict. They will also fail to understand what wartime readers knew from experience, that many ships will be sunk, and that the shipbuilding industry has to be mobilized to overcome those losses. Victory in the Battle of the Atlantic was won both at sea and in the shipyards; the United States actually suffered more industrial than military casualties during World War II. The production battle was a very real one.

Articles on the British and French navies emphasize the international quality of the Atlantic war. Nothing, however, appears on the Italian navy. Although the Italian fleet surrendered in September 1943, and although Italy became an ally, its fleet was laid up through much of 1944.

These magazines also highlight the strengths and weaknesses of wartime intelligence. Until well into 1944 the U.S. Navy had relatively little contact with the main Japanese fleet, and without such contact little was known of its wartime shipbuilding programs. Thus an article on the Japanese battle line mentions that Japan began the war with only two small battleships under construction. We now know that they were the *Yamato* and *Musashi*, the largest in the world, and we suspect that the article shows the success of prewar Japanese disinformation. The characteristics of these ships were not really known until after Japan surrendered.

One issue carries a dramatic photograph of the only really new type of Japanese fleet destroyer to enter service during the war, the *Akizuki* (called *Teruzuki* here). The photograph was, alas, misinterpreted; the ship is credited with 5-inch guns and a speed of over 40 knots. The reality was that she carried a new type of very high velocity 3.9-inch antiaircraft gun and that her speed was a more conservative 34 knots.

These pages also contain harbingers of the future. The newest British transport airplane is the anachronistic-looking York, the fruit of a decision that the United States would be responsible for most allied transport aircraft—and thus would dominate the postwar civil-aircraft market. No one comparing the York with the C-54, which became the standard early-postwar long-haul airliner (the DC-4), can doubt who would win that postwar economic conflict.

U. S. ARMY-NAVY JOURNAL OF
RECOGNITION

SEPTEMBER, 1943
NUMBER 1

RESTRICTED

QUIZ NO. 1—"ALL-IN RAID" (For answers see p. 50)

Courtesy AIRCRAFT RECOGNITION

U. S. ARMY - NAVY JOURNAL OF

RECOGNITION

SEPTEMBER, 1943   NUMBER 1

PUBLISHED BY THE BUREAU OF AERONAUTICS OF THE U.S. NAVY

COPYRIGHT 1943 BY LT. GEORGE H. FORSYTH JR.

NO MARGIN FOR ERROR

"The sky was graying just a little and we were within seven hundred yards of the objective when the party began. From the sea, over the stern, came the hum of planes.

"'Don't shoot, they're P-38's,' the spotter yells. Thrack, thrack, thrack! Bombs explode to port and up ahead of the bow. 'I was wrong, let 'em have it,' shrieks the spotter. Someone shouts, 'Timber,' and to a man we all duck down behind the splinter shield. A seaman rushes up and yells, 'We got hit, port side, amidships.' He adds, cheerfully, 'We're not sinking, though.'

"The planes come back, strafing. A seaman nudges me: 'Goddam her, mate, ain't this a mess.'"

This extract from a letter written by an officer in the amphibious landing force, who went in on the invasion of Sicily, is a good example of just what a mess faulty recognition of planes can lead to. The letter does not say whether anyone was killed because the appointed plane spotter could not distinguish between friendly and enemy planes, but the sober fact remains that the inability to recognize the enemy jeopardized the lives of the men in that landing boat and might possibly have led to the breakdown of the invasion at that one point.

Recognition is one of the best and most effective defense weapons any fighting nation has. And, at the same time, it is a potent, though intangible, offensive weapon. Knowing whether a plane, a ship or a tank is your own or the enemy's; knowing soon enough to give yourself time to shoot or formulate an attack is one of the fundamentals of war.

Mistakes are numerous, tragic

Recognition is too important a subject to be handled in an offhand manner. The attitude towards unidentified planes, for example, which says: "I don't know exactly what type it is but it must be one of our own," throws an advantage to the enemy for a cheap price, if that airplane turns out not to be on our side.

Since the war's beginning many mistakes have been made in recognition. Time and again we have had reports of near-sinkings of our own ships by our own planes. One of the classic examples of this took place in the North Sea when a flight of British torpedo planes sighted what they thought was the Bismarck. They closed in daringly and let their "fish" go. Luckily all of them were misses because the "Bismarck" turned out to be a British cruiser. Discovering his near-fatal mistake, the squadron leader flew over the ship and signaled laconically, "Sorry, pardon our kippers."

The enemy is just as susceptible to recognition mistakes as we are. One rather humorous mistake occurred when a flight of Italian bombers, operating over the Mediterranean, sighted a small freighter. Thinking it one of their own, they shepherded it along the way. The strange little convoy proceeded until R.A.F. planes happened along and chased the well-intentioned Italians off.

Recognition mistakes made by Americans are not as widely told as those of the British since the U. S. has been at war considerably less time. But our mistakes are piling up. One U. S. classic was made the day anti-aircraft crews on an American carrier in the South Pacific let Jap dive bombers get into the landing circle before they spotted them. This, quite likely, was a double-barreled error since it was apparent from their approach that the Japanese thought they were coming in on one of their carriers and didn't attack.

At Henderson Field on Guadalcanal there was one recognition boner that was a repeater. A lone Jap dive bomber several times sneaked into our landing circle at the tail end of a flight of U. S. planes landing at dusk. Circling the field with them, he would wait until the last plane hit the ground, then drop his bombs. His coolness prompted the Americans to cheer him, a sportsmanlike tribute. But mistakes do not pay off. Recognition must be one of the weapons with which we fight to win.

More training is needed

The accepted teaching methods of recognition place great emphasis on seeing an object as a whole and being able, through constant practice, to recognize that object (plane, tank, ship, etc.) from any angle. There are no short cuts to recognition.

To promote recognition three methods are used: small, handy manuals covering almost every operational ship, plane and tank either have already been published by one of the services or are forthcoming. In addition courses utilizing such teaching methods as movies, slides, silhouettes and photographs are produced for men in training. Lastly, in the field, on warships and at front line airfields are specially trained recognition officers.

This *Journal*, which will be published monthly, is a supplement to the methods now in operation. These methods form the backbone of this all-important subject; the *Journal's* function will be to bring out regularly the latest news. Being a monthly publication, it will emphasize last-minute changes in equipment and methods, both our own and the enemy's. The *Journal* will feature, as well as recognition, background material to enhance interest in ships, planes and tanks. Such interest leads to familiarity, and familiarity leads to instant recognition.

In publishing the *Journal*, a joint effort of the Army and Navy, we are following the well-established lead of the British. The editors of the *Journal* are grateful for the cooperation extended by the various branches of U.S. services and the R. A. F.

TRIPLE TAIL VERSION of the new York resembles the Lancaster (*below*) except for the number of fins. Note how wing has been changed to position level with top of fuselage in contrast to midwing arrangement on the parent plane. Triple tail structure makes hangar storage easier.

RAF'S YORK

BRITAIN'S NEWEST TRANSPORT

IS DEVELOPED FROM LANCASTER

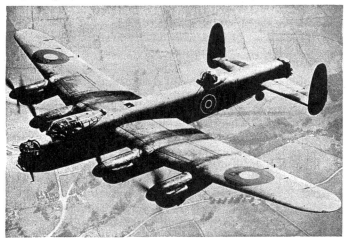

LANCASTER, England's great heavy bomber, is direct parent of new transport plane; endowed it with general shape, dimensions.

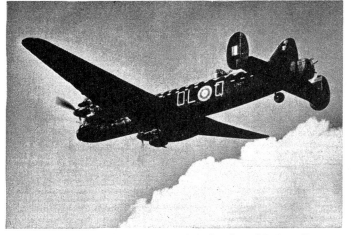

MANCHESTER, twin-engine bomber developed before Lancaster, is really York's grandfather, gave it characteristic triple fin.

The new RAF transport plane, the York, is recognitional news. Developed in the past year from the Lancaster and Manchester, the York has been, up until now, in a confidential category. Its flights have been kept secret for obvious reasons.

With the exception of the Ensign, the York is the largest transport plane England has ever built. It is the direct descendant of the famed Lancaster but has been slightly influenced by the Manchester (*left*). The line of descendancy has been Manchester (grandfather), Lancaster (father), and York (offspring).

From the Lancaster, one of the world's best bombing planes, it has taken its wingspread and the shape of the wing. However, where the Lancaster has the typically British "boxcar" fuselage, the York's fuselage is more capacious and is 9 ft. longer. In addition, the way in which their wings set is different; the York is a high-wing plane while the Lancaster is midwing. Like the Lancaster the transport has four Rolls-Royce Merlin engines.

From the Manchester, it inherited triple tail fins. Currently, the York has two tail versions, the double and triple fins. It seems likely, however, that the triple fins, which give more vertical surface and increase stability, might survive as the standard tail arrangement.

Because of its size, power, range and space the York might well be Britain's answer to postwar transoceanic cargo and passenger service.

RECOGNITION: The York has four engines, a deep-bellied fuselage, double or triple tail fins. Note odd shape of fins which look like guitar picks. York has high wing and tailplane. Might be confused with the B-24.

DOUBLE-TAIL YORK is the earlier version. Note how the shape of the fuselage of York differs from that of the Lancaster. York's fuselage fairs to a point astern while the Lancaster's has a tail gunner's position. Upper surfaces of the transport plane are painted with land scheme camouflage.

SEEN FROM THE GROUND the York looks very much like its parent, the Lancaster, except for the extended nose of the fuselage. The plane's wing tapers on both edges with rounded tips. The nacelles of the inboard engine extend to wing's trailing edge, the outboard engines only halfway.

NEW GERMAN SUBMARINES INCLUDE 1,600-TON LONG-RANGE MODEL, IMPROVED 740-TONNER AND NEW FAT-BELLIED "SEA COW" SUPPLY SUB

NEW SUBMARINE TYPES

GERMAN SUBS ARE EQUIPPED WITH AA GUNS TO FIGHT PLANES

Submarine warfare has taken a new turn. No longer do German U-boats dive frantically at the sight of Allied planes. Today, mounting anti-aircraft guns, they may prefer to stay on the surface and fight it out. Recently, they have frequently engaged fighters from our baby carriers.

The chief change in the new and re-fitted U-boats has been a new conning tower design which makes the German subs resemble our subsurface craft. In general, block conning towers have been replaced with towers having one or two steps called *Wintergarten*. On the first step is a quadruple mount of 20-mm. cannon; on the second step, two single 20-mm. guns; and on the conning tower fairing, four anti-aircraft machine guns. On the 740- and 1,600-ton U-boats, a 105-mm. anti-aircraft gun is also mounted forward of the conning tower.

Besides anti-aircraft defenses, the Nazis have developed a series of seagoing supply subs called *Seekühe* or sea cows. These carry fuel, torpedoes and other supplies to subs operating in the Atlantic and the Bay of Biscay. Both 740- and 1,200-ton models have been seen.

All types of German submarines are being used extensively for coastal minelaying operations. The mines are deposited through special mine shafts or through torpedo tubes. The new 1,600-ton minelayer, for example, has 30 mine shafts and carries 66 mines in its vertical hull chutes.

BROAD-BEAMED "OVERSEA COWS" are shown at Kiel base (1). Figure 2 indicates new Nazi torpedo boat; Fig. 3, 1,600-ton minelayer.

CONTRAST IN BEAM between "Oversea Cow" (A) and 517-ton U-boat (B) of same length is shown above at southern St. Nazaire lock.

MINELAYING 1,600-TONNER under attack by planes from a carrier of Bogue Class is shown in the three pictures on this page. Above, the U-boat has risen to the surface immediately after first depth bombing to prepare to repel the attacking aircraft. She obviously was soon sunk.

FULLY SURFACED, submarine reveals its anti-aircraft armament, big gun forward, 20-mm. guns aft and on conning tower. Below, half-naked crew members scramble towards their guns as depth bomb hits. Another depth charge can be seen about to hit water at bottom center.

PEARL HARBOR FLAMES
MODERNIZED DESIGN
OF U. S. BATTLESHIPS

U. S. S. ALABAMA, FIRST AMERICAN BATTLESHIP LAUNCHED AFTER PEARL HARBOR, HAS NINE BIG GUNS, FOREST OF ANTI-AIRCRAFT GUNS

OUR BATTLESHIPS

NEW AND RECONDITIONED SHIPS GIVE U. S. MORE POWER

The modern warship is the lineal descendant of the ship-of-the-line. Since guns first went to sea, the navy which could get the greatest weight and volume of fire into action most quickly and effectively has carried the day. The guns of the Spanish galleon ruled the sea from the conquest of Mexico till 1588, when the faster, more maneuverable ships of Sir Francis Drake were able to bring their guns more tellingly to bear and sweep the Armada from the seas. In the same way, the British frigates were unchallenged until the swift ships of Jones and Perry out-sailed and out-fought them in individual actions.

The modern battleship really began to evolve in the mid-19th Century with the development of steam drives, turret guns and armored hulls. Steam engines were first added to sailing ship designs as an auxiliary drive. As better engines were developed, steam became the main drive and sail was finally eliminated completely.

In America, armor was first used during the Civil War in the celebrated encounter between the Monitor and the C.S.S. Virginia. These ships, however, had little effect on battleship development. They did stimulate American interest in armored vessels and the Monitor demonstrated the advantages of mounting guns in rotating turrets, but both were poorly de-

signed warships. The Virginia was little more than an ironclad shed erected on the lower hull of the steam frigate Merrimac. The Monitor was also clumsy and unseaworthy, having very little freeboard, but it had a very shallow draft and, as a military expedient, satisfactorily performed its job of attacking Confederate fortifications and shipping in Southern harbors.

By the end of the 19th Century the pre-dreadnought battleship was standard throughout the world. The old sailing gear had disappeared and powerful multiple-screw steam drives had taken its place. Belts of heavy armor were installed amidships, with lighter armor fore and aft and on the decks. The main guns were mounted in two turrets, one placed at each end of the ship. In 1906, with the advent of H.M.S. Dreadnought, a main battery of uniform caliber was adopted, and accurate fire control became possible.

From then on, the story of battleship development was largely a story of more powerful drives, heavier armor and increased firepower. Heavy main batteries and armor kept the speed of the battleship at a low level. To attain high speed, a new ship with a reduced main battery and lighter protective armor was developed. This type, the battle cruiser, is best exemplified by H.M.S. Renown.

The Washington Naval Treaty of 1922,

with its limits on the size and number of battleships, suspended the building of capital ships until the preparations for the present war got under way. Instead, the major powers turned to the development of the aircraft carrier, which, with its torpedo and dive bombers, has itself influenced the design of modern battleships. No longer is it sufficient for a warship to meet enemies on the surface and below the sea. It must now be prepared to repel attacks from the air above.

When the Japs struck at Pearl Harbor, the U. S. had 17 battleships in service. On Dec. 8, only nine of these were still capable of action. Since then five have returned to the fight while only the Arizona will probably never sail again. The story of how Pearl Harbor made possible the modernization of these ships will be found on pages 12–13.

Fifteen new battleships were building or on order before the U. S. entered the war. A number of these are now at sea, the others are being rushed to completion. Photographs and recognitional detail on those which can be released follow on pages 14–15. The nature of our newest and most powerful ships must be withheld from publication for obvious reasons. Four of our new aircraft carriers are pictured on pages 16–17.

9

U.S.S. TENNESSEE before the war was a typical oldline battleship. Old-fashioned cage masts supported duplicate spotting tops and "clock face" of the range coordinator, clearly visible to other ships. The secondary guns and anti-aircraft batteries were virtually without protection.

THE REFITTED TENNESSEE, rushed back into action after being hit at Pearl Harbor, Dec. 7, was better able to defend herself against air attack. Anti-aircraft guns could be fired over a wide arc of sky where the old cage mainmast had towered. Catapult was kept on No. 3 turret.

CLUSTERS OF MACHINE GUNS and twin dual-purpose gun houses make the rebuilt battleship a seagoing fortress, more immune to air assault. The pyramidal tower houses elements of her fire and ship control systems. All exhaust uptakes discharge through a single broad stack.

MODERN SHIP GROWS OUT OF PEARL HARBOR WRECKAGE

After Pearl Harbor, a new span of fighting life was given the U. S. S. Tennessee, a typical pre-Washington Treaty battleship. From the battering she took on Dec. 7 has arisen a powerful fighting ship. Originally commissioned in 1920, the ship went through the long days of peace without alteration. She displayed the cluttered superstructure of the period (*see top left*)—tall cage masts, a high boxlike bridge, insignificant stacks, and upperdeck casemate batteries.

It was not until after the Tennessee was bombed at Pearl Harbor that she began to assume her present form. To reduce her

silhouette and provide greater arcs of fire for her AA batteries the cage mainmast was removed, leaving only a stump tower and light pole mast. The ship's boats gave way to batteries of single dual-purpose guns to supplement the open secondary batteries. Splinter shields were set up at all gun positions and a number of anti-aircraft machine guns were added to both towers.

This refitting gave the Tennessee some protection against air assaults but by no means made her a modern ship. In the fall of 1942 she was returned to the yard for further refitting. For increased protec-

tion against underwater damage huge blisters were added giving her a broader beam. A short deck has been added amidships to support several enclosed twin dual-purpose mounts. Both uptakes have been combined into a single broad stack. Forward cage mast has been removed and fire and ship control elements housed in tower. AA machine guns have replaced the plane catapult on top of No. 3 turret. All exposed gun positions were shielded.

The present superstructure of the Tennessee has a long pyramidal shape, which makes it difficult for enemy ships to judge her target angle at any speed.

NEVADA

CLINKER SCREEN on stack and stump mainmast help identify the rebuilt Nevada (*below*). Twin dual-purpose guns have replaced casemate guns. Notice also the shielded machine-gun mounts on the stern, forward, and all over island and tower.

BATTLESHIPS GET NEW PUNCH IN PEARL HARBOR REFITS

Some idea of the service the Japs performed for us in their treacherous attack on Pearl Harbor can be obtained from a study of the pictures on this and the opposite page. Here, in before-and-after terms, is told the story of a masterly job of ship modernization.

The ships shown here are only three out of a large number which are undergoing a thorough rebuilding in American Navy yards, but the pattern displayed in their refitting will help you to recognize old and new U. S. Navy capital ships when you encounter them at sea. All show the influence of changing conditions in modern sea warfare.

The airplane has been a great factor in altering the appearance and performance of surface craft. Indeed, strong believers in airpower have repeatedly asserted that the battleship is an obsolete weapon, itself highly vulnerable from the air, and its heavy striking power superseded by the bombs and torpedoes of carrier-borne and shore-based aircraft. Recent naval actions have shown, however, that with increased anti-aircraft firepower and fighter plane protection, the capital ship is still making its presence felt.

As is apparent from the lower picture

in each of these three groups, a great many anti-aircraft guns have been added during their refits. Their AA batteries are of two general types: heavy AA guns in single or twin shield or enclosed mounts, and single and multiple machine guns placed wherever convenient. Modern naval AA guns are dual-purpose and can be used against surface or aerial targets. Heavy AA guns are most effective at high altitude and long range, while machine weapons constitute the principal defense at short range.

In order to be most effective, these guns must be able to train and elevate through a wide arc in following the course of the attacking plane. This means that as little of the superstructure as possible should mask their field of fire. This consideration, together with an attempt to reduce the ship's silhouette, has resulted in striking all unnecessary superstructure elements, such as bulky mainmasts, boatcranes, boats, etc., and in streamlining foremast bridge structures. The island has a less separated appearance and tends to form a solid block amidships. It is now in fact an anti-aircraft fortress protecting the vital parts of the ship: fire-control apparatus, the steering and navigational controls and locating devices.

In many cases the old secondary batteries have been removed to make way for more effective dual-purpose guns. In all cases, splinter shields have been fitted to exposed gun positions.

A few of the ships have been fitted with large blisters along the sides of the hull as additional protection against underwater attack. The Tennessee is an out-standing example (*see pp. 10–11*). These blisters—which in effect form a second hull—cut the speed of the ship but more than make up for this loss in reduced vulnerability.

All of these refitted ships do not show all of these features. The assault on Pearl Harbor left our West Coast open to attack and it was necessary to get as many ships back into action as possible. Ships which were badly hit in the Dec. 7 attack and subsequent actions needed more rebuilding and offered a chance for greater modernization.

The captions to the pictures on these pages point out particular recognition features for battleships Nevada, Pennsylvania and Colorado. The Maryland has been changed so that it resembles the Colorado, and the California will be much like the Tennessee when completed.

PENNSYLVANIA

MACHINE GUN MOUNTS on bow and No. 2 turret and two banks of raised twin guns mark the modernized Pennsylvania

(*below*). From abeam, the rebuilt ship has a very low silhouette. Open work on bridge, a recognition feature, was kept in refit.

COLORADO

SHORT CAGE MAINMAST and both stacks were kept in modernizing the Colorado (*below*). Three machine-gun mounts

replace catapult on No. 3 turret. Heavy AA guns are above the deck in separate "bandstands." Maryland will be similar.

NEW WARSHIPS SWELL U.S. FLEET

New American battleships built, building, or on order will more than double the strength of our main offensive lines at sea. The few minor changes suggested by battle experience are being made when the ships return to their bases for overhaul and are being added in our new designs.

The North Carolina was the first of the new line to take to sea. In her was incorporated the tower foremast construction typical of many European ships to which she has a certain resemblance, most particularly the Italian Littorio class. Having been on the drawing boards long before the war, the North Carolina does not represent so great a departure from the pre-Washington Treaty ships as the Iowa and South Dakota classes.

Since her commissioning, the North Carolina has undergone some refitting, chiefly the addition of a great many light anti-aircraft guns. The ship's boats and boat cranes have been replaced by life rafts, which are less cumbersome and easier to launch.

The experience gained with the North Carolina influenced the construction of the South Dakota class, a shorter, more compact and handier ship. To increase her seakeeping qualities, the freeboard has been increased. Her broad single stack is faired into the tower to form a solid pyramidal island. This should make it difficult for the enemy to judge her course or the target angle. At a distance the South Dakota has a superficial resemblance to Germany's Tirpitz.

Long clean lines make the Iowa one of the handsomest and fastest ships afloat. From the air, her long narrow bow makes her unmistakable. A high speed version of the earlier South Dakota, she is greatly enlarged and lengthened. The Iowa thus completes the transition from pre-war designs.

NORTH CAROLINA

FROM THE AIR, North Carolina has a balanced deck plan. Symmetrical arrangement of five dual-purpose mounts each side of island are distinctive recognition feature of the ship.

FROM ABEAM, North Carolina has long, low silhouette with two stacks and high tower rising cleanly above the island. Boats and boat cranes visible in both views have since been replaced by life rafts. Many anti-aircraft machine guns have also been added since she was commissioned.

SHIPS OF THE SOUTH DAKOTA CLASS, like the Indiana, are distinguished by the pyramidal island and single broad stack faired into the tower mast. Beam view of this class resembles refitted Tennessee. Note also the two splinter-shielded machine-gun mounts which overhang stern.

PRIDE OF U.S. FLEET is the new Iowa class. Superstructure is very clean, with broad forward stack faired into the tower. The deck plan is like no other, tapering sharply from No. 1 turret to long sharp bow. Symmetrical staggered mounting of dual-purpose guns is typical of new ships.

CARRIERS

LATEST CARRIER CLASSES

INCREASE NAVY'S PUNCH

Since Jan. 18, 1911, when Eugene Ely landed his flying bird-cage on a platform on the deck of the old U. S. S. Pennsylvania (*right*), the use of ship-borne planes has come a long way. Big fast ships like the Essex, carrying a large complement of fighters, dive bombers and torpedo planes, now set out to sea behind a screen of destroyers to seek out the enemy and destroy him. Though lightly armored and vulnerable, the carrier's defensive planes and heavy anti-aircraft fire make it a deadly ship to approach mistakenly and unidentified.

To supplement these great task-force weapons, a large number of small converted carriers have been built. Converted cruisers like the Independence can race into action at great speed. Numerous adaptations of the Maritime Commission's

ESSEX CLASS

PYRAMIDAL ISLAND of Essex Class is narrow and rectangular when seen fore and aft. Twin dual-purpose guns are at each end of the island, with AA stepped up to stack. Seen from above, hull has smooth line along island side but flight deck is indented sharply at both ends. Elevator opposite island makes additional cut-in when vertical, projects beyond deck line when down. Hangar deck is screened when not in use.

SANGAMON CLASS

CONVERTED OILERS which make the Sangamon Class are relatively long narrow ships, faster than other conversions. Flight deck is symmetrical, tapering forward of forward elevator. Numerous gun platforms extend from gallery walkway. Island is small and rectilinear with an antenna tower rising from it. Two radio masts on starboard side aft will be vertical while cruising, project horizontally when carrier is in action.

C-3 hull escort convoys or carry planes to the front. Converted oilers—long, lean ships that lie low in the water—can be used on limited combat missions as well as being supplementary fuel ships. The newest class—the Casablanca—has slightly more speed than other converted merchant vessels. Otherwise it greatly resembles the Bogue Class.

Recognition-wise, the major carriers of the American fleet are marked by the tower island on the starboard side amidships. The Independence Class has four prominent stacks just aft of a small island. All of the smaller carriers, with islands well forward, may easily be mistaken for Japs of similar size. Specific recognition details on these ships should be studied carefully. Deck plans, gun sponsons and exhaust stacks are significant details.

EUGENE ELY LANDED, took off from battleship Pennsylvania, Jan. 18, 1911. On Nov. 14, 1910 he had successfully landed on Birmingham.

INDEPENDENCE CLASS

FOUR STACKS protruding from starboard side immediately identify ships of this class. Long, narrow cruiser hull is unusually fast. Flight deck is symmetrical but small island tower overhangs the sea. A large boat crane is just forward of island. Machine-gun mounts ring the deck and single dual-purpose guns are forward just below the flight deck and on transom stern. Five antennae can be lowered when ship is in action.

BOGUE CLASS

SMALLEST OF OUR CARRIERS now in action, the Bogue Class is being produced in large numbers. Single stacks project from each side and extend up flush with the deck. Gun blisters have been built along what would be the weather deck of the merchant ship. Flight deck presents rectangular surface to the incoming pilot. A small island structure is outboard of flight deck proper well forward on starboard side.

MEDIUM TANKS

BRITISH

THE CRUSADER IS A CRUISER TANK

The British Army uses two types of tanks: infantry and cruiser. Former is heavily armored, slow and is used in close cooperation with troops. The cruiser, faster but less well armored, plays the role of modern cavalry doing reconnaissance in force, exploiting break-throughs.

The Crusader, a medium cruiser, first appeared in 1941 in Africa where it had some success. It is now being replaced by a later type, the Cromwell. Crusader carries a 40-mm. gun and two 7.92 machine guns.

RECOGNITION: Head-on the Crusader looks diamond-shaped, has a large bulbous mantlet from which her gun protrudes and narrow track plates. Side view of the Crusader shows streamlined, undercut turret, prominent driver's cab and two radio masts. From the air her turret, six-sided and kettle-shaped, set well forward, is her most recognizable feature.

LIKE ALL BRITISH TANKS, except Churchill, the Crusader has only driver sitting in hull. Front armor is 50-mm. thick; armor on sides and turret 30-mm. and 40-mm. respectively.

BATTLE RECORD of Crusader is fair but not as good as German medium or U.S. General Sherman. Note: smoke dischargers on side of turret.

SAND GUARDS protect bogie wheels. The Crusader weighs 19 tons, carries crew of five, can make 25 m.p.h. on roads, 23 m.p.h. cross country.

TWO RADIO MASTS, one "fishing rod" type, one "peg" type protrude from turret. Tank's drive comes from sprocket wheel in rear of track.

ANGULAR TURRET helps deflect enemy projectiles. Crusader's speed comes from five large bogie wheels which touch track top and bottom.

SOVIET

T-34 IS GREAT FIGHTING TANK

The T-34 medium tank is the backbone of all Soviet armored equipment. It is considered by the Germans who have fought against it to be the most formidable tank in the Soviet arsenal.

The T-34 first appeared after the start of the Russo-German war. Built by men who are considered among the top tank experts in the world, it represents some of the best features possible in a tank; a low silhouette, broad track plates for snow work, lack of protrusions by which tank destroyers can climb aboard. The T-34, in addition, is highly maneuverable, has excellent fire power and high quality armor.

RECOGNITION: Viewed from the front and sides the T-34 has a roughly triangular shape. It has a low silhouette, wide (24 in.) tracks and five large, Christie type bogie wheels. From the air it is recognizable by turret set well forward. Its long barrelled 76.2-mm. gun extends beyond tank nose.

TOP OF TURRET opens forward only. The turret has small cupola. The T-34 is 19 ft. 4 in. long, 9 ft. 10 in. wide but only 8 ft. high. It weighs 26 tons and carries 45-mm. armor.

T-34'S TOP SPEED is 33 m.p.h. Because of her low, squat silhouette the tank can easily be dug into the ground, used as stationary pillbox.

TURRET GUN has full 360° traverse. Tank also has two 7.62 machine guns. It carries a crew of three and has a maximum range of 200 miles.

CAMOUFLAGED with white paint, T-34 operates in deep snow. In operation on all Russian fronts, the T-34 often carries troops into battle.

HIGH CLEARANCE under hull makes snow work easy for T-34. Lack of projections on plates eliminates possibility of snow clogging tracks.

ALL FIVE CREWMEN can be seen in this Mark IV. This tank has short barreled 75-mm. gun, now being replaced. In addition, Mark IV's carry two machine guns.

GERMAN
ROMMEL MAINSTAY
WAS THE PZKW IV

DOUBLE MUZZLE BRAKE

The PzKw Mark IV is one of the most popular and effective German tanks. Used widely by Rommel in Africa it has been a standby of Germany's mechanized Army since 1940.

Before the Mark VI or "Tiger" tank was introduced the IV was the heaviest German tank. It weighs 22 tons, is 19 ft. 4 in. long, 9 ft. 7¼ in. wide, 8 ft. 6 in. high, has a 360° turret traverse and carries a crew of five. Its range is 100 miles. Mark IV was first used in France in 1940 and since then the gun and armor have been modified and the turret has been made more squat, resulting in a lower silhouette. The tank has had seven models, A to G.

Originally the Mark IV had 30-mm. armor in front which was improved by adding an outer layer of 30-mm. armor with an air space between to help deflect projectiles. This was improvised after tank was in action. Later a solid sheet of 50-mm. was used. The sides of the tank have 20 plus 20 mm., the turret 20 plus 30 mm.

The tank's armament varies. It can carry a short, thick-barreled 75-mm., now being replaced (*see top left*), a long barreled 75 or, in the Mark IV Special, a long barreled 75 with an oddly shaped double baffle muzzle brake (*see inset*). Muzzle brake disperses muzzle gases, cuts down recoil and reduces flash.

Allied experts consider the Mark IV a good tank but inferior to the U. S. General Sherman. Tactically the Germans are smart tankmen. They usually operate by proceeding slowly over the terrain, hillcrest to hillcrest. Sighting anything suspicious they lead onto it with their machine guns, then open up with their 75 if it looks like paydirt. They are clever at improvisation, often turning damaged tanks into assault artillery by using chassis as mobile gun mount.

RECOGNITION: Most salient features of the Mark IV are eight small bogie wheels and four return rollers, the angular slabsided turret with small round cupola. Noteworthy also are gun in its different lengths, muzzle brake and the odd horseshoe-shaped extension on turret. Radio mast is retractable, is mounted to right of turret.

TANK TREADS and extra bogie wheels are piled onto hull of tank to give extra protection. The Mark IV has been used both in Africa and on the Russian front.

FROM THE AIR Mark IV shows the small, round cupola, rear of turret. Beyond the cupola is a horseshoe-shaped extension.

SMALL BOGIE WHEELS, mounted in tandem, are prime recognition features. Note how long-barreled gun with muzzle brake extends well beyond tank's nose.

AMERICAN

SHERMAN WAS BEST IN NORTH AFRICA

IN TANK TRAP on maneuvers an M-4 shows clearly its twin-suspended bogie wheels. Various models of the tank can cross trenches from 6 to 7½ ft. in width.

With an impressive battle record behind it in Tunisia, the U. S. Army's medium tank, the M-4, is now operating in Sicily. Reports from the new front are as yet meager but it can be expected that the General Sherman will once more prove its fighting ability.

The Sherman is actually five tanks; i.e. there are five models of it built by four different manufacturers, M-4 to M-4-A4. They are generally similar except in minor details. In addition two types of hulls are used: cast and welded. The tanks shown on these pages are welded, except center right. Cast hulls are less angular, have rounded contours. The Sherman is well gunned, carrying a 75-mm. high velocity gun in a full traverse, power-operated turret, a .50-cal. machine gun for AA mounted on turret hatch and two .30-cal. machine guns, one in turret, one in hull. From 90 to 98 rounds of 75 ammunition is carried and 5,650 machine-gun rounds.

The M-4 is 18 ft. 7 in. long, 8 ft. 7 in. wide and 9 ft. high. It weighs from 30 to 33 tons, can go from 22 to 27 m. p. h. It carries a crew of five and has a maximum cruising radius of 150 to 200 miles. It has three pairs of small bogie wheels. The driving sprocket is in front, the idler in the rear. In addition to its guns, it also carries hand grenades, smoke and thermite grenades. Its radio mast is mounted on the left rear of the turret. The Sherman was first introduced in the spring of 1942.

Although the British had a few models of the General Sherman in North Africa earlier, the tank was first used in force when Montgomery's desert-wise Eighth Army broke through Rommel's lines at El Alamein and started on their victorious route to Tunisia.

After their experience with the Sherman in North Africa the Germans have a high opinion of it. In fact, according to captured documents, it seems likely they already have plans to produce an imitation.

RECOGNITION: Basically the General Sherman looks like no other tank in existence. Its turret is completely round, its lines are clean and not sharp and angular. The 75-mm. gun projects beyond front of the tank. Twin-suspended bogie wheels in three pairs are characteristic. Painted on turret is a 20-in. white star and on the engine cover a 36-in. white star. Seen head-on the Sherman is deep, full-bodied although actually it has well over 1½-ft. clearance underneath hull. Seen from the air its most obvious characteristic is the rounded turret.

CAST HULL TANK presents fewer angles and can deflect projectiles easier than welded version. Note how the gun turret has swung around, is facing backwards.

ON STEEP HILLSIDE a General Sherman shows its great climbing ability. Note tank's deep-bellied look in front view.

PILOT'S EYE-VIEW of the General Sherman shows the rounded turret, prime recognition feature from air. Note that high velocity gun projects beyond tank.

HEAD-ON, MOSQUITO HAS TWO UNDERSLUNG NACELLES, MIDWING FUSELAGE ON SLENDER TAPERING WING. FIN RISES HIGH ABOVE FUSELAGE

THE MESSERSCHMIDT 210 IS LOW-WING PLANE WITH UNDERSLUNG NACELLES. ITS KEYHOLE-SHAPED FUSELAGE IS BI-SECTED BY TAILPLANE

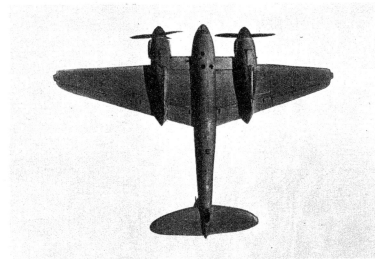
BROKEN LEADING EDGE AND ELLIPTICAL TAILPLANE MARK MOSQUITO

ME-210 HAS LONG THIN FUSELAGE AND PROMINENT ENGINE NACELLES

DON'T CONFUSE MOSQUITO WITH MESSERSCHMIDT 210

The De Haviland Mosquito does not look like the Messerschmidt 210. They have been confused, but you will not do it if you appreciate their different lines, the way they "sit" in the air, their overall appearance. Though they have similarities, their personalities are entirely different.

The Mosquito is a beautiful plane whose beauty has paid off in high performance. The Me-210, like so many German planes, is ugly but a good fighting craft. Both are used for similar military tasks: fighting, attack bombing, high-speed photographic reconnaissance.

Recognitionally, the chief differences include the bulbous greenhouse of the Messerschmidt which makes a pronounced hump in both side and head-on views, while the Mosquito cockpit fairs smoothly into the fuselage. In plan view, the main taper of the wing of the Mosquito is on the trailing edge, the Messerschmidt wing tapers equally. The Mosquito's leading edge is a broken line; between the nacelles the radiators cause it to project farther forward than the outboard sections. The tail structures also differ. The rudder on the Messerschmidt ends flush with the fuselage; on the Mosquito, the fuselage extends to a point well beyond the rudder.

Four models of the Mosquito are currently important for recognition. The earliest, Mark 1, served as the prototype and required little modification. Later three specialized versions were developed. The Mark 2, the fighter model, has a solid nose in which the machine guns are mounted. The Mark 3 is used for operational training and Mark 4 is the unarmed day bomber. On the Mark 2, 3 and 4, nacelles project beyond trailing edge.

GRACEFUL CONTOURS OF MOSQUITO FUSELAGE ARE UNMISTAKABLE

FROM SIDE, FUSELAGE OF ME-210 LOOKS LIKE AN AERIAL POLYWOG

QUIZ NO. 2: FIGHTER TYPES OF NATIONS IN THE WAR

For answers see p. 50

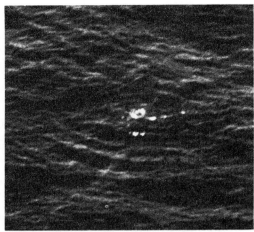
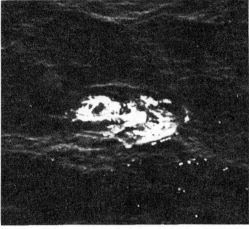
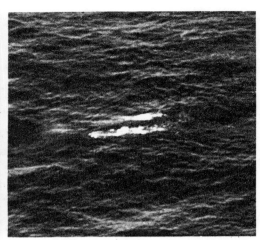

CARELESS "ENEMY" SURFACES BELOW PILOT   PILOT DECIDES THE SWIRL IS SUSPICIOUS   CIGAR SHAPE COMPLETES IDENTIFICATION

"SIGHTED SUB, SANK WHALE" PILOTS GET NEW MEDALS

Whales are peaceable mammals by nature. But like most other living creatures they are finding it impossible to escape the effects of the war. At first there were the escort ships to cope with. Many a whale got in the way of the sound beam. Corvettes, destroyers and PCs pursued them mercilessly with depth charges.

Now the unfortunate beasts find it unsafe to come up for an occasional breath of air lest they meet an honorable member of the Royal Order of Whale Bangers.

Historical records fail to identify the original whale bomber but nevertheless there are now enough pilots who have the distinction of wearing the medal (*center*) to place Whale Bangers on a par with Short Snorters and Caterpillars.

The following is one of the latest case histories: "Recently, a naval pilot was fly-

MEDAL IS PRESENTED TO WHALE BOMBERS

ing a Kingfisher observation scout plane on anti-sub patrol. In response to radio orders he sped to the spot from which a 'sub sighted' report had been flashed. Arriving there the pilot quickly located a suspicious swirl. There was no time for thoughtful identification. Going into a dive, the pilot released his depth charges. Direct hits, right on the target!

"Dark objects bobbed up to the surface. A Coast Guard cutter arrived, her crew started dragging objects onto the cutter's deck. The anxious pilot signaled.

" 'What is it?' he asked.

" 'Whale meat,' came the reply from the cutter, 'but good!' "

The picture at the bottom of the opposite page shows the difference between a feathering periscope and a feathering whale. However, when in doubt as to whether you are meeting an enemy submarine or a neutral whale, let the depth charges drop. Remember a whale filet looks like beef, tastes like beef and has the added advantage of being 20 ft. long.

PILOT DROPS DEPTH CHARGE ON ALLEGED SUB SHOWN IN PICTURES AT TOP OF PAGE. PROUD PILOT WAS SURE HE HAD SCORED A DIRECT HIT

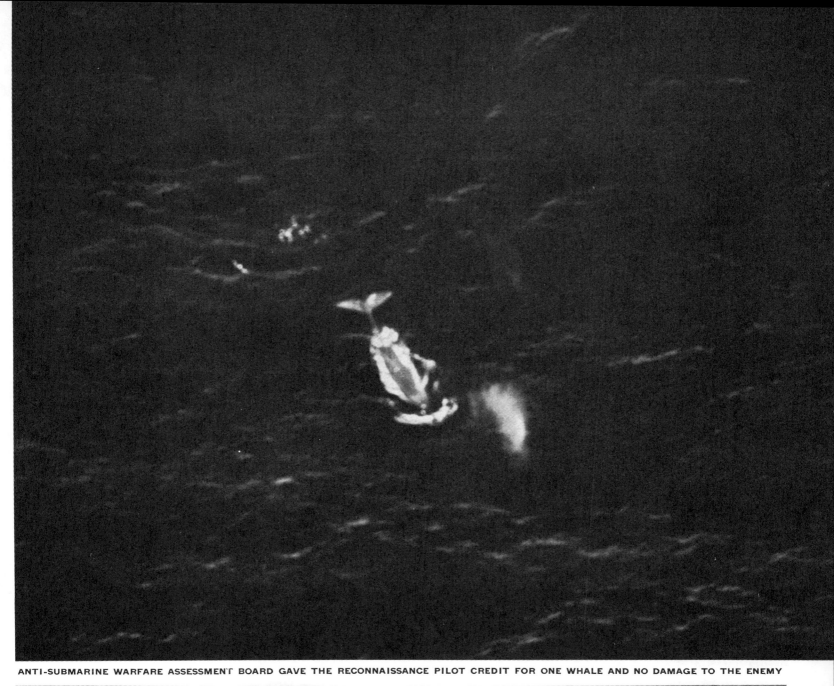

ANTI-SUBMARINE WARFARE ASSESSMENT BOARD GAVE THE RECONNAISSANCE PILOT CREDIT FOR ONE WHALE AND NO DAMAGE TO THE ENEMY

SUB WAKE (ABOVE) IS LONGER THAN WHALE WAKE, MAKES A SINGLE WHITE LINE. WHALE STIRS UP WATER AT SIDES, LEAVES LITTLE WAKE

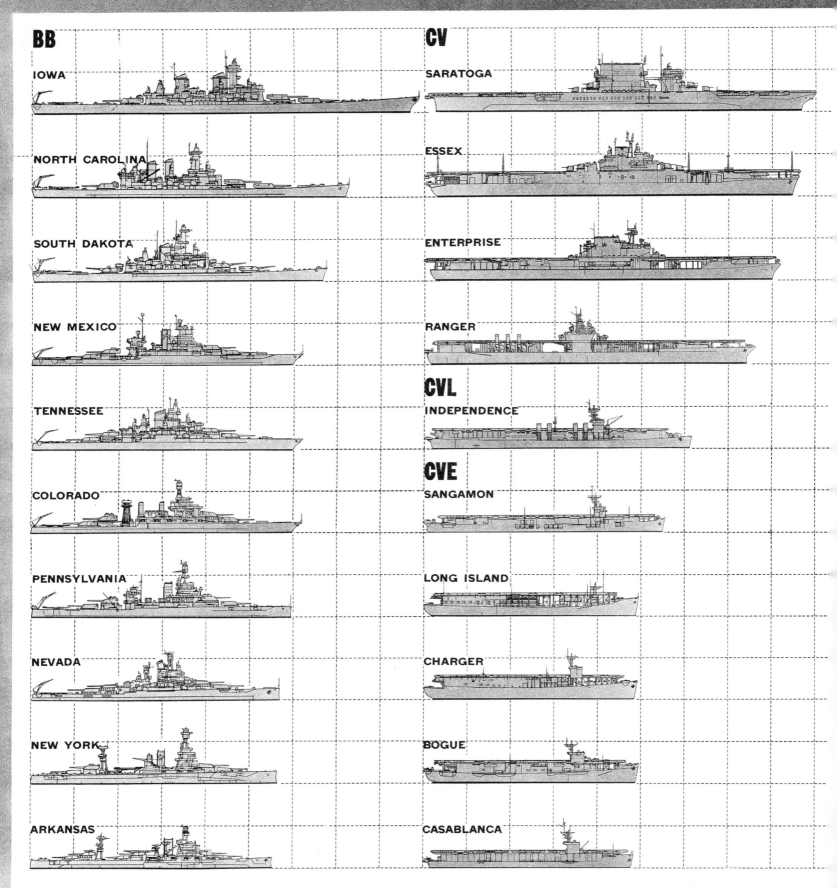

BB

- IOWA
- NORTH CAROLINA
- SOUTH DAKOTA
- NEW MEXICO
- TENNESSEE
- COLORADO
- PENNSYLVANIA
- NEVADA
- NEW YORK
- ARKANSAS

CV

- SARATOGA
- ESSEX
- ENTERPRISE
- RANGER

CVL

- INDEPENDENCE

CVE

- SANGAMON
- LONG ISLAND
- CHARGER
- BOGUE
- CASABLANCA

Here on these pages are silhouettes of 42 classes of fighting ships of the U. S. Navy. Ranging in size from the huge battleship *Iowa* which stretches a majestic and deadly 887 ft. and displaces 45,000 tons to the old flush-deck destroyers of World War I vintage which are only 314 ft. and displace 1,190, these silhou-ettes are drawn to accurate scale. Also included are two of the newest additions to the Navy's destroyer-escort class.

A quick glance will tell the recognitional characteristics of each class. By tracing the development within the broad types (i.e. battle-ships, cruisers, etc.) the changes in the grouping of structures and the placing of guns can be seen. This chart, with each square equalling 100 ft., also tells the relative size of each class. It can be taken out of the *Journal* and pinned up on a wall or bulkhead. It is hoped that in the near future scale silhouettes of a[ll] navies, both Allies and Axis, can be publishe[d]

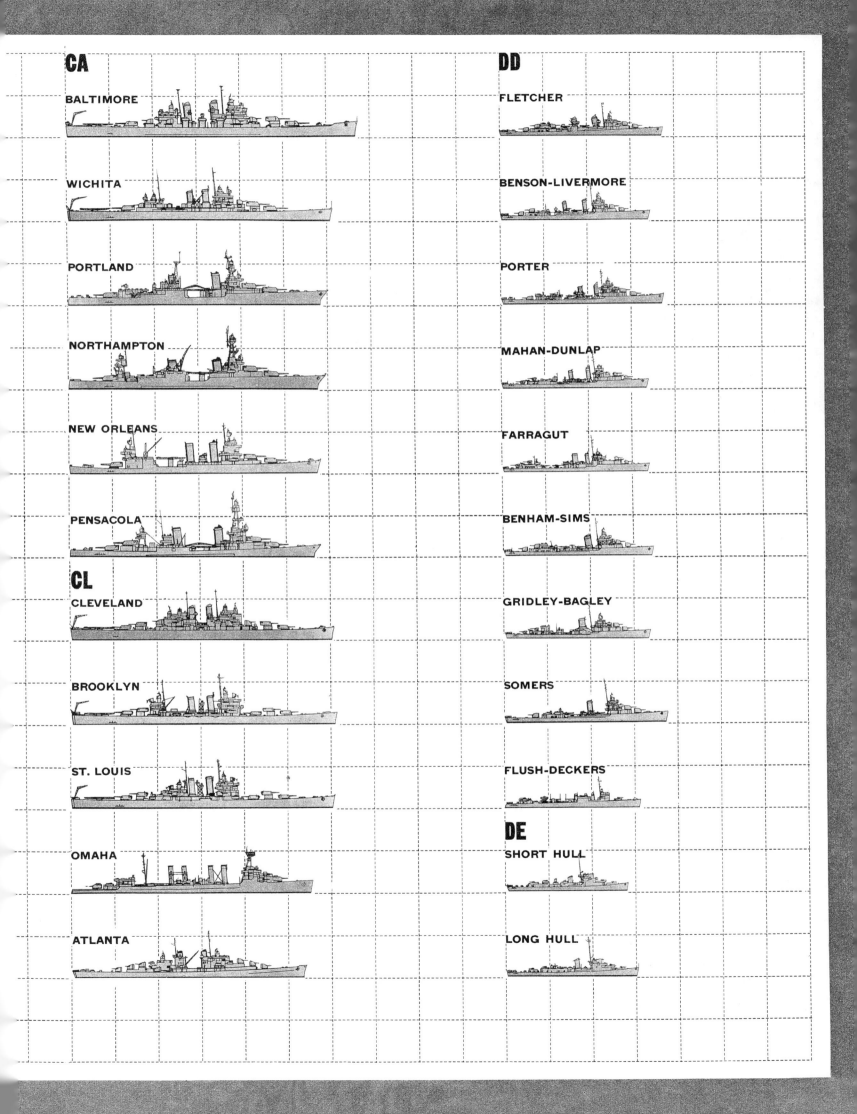

CA

BALTIMORE

WICHITA

PORTLAND

NORTHAMPTON

NEW ORLEANS

PENSACOLA

CL

CLEVELAND

BROOKLYN

ST. LOUIS

OMAHA

ATLANTA

DD

FLETCHER

BENSON-LIVERMORE

PORTER

MAHAN-DUNLAP

FARRAGUT

BENHAM-SIMS

GRIDLEY-BAGLEY

SOMERS

FLUSH-DECKERS

DE

SHORT HULL

LONG HULL

VAL, TOP JAP DIVE BOMBER, ATTACKS HORNET DURING SANTA CRUZ BATTLE. LATER, DIVING PLANE HIT HORNET'S ISLAND, CRIPPLED HER

JAP AIR FORCE

IN 22 MONTHS IT HAS PROVED A FORMIDABLE FOE

On Dec. 7, 1941, the Japanese air forces played their trump card. In the attack on Pearl Harbor they displayed their fighting temperament, they showed that they would risk any loss to inflict an appreciable amount of damage on the enemy. Such a philosophy of fighting is a paradox, at once a weakness and a strength.

For many years the Japanese were underestimated. Their air power, in particular, was never followed closely enough in China. And, at the same time in China, it is likely that they withheld their best planes preferring to develop them secretly. Hence, when war started, we were at a loss. We did not understand the integral makeup of their air forces nor did we have enough respect for their planes or pilots. We know now that despite some fighting qualities we consider questionable (i.e. lack of individual initiative), the enemy is a skilful, daring flier. The equipment he fights with, though it seldom approaches the rigid standards of our air forces, does the job it is designed to do.

Japan's aviation history began just before World War I, when several Army and Navy officers were sent to France to investigate the possibilities of aerial warfare. In 1919 an Aviation Section was set up in the War Office in Tokyo. In 1921 a British civil air mission brought flight instructors, engineers, designers and planes to Japan. Even at that early date the British were impressed with the Japanese approach to flying; it showed energy, ability and determination. In addition, the Japanese quickly realized the immense potentialities of air power and explored every possibility. As early as Dec. 7, 1922 they commissioned their first aircraft carrier, the Hosho, and put plane catapults on warships.

Today the Japanese air forces can be considered one of the

That part of the graphic material in this article, as noted on certain pictures, is from the forthcoming manual ONI 232—Japanese Military Aircraft which is a standard ONI manual of similar character to those which have already been issued by the Division of Naval Intelligence on the navies of the world.

most potent weapons in the war. They do not constitute an independent air force; instead, each of the services has its own air force. However, within each service the air arm plays a relatively large role. Thus the head of Naval Aviation Headquarters, who corresponds to our Deputy Chief of Naval Operations for Air, together with the Navy Minister and the Chief of the Naval General Staff, constitutes the high command of the Japanese Navy. The head of Army Aviation Headquarters, with the War Minister and the Chief of the Army General Staff, constitutes, in a similar manner, the Army's high command. This increased recognition of the importance of air power resulted from the complete reorganization of both air forces which took place in 1942.

The Japanese Army and Navy air forces are about the same size. The Army has fighters and bombers; the Navy has fighters, dive bombers, torpedo planes and long range patrol planes. A surprisingly small number of the Navy's planes are carrier based, and an exceptionally high number are land based.

The functions of the Army air force are bombing, fighter protection, close support of ground troops. The Navy handles long range bombing, reconnaissance, anti-shipping strikes and carrier actions. On the whole the Navy is a better-trained, better-equipped force and has borne much of the brunt of the fighting in the South Pacific. The Army's role has been mainly support.

Most important cog in the Jap air forces, and in every air force, is the individual pilot (see inset). In the case of Japan the pilot situation is a complex one. Of the first-line pilots only one-fourth are commissioned officers, the rest enlisted men. This division is further accentuated in the methods of training and in the combat results of that training.

In Japan there are both Army and Navy training schools for

FLIGHT OF JAP PLANES OF "BETTY" TYPE COMES IN LOW OVER THE WATER ON A TORPEDO ATTACK AGAINST SHIPPING OFF GUADALCANAL

fliers and the course is long and thorough. On the whole, however, little was known of Japanese training, either from the viewpoint of quantity or quality, before the war. Now it is believed that primary and intermediate training are conducted in Japan, while advanced operational training takes place in the field.

The flight course differs for officers and enlisted pilots. Both undoubtedly get the same basic flight training but it appears that the enlisted men get less tactical training. Before a bombing flight, for example, only officers are briefed. The rest of the pilots on the mission make the flight "blind."

Always anxious to secure results even at the cost of high losses, the flight flies over the target in close formation for a better bomb pattern despite anti-aircraft fire. On such a flight the commissioned pilot leading the flight gives the signals to drop bombs, sometimes by blinker or wing-wagging. It is possible that only his plane is fully equipped with radio. In case he is shot down the flight is liable to disintegrate.

Such disintegration has happened enough not to be unusual. On all combat flights most of the pilots are trained to do a specific job and do it well. They will adhere to a plan and follow it through to completion or death. However, if anything goes awry with the plan the Japanese aviator does not have the initiative to work out an on-the-spot scheme of continuing the fight on his own.

The Japs have fast, maneuverable fighters and they know how to use them. U.S. pilots have been able to out-fight them but the Japanese are determined, seasoned fighters. They are improving their planes constantly and building new ones which incorporate lessons already learned. (*See Tony, Hap— pp. 30–31.*)

Their dive bombers and high level bombers are below U.S. par. Val, their first dive bomber, is not structurally strong enough for steep dives of long duration and was not even in production until 1939 after the German success in Poland. The most effective use of Jap planes and pilots has been with the torpedo plane. The training period for torpedo combat crews is long and hazardous, has paid off well with successful

TYPICALLY DETERMINED PILOT ties a Rising Sun flag around head before combat.

sinkings of U.S. warships and merchant vessels. Lastly, the Japanese have worked out a good reconnaissance system and have stalked our task forces with remarkable skill. For details on each important Jap plane, see following pages.

Losses have been high, but not crippling

In task force operations, carrier-based planes are sometimes sent out late in the afternoon to attack the enemy which means risky night landings, losses through faulty navigation. The Japs may also, if absolutely necessary, send most of the fighters from a carrier beyond their fuel range to convoy a flight of dive bombers and torpedo planes over their target. Again, this is the Japanese practice of paying a high price in men and materiel for results.

Most Jap pilots follow the exact blueprint of a method once they have accepted it. They will attack time and again in the same way at the same hour day after day as they did at Guadalcanal despite the most shocking losses. Their lack of pilot individuality and their dogged acceptance of blind orders makes them as dangerous an opponent as it does a vulnerable one. When they do change their tactics they change them abruptly and with great originality.

They have been hit hard by U.S. fliers and hurt badly, losing many hundreds of planes. But as yet there is no conclusive evidence that their airpower has been seriously cut. Their pilot losses have been heavy and some observers think we are now fighting the second team; but other U.S. fliers believe the Japs have not deteriorated, but rather that we have improved.

It is estimated that the production rate of Japan's plane industry is considerably higher than it was expected to be. New types will have increased horsepower, better armament, better streamlining, self-sealing tanks, and possibly armor for the pilot. Though the Japanese are commonly accused of imitating the planes of other nations, it should be remembered that this does not necessarily indicate a weakness; they are incorporating proven features and adapting them ingeniously to their own use.

LIKE MANY JAPANESE PLANES, TONY'S FUSELAGE TAPERS TO A SHARP CONE. NOTE THAT THE PLANE HAS A VERY LARGE AIRSCREW SPINNER

TONY

IS NEW JAP FIGHTER PLANE

HEAD-ON, Tony is a low-winged monoplane which resembles RAF's Hurricane. Note bulges under wings, almost to wing tips.

DIVING, Tony shows high tail structure. Below, from quarter view the dihedral of the wings from the wing roots can be seen.

The first Japanese fighter plane to be equipped with an in-line, liquid-cooled engine has recently appeared in the combat areas of the Pacific. Listed operationally as Tony, the combat data on the plane (speed, rate of climb, service ceiling, armament, possible armor, etc.) has not yet been released. Nor has the plane's primary function been established. Because of the bulges, visible in the pictures to the left, on the lower surface of the wings, there are two possibilities.

First, the plane might be a long range fighter equipped with jettisonable gas tanks; second, these bulges might well be light, anti-personnel bombs which would make the plane's main job ground attack.

Little is known at the present time about Tony. However, as soon as more reports from the field come in, the *Journal* will endeavor to put Tony into its proper niche in the Japanese scheme of combat.

RECOGNITION: Tony's wing has the same general outline as Zeke's (*see p. 33*). The wings have a dihedral from the roots with a nearly equal taper on both surfaces. The wing tips are rounded. Tony's fuselage tapers to a cone aft, somewhat like Germany's Heinkel 113. From a head-on view, Tony looks something like the RAF's Hawker Hurricane.

DIRECTLY OVERHEAD, Tony shows its resemblance to both the Heinkel 113 in the general contour of its fuselage and to Zeke by the outline of the wing.

HAP LOOKS LIKE GRUMMAN PLANES BUT HAS THINNER, MORE TAPERED FUSELAGE.   THIS ZERO, MARK 2, HAS SERVICE CEILING OF 40,200 FT.

HAP

FIGHTER IS IMPROVED ZERO

Hap, the newest Jap fighter plane, is an improved model of Zeke. In fact, it is Zeke with the following changes: 1) it has squared-off wing tips which give it a 3-ft. shorter wing span than Zeke; 2) engine cowling has smaller diameter; 3) airscoop is atop cowling instead of below like Zeke's; 4) it has shorter ailerons; and 5) has a new engine with 100 more h.p.

Hap is widely used in the South and Southwest Pacific both as a land-based and carrier-based plane. Like many Jap planes it is light with no pilot armor or self-sealing gas tanks. Its low wing loading gives it great maneuverability. The use of square wing tips might possibly be a production expediency.

Hap's all-around flying abilities are greater than Zeke's. Her maximum speed is 350 m.p.h. at 17,000 compared to Zeke's 328 at 16,000 ft.; however their rates of climb are about equal.

RECOGNITION: Square wing tips which might easily lead to mistaking Hap for a Grumman plane. The wings are evenly tapered. It has same fuselage appearance as Zeke with a high-set cockpit enclosure. Wings have pronounced dihedral, with the greater taper on trailing edge.

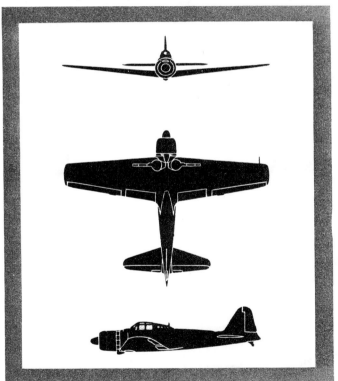

HAP'S LANDING GEAR retracts inward towards the fuselage of the plane; tail wheel also retracts. The plane's span is 36 ft. 6 in.; its length is 29 ft. 8 in.

HUMPBACK COCKPIT enclosure is typical of Zero models. Note the stubby radio mast projecting aft of the greenhouse.

FIGURE EIGHT PATTERN of a model of Rufe in flight gives a clear idea of what the plane looks like in various attitudes of flight. For a float plane Rufe is remarkably fast (279 m.p.h.) and has high maneuverability. Rufe may occasionally carry small bombs under her wings.

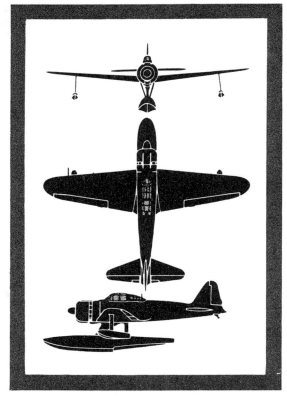

RUFE

JAP FLOAT FIGHTER IS EFFECTIVE

The third Zero used by the Japanese is a single-engine float plane known as Rufe. Rufe is basically the same plane as Zeke with the addition of a single float. Rufe can operate from seaplane tenders or from island bases.

Many float Zeros are based at Rekata Bay in the Solomons area and around the Shortlands just below Bougainville. They have been used largely as defensive fighters rising to combat only when their bases or near-by concentrations have been attacked. Ordinarily their function is reconnaissance work close to their base of operations. They prey on lone U. S. patrol planes. Rufe has also been reported in the Aleutian theater.

In combat Rufe is very maneuverable and is considered to be an excellent float fighter. It has fired explosive 20-mm. shells which indicates that the armament is probably the same as Zeke's: two 7.7-mm. machine guns mounted in the fuselage and two 20-mm. guns in the wings.

RECOGNITION: Prime recognition feature is long single float under the fuselage attached by two large faired struts. Almost one third of the float extends beyond nose. Plane's fuselage has the same general outlines as Zeke's. There are two small outboard stabilizing floats, each fitted to the wings by faired struts.

RUFE'S CLEAN LINES show clearly in head-on view of model. Note that cockpit projects from fuselage almost as high as tail.

PLAN VIEW OF RUFE shows great forward thrust of the single float Rufe uses a Nakajima 14-cylinder, air-cooled, radial engine with 955 horsepower.

ZEKE IS TRIM, clean-lined plane with a service ceiling of 38,500 ft. The rounded wing tips unhinge 2 ft. from end, fold up for stowage aboard carrier.

ZEKE'S SPEED is 328 m. p. h. at 16,000. Flying high cover for bombers it sometimes flies well above, does wing-overs and loops.

ZEKE

ONE OF JAPAN'S BEST FIGHTERS

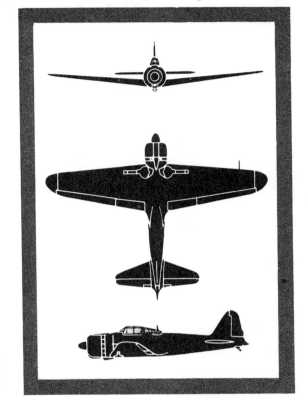

One of the most widely used Jap planes is Zeke, a carrier-borne Zero, Mark 1. Because it has been used in all combat areas in the Pacific theater of war it is one of the best known planes in the Japanese arsenal. This single engine, low-wing monoplane has been encountered in numbers on all Pacific fronts, is noted as a fast, highly maneuverable fighter. It has a metal skin with smooth flush riveting which gives it a clean appearance.

The pictures of Zeke on this page were made in the U. S. when a crashed plane, captured in the Alaskan campaign, although severely damaged, was restored and flight-tested by the Navy. When operating from carriers, Japanese dive and torpedo bombers are usually provided with strong cover of Zeke fighters. A sharp lookout for Zeke should be kept by carrier pilots and anti-aircraft crews, also by land-based pilots in the South Pacific and Aleutians.

RECOGNITION: Wings have a pronounced dihedral and moderate taper. Fuselage is oval-shaped, tapers to cone. Landing gear and tail wheel retract. High-set transparent cockpit enclosure. Fin and rudder have round top, pronounced taper on leading edge, slight taper on trailing edge. Zeke has round nose with medium large spinner. Air scoops for oil cooler, carburetor show below cowling.

LAST SUMMER, flown by a U. S. Navy pilot, Zeke crossed the country from California to Anacostia without once being reported by a plane spotter. Although the plane did wear a white star for safety's sake, its unusual shape should have made it an easy "spot" for alert observers.

OSCAR

THIS PLANE HAS FOUGHT IN
BURMA, CHINA AND PACIFIC

One of the most widely used Japanese fighter planes is Oscar, known as the Type 1. Oscar's fighting experience has been widespread over all theaters in the Pacific and Asiatic areas. It is slower than the later Japanese types, having a maximum speed of 317 m.p.h. at 16,000 ft.

It is believed that there might be a later version of Oscar in operation fitted with a two-speed supercharger which might increase the maximum speed to about 350 m.p.h. at 20,000 ft.

A new version of Oscar has a more powerful engine and has Fowler-type flaps which increase wing area making the plane more maneuverable. It is the first known Japanese fighter on which an attempt has been made to use self-sealing gas tanks. The attempt, however, has not been a success since it is not effective against .50-cal. bullets. Oscar should be watched for by fighters and bombers and, since it might be used for ground attacks, by anti-aircraft crews.

RECOGNITION: Oscar is a single engine, low-wing monoplane. It has a 14-cylinder, twin row, air-cooled, radial power plant. The wing's leading edges are straight, the trailing edges are tapered and tips rounded. Oscar's cockpit enclosure is high-set, transparent. Fin is large with straight leading edge and rounded top; rudder is rounded and extends to bottom of fuselage. Elevators have V-shaped cut-out for rudder movement. Landing gear is retractable.

FROM ONI 232—JAPANESE MILITARY AIRCRAFT

OSCAR'S SLENDER FUSELAGE ENDS FLUSH WITH THE RUDDER.   NOTE THE CHARACTERISTIC HIGH-SET, SLAB-SIDED COCKPIT ENCLOSURE

NATE IS SLOW BUT IS HIGHLY MANEUVERABLE AIRPLANE AND HAS A VERY GOOD RATE OF CLIMB. IT CAN CLIMB TO 20,000 FT. IN 7.4 MINUTES

NATE

FIRST USED IN 1937, NATE

IS STILL ON LIMITED DUTY

Nate is one of Japan's oldest fighter models, was introduced in 1937. Since then it has seen much service as a fighter and ground attack plane in China, Burma and the Pacific.

For a fighter it is slow, making only a maximum speed of 284 m.p.h. at 13,000. It has no armor and carries its gas tanks in the wing roots. It sometimes carries jettisonable tanks attached to the wings. These tanks are half-egg shaped. Although Nate is an old plane it is considered to be highly maneuverable and easy to fly. Like many Jap planes it usually carries no radio but sometimes has a two-way radio telephone.

RECOGNITION: Nate is single engine, low-wing monoplane. Wings have straight taper to rounded tips and large wing-root fillets. Note that some models have open cockpit, others have closed cockpit. Fin is large with straight leading edge, rudder has curved trailing edge. The landing gear is fixed, has a single strut and wheel spats.

NATE, IN HEAD-ON VIEW, LOOKS A LITTLE LIKE THE DIVE BOMBER, VAL

THE COCKPIT IS HIGH, HAS TRANSPARENT FAIRING BEHIND PILOT

VAL 1 & 2

JAP DIVE BOMBERS ATTACK

TARGET AT SHALLOW ANGLES

The dive bomber, latest addition to Jap plane types, was first adopted by the Japanese after the German successes in Poland and The Netherlands. Val, Mark 1, the first Jap dive bomber, was used in the attack on Pearl Harbor.

Val is an effective but not exceptional plane. It is used in rather shallow dives, 50 degrees being the customary angle. Short dives of 70 degrees are possible but are not usually attempted.

Nine, 18 or 27 Vals may attack at once, coming in at 18,000 ft. and gliding to a push-over at 6,000. Pilots push the attack home with determination; they will even crash the plane into the target to make a hit. They like to come in from up-sun, from direction of lowest visibility, or in line of weakest anti-aircraft fire. The bridge or the central anti-aircraft fire director is the favorite target.

RECOGNITION: Val has fixed landing gear with large faired struts and wheel spats, is a single engine, low-wing monoplane. Greenhouse stands out prominently centered over wing. Wings are elliptical with sharply rounded tips. Fin has long fairing extended well forward on the fuselage.

Val Mark 2 (*see below, right*) is a new model of Val. It has a more powerful engine and a longer cockpit enclosure faired smoothly into the fuselage. A large spinner has been added to the plane's nose. The vertical tail surfaces, which are not so broad fore and aft as those of Val 1, resemble stack of wheat straw.

CRIPPLED VAL plunges in flames toward the sea. Elliptical wing and tailplane and slender landing gear help identify Val in the view above.

EVEN IN BLURRED OUTLINE, long fairing on fin, greenhouse and dive brakes make Val easily recognizable. Its fin and rudder stand out.

VAL FLIES IN THREES or multiples of three, dives at less than 340 m. p. h. at intervals as low as 5 seconds. Like most Jap planes it is an ag-glomeration of features from other planes: fixed landing gear and pronounced dihedral from Stuka, fuselage shape from U. S. Navy planes.

VAL, MARK 2

SECOND VERSION of this Japanese dive bomber has improved performance, cleaner lines. Chief recognitional differences are streamlined cockpit and narrower rudder. Though Val 2 still has no armor or fuel tank protection, construction may be sturdier to stand steeper dives.

KATE'S LANDING GEAR FOLDS INWARD FLUSH WITH FUSELAGE

KATE

POTENT JAP WEAPON IS

THIS TORPEDO BOMBER

Torpedo bombing is the favorite Japanese form of attack on Allied shipping. The do-or-die nature of the attack and the devastation caused by successful torpedo runs have a great appeal to the Japanese spirit. The long, hard training of the pilots who fly these planes has paid off heavily as the Pearl Harbor wreckage will testify. Land-based medium bombers are often used, but the only operational carrier-based torpedo plane is Kate.

RECOGNITION: Kate was developed from our TBD which it very much resembles. Snap recognition is difficult, so close attention must be paid to points of difference. Kate's wings taper on both edges; the TBD has a straight leading edge with a slight projection close to the fuselage. TBD's greenhouse fairs into fuselage; Kate's has straight upper surface. Trailing edge of TBD rudder has a full curve.

JAPANESE TORPEDO PLANES COME IN FAST AND LOW FOLLOWING FIGHTER OR

KATE MAY APPROACH SHIP PARALLEL TO LINE OF BEARING, TURN SHARPLY

DIVE-BOMBING ATTACKS, DROP THEIR "FISH" FROM 50 TO 250 FT.

WHEN ABREAST OF SHIP. TORPEDO IS SLUNG BELOW FUSELAGE

JAKE, PHOTOGRAPHED AT KISKA, IS NEW JAP DIVE BOMBER ON FLOATS

JAKE

FLOAT DIVE BOMBER SEEN

IN ENTIRE PACIFIC AREA

Jake was originally thought to be a float version of Val, the standard Jap dive bomber. Recent photographs have shown it to be a different plane. Jake carries a bomb load of about 480 lb.—two 140-lb. bombs being carried in the bomb bay, and two 100-lb. bombs on outboard racks.

RECOGNITION: The confusion between Jake and Val becomes very understandable when pictures of the two planes are placed next to each other. They are very similar. Each has an elliptical wing, but the leading edge on Jake is somewhat straighter. The vertical tail surfaces are the same shape, but Val's rudder has a long, low fin fairing into the fuselage.

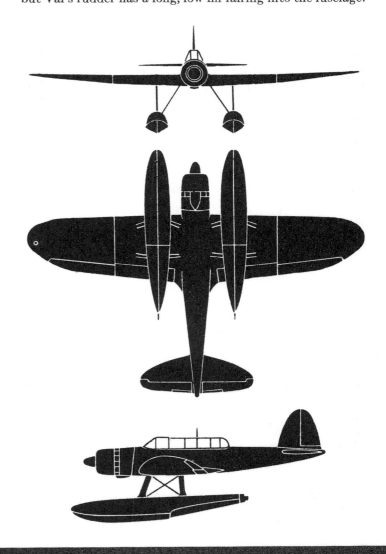

DAVE IS ARMED with three 7.7-mm. machine guns, two fixed and one flexible. For short runs it can carry up to 500 lb. of bombs though the usual bomb load is two 132-pounders. However, its guns are only protective armament; bombing is secondary to its reconnaissance work.

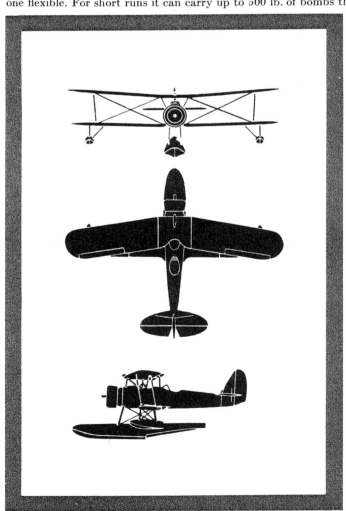

DAVE

THIS EARLY SCOUT PLANE HAS

MADE AN EXCELLENT RECORD

The reconnaissance system of the Japanese Naval Air Force is second only to its torpedo bombing in efficiency. With patrol planes flying in patterns from a long string of bases from the Empire to New Guinea, their lines of supply are protected from surprise attacks by our surface craft and bombing squadrons.

As an offensive measure, the Japanese have developed great skill in ship shadowing. When Allied shipping is discovered by the land-based planes or by Jap submarines, a shadow plane is sent out to follow the ship just out of visual range, the plane being able to follow the ship by its smoke or wake. Thus the reconnaissance plane can maintain a report on the ship's position until the bombers can attack. As the bombers approach, the "shadow" often makes a real or simulated bombing run on the ship to distract AA fire from the real attack which is forming in another direction.

Dave is one of the older scouts in the Jap Air Fleet. It is becoming obsolete and Pete (*see opposite*) is replacing it. It is still active enough, however, to warrant recognitional attention.

RECOGNITION: The swept-back upper wing, the prominent nose cowling and the N-struts between the wings will help identify Dave. Engine cowling is short, not faired into fuselage. Dave is launched from a warship catapult so it may be found in entire Western Pacific area.

CLEAN LINES and elimination of some external struts are made possible by Pete's stressed-skin construction. This makes it easy to distinguish from Dave or such other operational biplanes as the British Albacore. Dave and Pete are Japan's chief operational single-float biplanes.

PETE

NEW SINGLE-FLOAT BIPLANE

HUNTS DOWN ALLIED SHIPS

The Japanese Navy has based a great deal of its air strategy on the use of warship and tender-based float planes. Before they built any carriers, catapults were installed on their larger warships and a number of cargo ships were converted to use as seaplane tenders. Though float planes like Pete and Dave (*opposite*) have a limited range, they are given great strategic mobility by the range of their ship bases. In this regard, the Japanese fondness for diminutive ingenious devices has found expression in two small float planes, Slim and Glen, which are believed to be based on submarines.

It is expected that Pete will eventually replace Dave for this sort of naval reconnaissance. In its appearance and performance, it is a more modern airplane. Its lines are cleaner; fewer external struts are used, it is more powerful. These improvements are reflected in better performance. Pete is about 50 m.p.h. faster than Dave and has a ceiling of over 33,000 ft. as against 20,000 ft. for the older plane. Pete's climbing speed more than doubles that of Dave. The range of both is about the same.

RECOGNITION: Since few single-float biplanes are currently used by the Allies, Pete and Dave are easily spotted as enemies. Elliptical wings and cowling faired into barrel-type fuselage differentiate between them. Closer view shows single wing strut, heavy float strut.

NELL

DUAL-PURPOSE BOMBER

HAS TAKEN HEAVY TOLL

Nell is one of the planes known to the soldiers and Marines on Guadalcanal as Washing Machine Charlie. Every night on schedule it made nuisance raids on Henderson Field, dropped bombs. Early in the Malayan campaign, Nell did its greatest service to our enemies when it destroyed the British warships Prince of Wales and Repulse in an intense high-level and torpedo bombing attack.

Though Nell is reported to have been developed from the Ju-86, there is little resemblance aside from the angular outlines favored by the Junkers' designers. This is in line with other Japanese imitations. They have not blindly copied a foreign operational type but have improved and adapted the plane to their tactics.

By European and American standards, Nell does not have very high performance. Its top speed of 230 m.p.h. is well below our best medium bombers. It has a service ceiling of 24,800 ft. and a maximum bomb load of 2,200 lb. or one 1,760-lb. torpedo. It has two fixed 7.7-mm. machine guns in the nose, three in single mounts in top and side blisters, one in both the tail and the belly. A 20-mm. cannon is mounted in the top turret.

RECOGNITION: Nell has several marked features of recognition. Most prominent of these is the upper surface of the fuselage which is broken by a round astrodome and hump-shaped gun blister. Unlike other Jap medium bombers, Nell has staggered side blisters. The lower surface of the fuselage is broken just aft of the trailing edge to form a slight step. This might cause confusion with the Martin Baltimore but the likeness is otherwise meager. The wheels are retractable into the engine nacelles but are not completely enclosed. Both the main and tailplanes, as well as the twin fin and rudder, are very angular in appearance. The greatest taper is on the wing trailing edge.

NELL, like most of the Japanese bombing planes, usually appears in flights of three or multiples of three. They hold to a close formation over the target, both to form a tight bomb pattern and to assure that the enlisted pilots can see the flight leader's signals. Only the leader knows the full flight plan.

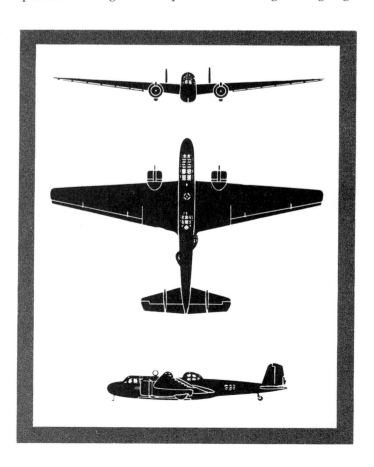

INTERMEDIATE STAGE OF SALLY, MARK 1, HAS ONE STINGER MACHINE GUN IN THE TAIL. IN SALLY, MARK 2, A TOP TURRET HAS BEEN ADDED.

SALLY

NEW LAND-BASED

BOMBER IS ACTIVE

IN BURMA, CHINA

Japanese bombing squadrons are now being augmented by new models of this fast medium bomber. All are generally similar to the planes shown on these pages but continual improvements are being made in performance and armament.

Sally, Mark 1, is still the chief operational type, but the Mark 2 is appearing in sufficient numbers to make it a highly important plane. The Mark 2 is slightly larger than the Mark 1, is 40 m.p.h. faster, and has about 6,000 ft. additional ceiling. A turret mounting a 12.7-mm. gun has been added at the rear end of the greenhouse. This gun replaces two of the plane's normal complement of seven 7.7-mm. guns. The Mark 2 has a stinger in the tail.

RECOGNITION: Sally has a superficial resemblance to the Douglas A-20, but can be differentiated from it by the tail structure. Sally is also somewhat larger and much slower. Elliptical wing tips give both the main and tailplanes a very clean appearance. The most pronounced taper is on the trailing edge of the wing and leading edge of the tailplane. Dihedral starts close to wing root.

HIGH-LEVEL BOMBING is considered by the Japanese to be the least effective sort of attack. Hence, bombers like Sally are also used in torpedo runs.

LILY

ARMY BOMBER APPEARS IN CHINA AND BURMA

This medium bomber has been known to exist for some time, but it has seen little combat until recent operations in China and Burma. It is used as a medium bomber and a reconnaissance plane. Lily has been compared with the Martin Baltimore and British Blenheim bombers. The differences between Lily and these planes should be studied carefully.

RECOGNITION: Though the resemblance between Lily and the A-30, or Baltimore, at first seems quite marked; the differences are equally prominent. Both planes have transparent noses and prominent bomb bays but Lily's engine nacelles are small and underslung, the A-30's large and centrally mounted. Lily's fuselage is almost round; the A-30, deep and narrow. Sharp taper on the stabilizer's leading edge and large fillets on wing distinguish Lily.

SIDE VIEW of the plane shows clearly the deep-bellied bomb bay which extends well beyond the end of the cockpit enclosure.

GLASS ENCLOSURE for bombardier projects beyond engine nacelles. Greenhouse is separated type with solid section between pilot's seat and top turret.

CHARACTERISTIC STEP in bottom of fuselage holds machine gun for protection against attacks from below. 1,500-lb. bomb load is carried in bomb bay.

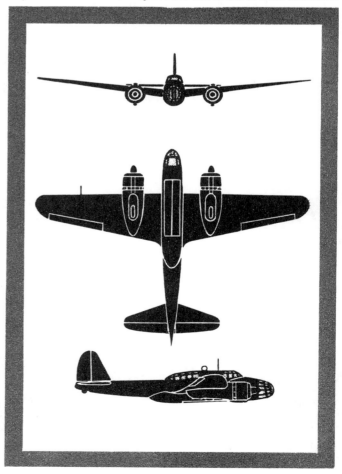

BETTY IS SHORE-BASED Naval plane used for much Jap high-level and torpedo bombing in the Southwest Pacific. It usually appears in flights of nine or 27 planes. The plane above was shot down when the pilot tried to suicide crash his damaged plane into one of our carriers.

BETTY

HAS FIRST ATTEMPT AT ARMOR

In Betty, fast medium high-level and torpedo bomber, the Japanese are now incorporating light armor for the tail gunner and rubber shields for the fuel tanks. Both are relatively ineffective but indicate a break with the Jap idea that all planes and men are expendable.

RECOGNITION: Betty has a unique cigar-shaped fuselage with glass enclosures at both ends. The tail surfaces look light against the bulk of the fuselage. Gun blisters are built at the rear of the greenhouse and on the sides just aft of the trailing edge of the wing. Both the main and tailplane are double-tapered, have smoothly rounded tips.

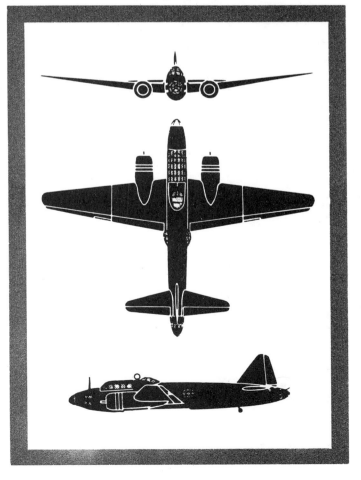

ROUNDED TRIANGULAR FIN rides high on the fuselage. Wheel is forward of tail assembly. Note indentation under fuselage which is open bomb bay.

45

DINAH'S GREENHOUSE IS LONG, EXTENDS HALF THE LENGTH OF FUSELAGE. DINAH CARRIES TWO MEN ON SCOUTING AND BOMBING MISSIONS

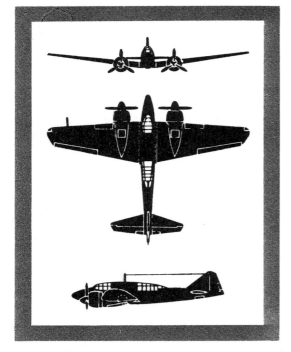

DINAH

TWO-PLACE ARMY RECON PLANE

Dinah, a two-engine, low-wing monoplane, is used for photographic reconnaissance missions and can be used as a fighter. Though designed primarily to do special reconnaissance work it is quite likely that Dinah is capable of other jobs. Specifically, it might be equipped for bombing missions or for ground attacks against troops.

Dinah may carry one 20-mm. cannon and two 7.7-mm. machine guns in fuselage, firing forward. Two more 7.7-mm. machine guns may be located in cockpit. Dinah's engines are probably 14-cylinder, air-cooled radials which produce assumed horsepower of 1,060.

The plane has good speed at high altitude (324 m.p.h. at 17,000 ft.) and good rate of climb (3.2 minutes to 10,000 ft.) for a reconnaissance plane. It is believed that Dinah may also be the fighter known as Type 45, Nick.

RECOGNITION: A twin engine, low wing monoplane with deep, narrow fuselage, sharply pointed nose. Wings taper sharply, taper is more pronounced on trailing edge. Wing tips are rounded. Single fin and rudder with angular top. Leading edge of the fin is sloped. Retractable landing gear and tail wheel.

DINAH RESEMBLES Germany's Me-110 except for the single fin and rudder. It carries no armor, has no self-sealing gas tanks. The sketches of Dinah on this page were made from combat reports, therefore they differ in detail. A Jap prisoner recognized them immediately as Dinah.

MAZE OF STRUTS SUPPORTING THE PARASOL WING AND BOTH TAIL SURFACES QUICKLY IDENTIFY MAVIS. NOTE ALSO FIXED WING FLOATS

MAVIS

TOP JAPANESE

PATROL PLANE

Mavis, Japan's biggest airplane and its chief four-motored plane currently operational, can fly over 5,000 miles when equipped with auxiliary fuel tanks and carrying no bomb load. This flying boat is in wide use and should be looked for over all western Pacific waters as well as in the Aleutians. Since it can be refueled from a mother ship, it can range the entire Pacific Ocean. After Dec. 7,

Mavis was frequently seen near Midway.

Mavis has also been used as a horizontal and torpedo bomber and at least once attacked one of our patrol planes. The plane carries a maximum bomb load of 3,300 lb. or two 1,760-lb. torpedoes.

RECOGNITION: The external bracing on the very long wing is an obvious telltale. The centrally located wing floats and small vertical tail surfaces also help.

TAIL TURRET AND TOP TURRET just forward of tail guard against rear attacks. Plan view (*left*) shows long straight wing, tailplane center section.

For answers see p. 50

QUIZ NO. 4: BATTLESHIPS, THE WAR'S HEAVIEST WEAPONS

For answers see p. 50

NEWS & MISCELLANY

COMMUNICATIONS

Comments relative to recognition materi-al contained in the Journal *will be pub-lished if of general interest. Inquiries as to materials, sources, methods, etc. will be accepted. Such communications should* *be addressed to the Recognition Sub-Sec-tion of Gunnery Training, Bureau of Aer-onautics, Navy Department, Washing-ton, D. C., and should be signed with the name, title and activity of the writer.*

NEWS

According to the latest information available the enemy aircraft likely to be encountered over the United Kingdom are as follows:

PROBABLE	POSSIBLE	UNLIKELY
Ju-88	Do-17	Ju-52
Do-217	He-177	He-115
He-111	Ju-86	Do-18
Me-410	Me-110	FW-200
FW-190		Do-24
Me-109G		BV-138

In flying over continental Europe other planes may be encountered and new planes should al-ways be expected.

Halifaxes may now be seen with three dif-ferent types of noses. The first modification, Halifax II, has the nose turret removed and the lines curved down from the pilot's wind-screen to the bomb aimer's position. The sec-ond modification has a remodelled nose some-what similar to that of the Hampden and mounts a single hand-operated 4-gun dorsal turret Vickers machine gun.

The Spitfire V may now be seen with square clipped wings which reduce the span from 36′ 10″ to 32′ 2″ and increase the maneuvera-bility.

Minor changes may be noted in the Port-land Class (U.S.-CA). The mainmast has been changed from stick to tripod and moved just forward of the afterstack.

The Japanese destroyer class hitherto listed as Jap-Un-One (*see ONI 41-42*) is now prop-erly titled the Teratsuki Class.

The French aircraft carrier, Bearn CVI, has a very distinctive appearance for an island type aircraft carrier. From the air it has a wide flight deck with narrower, tapering bow and stern extensions. The taper to the stern end of the deck is unusually sharp. Sections of the deck fold up when raising or lowering aircraft to hangar spaces.

SOURCE MATERIAL

Official list of recognition publications in use by the U. S. Navy:

Joint Army-Navy Pictorial Manual
Recognition Instructor's Handbook

SPECIAL DEVICES

Device 51-11a—Recognition Posters

ONI—(RESTRICTED PUBLICATIONS)

201	British Naval Vessels
54-R	U. S. Naval Ships and Aircraft
203	French Naval Vessels
220-M	Axis Submarine Manual
249	Japanese Aircraft Manual
204	German Naval Vessels
41–42	Japanese Naval Vessels
223	Ship Shapes—Anatomy and Types of Naval Vessels
206	Warships of the Minor European Navies
202	Italian Naval Vessels
222	Statistical Data on Navies
223-K	Warships in Code
209	Confidential—July 5, 1943
225-J	Japanese Landing Operations

ONI CHARTS

A-1-43	U. S. Army Aircraft
B-1-43	British Aircraft
I-1-43	Italian Aircraft
J-1-43	Japanese Aircraft
N-1-43	U. S. Navy Aircraft
G-1-43	German Aircraft
GF-1-43	Minor German Aircraft and French Aircraft under German control

Photo File No. 1—U. S. Naval Vessels

Photo File No. 2—Japanese Naval Vessels

Pictorial Manual, Instructor's Handbook and Special Devices posters may be ob-tained only through regular channels ad-dressed to the Chief of the Bureau of Aero-nautics. ONI publications may be requested from the Office of Naval Intelligence, Mail and Despatch Section, Navy Department, Washington, D. C.

TEACHING AIDS

Many variations of teaching procedures are found at different Naval activities through-out the country in connection with Recogni-tion Training. Many of these are suitable only to local conditions but such novel meth-ods of presenting subject matter help to "pep up" the instructional program.

NAS, Jacksonville, in practicing knowl-edge of ship recognition, places models on a blue painted table in a room around which is a balcony. Students then view this table from the balcony, thus getting a simulated long-range aerial view of an ocean scene. Another technique is to hang models on wires so con-trolled by pulleys so that the plane may be moved into view at a fairly rapid rate and in flight positions. A similar method is used at the Gunnery School at Yellow Water.

NAS, Corpus Christi, Texas, reports that wide use is made of ballopticans equipped with flashmeters so that new material not yet used in slides can not only be projected but also can be used in connection with other flash material. In order to solve the problem of using a projector and a blackboard in the same room at the same time, they have set up a system of screened lights so that their blackboards are illuminated while the re-mainder of the room is in sufficient darkness for projection.

NOTE: on opposite cover are two Soviet planes to be added to the already issued *Joint Army-Navy Pictorial Manual*. This page, and subsequent addi-tions, are to be cut along dotted lines and inserted in the *Manual*. Three black dots mark the point of perforations.

QUIZ ANSWERS

QUIZ NO. 1

1. Halifax
2. Lancaster
3. Mitchell
4. Sunderland
5. Do-24
6. Wellington II
7. Battle
8. Halifax
9. Boeing 247D
10. Me-109E
11. Stirling
12. Hurricane
13. AT-6A
14. Moth Minor
15. Lancaster
16. Me-108 "TAIFUN"
17. Anson
18. Condor
19. Ju-88
20. Harrow
21. Ju-52
22. Airacobra
23. GAC Monospar
24. Spitfire
25. Whitley
26. Fairchild 28W
27. Battle
28. AT-6A
29. P-51
30. AT-6A
31. Master II
32. Me-109
33. Me-109E
34. Wellington II
35. Wellington
36. F4F
37. Battle
38. Liberator
39. Audax
40. A-20
41. Battle
42. Hurricane
43. Master II
44. Airacobra
45. P-40
46. Airacobra
47. AT-6A
48. A-20
49. AT-6A
50. F4F
51. Master II
52. A-20
53. Battle
54. F4F
55. Me-109
56. Master
57. Beaufighter
58. P-51
59. Liberator
60. P-51
61. AT-6
62. F4F
63. P-51

QUIZ NO. 2

1. Me-109
2. Thunderbolt
3. Barracuda
4. Lightning
5. Typhoon
6. Hurricane
7. Zero
8. Ju-88
9. Nate
10. Mosca
11. Ju-88
12. Hurricane
13. Spitfire
14. Mustang
15. Rufe
16. Corsair
17. Macchi 202
18. Mustang
19. Warhawk
20. Airacobra
21. Wildcat
22. Fiat G-50
23. Focke-Wulf 190
24. Beaufighter

QUIZ NO. 3

1. Coronado
2. SM-79
3. Marauder
4. Nell
5. Mosquito
6. Beaufort
7. Halifax
8. Stirling
9. Mariner
10. Cant Z-1007 bis (Modified)
11. Mitchell
12. Sally
13. Commando
14. He-111
15. Skymaster
16. Liberator
17. Lancaster
18. Ju-52

QUIZ NO. 4

1. King George Class
2. Tennessee Class
3. Gneisenau—Germany
4. Iowa Class
5. Tirpitz—Germany
6. New York Class
7. Richelieu—France
8. Kongo Class
9. South Dakota Class
10. Iowa Class

IL-2 "STORMOVIK"

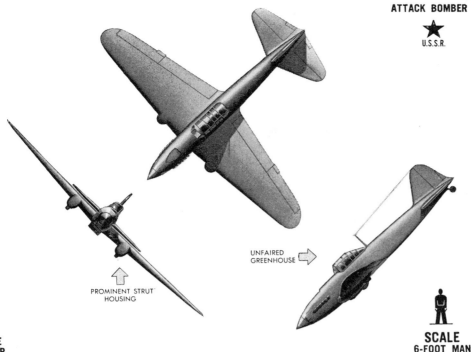

PROMINENT STRUT HOUSING

UNFAIRED GREENHOUSE ⇨

SCALE
6-FOOT MAN

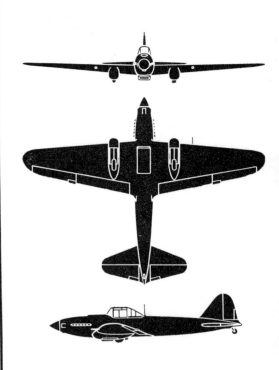

**STATE
U.S.S.R.**

DISTINGUISHING FEATURES: Single inline engine, low-wing monoplane. Wing has pronounced taper and trailing edge fairs into fuselage. Prominent fairings for landing gear beneath wings. Fuselage has rather long nose and pointed spinner. Radiator beneath fuselage. Cockpit canopy sits on top of fuselage. Fin and rudder have rounded top. Diamond-shaped tail plane with round tips.

INTEREST: The Stormovik is said to be so heavily armored for strafing work, that light cannon fire has small effect on its sides. It is in its element when flying low, attacking German tank and mechanized columns.

The engine cowling is composed of steel plate 6- to 8-mm. in thickness. Even parts of the plane which are the least vulnerable have protecting armor of 4-mm. thickness. With a phenomenal armament of two 20- or 37-mm. cannon, plus machine guns, the plane is designed especially to be a "flying anti-tank battery." Two improved versions of the Stormovik, the IL-3 and the IL-4, have recently been reported.

SPAN: 47 ft. 11 in.
LENGTH: 38 ft.
MAX. SPEED: 275 m. p. h. at 8,000 ft.
SERVICE CEILING: 28,000 ft.

RESTRICTED

"I-16" & "I-16C"

⇦ LARGE FILLET

SHORT, STUBBY FUSELAGE

SCALE
6-FOOT MAN

**STATE
U.S.S.R.**

DISTINGUISHING FEATURES: Single radial engine, low-wing monoplane. Trailing edge tapers to rounded tip. Wing fillets extend deeply back toward tail. Fuselage very short and stubby with large circular nose. Small cockpit set well back with head fairing extending to fin. Rudder has round trailing edge. Stabilizer has leading edge tapered forward. Elevators have cut-out in center.

INTEREST: This monoplane received a thorough testing in the Spanish Civil War, when it was extensively used. As a fighter it has been handicapped in maneuverability due to high wing loading. As used in Spain, the I-16 has a curved armor plate of 7-mm. thickness, which protected the back and head of the pilot. This plane, although becoming obsolete, is still being used in quantity as a fighter and advanced trainer. The current model, the I-16C or "Super Rata," is equipped with a 1,000-hp. engine. The older I-16 is sometimes called the "Rata" or "Mosca".

SPAN: 29 ft. 2 in.
LENGTH: 20 ft. 4 in.
APPROX. SPEED: 300 m. p. h. at 15,000 ft.
SERVICE CEILING: 32,000 ft.

RESTRICTED

 A

 C

 B

 D

STORMOVIK, Russia's "flying anti-tank battery" is designed and armored to sweep low over enemy tank columns and troops. Nazis call this highly successful plane "Black Death," try to ward off its low level attacks with flame throwers and thermite guns.

RATA, known also as Mosca, is one of Russia's older fighters. It was first used in the Spanish Civil War and is rapidly becoming obsolete though still used as both a fighting plane and advanced trainer. Successive models have stepped up power, speed and armament.

 A

 C

 B

 D

U. S. ARMY-NAVY JOURNAL OF
RECOGNITION

OCTOBER, 1943
NUMBER 2

QUIZ NO. 1: FORMATIONS

(For answers see p. 50)

1

2

3

4

5

6

7

8

9

10

11

12

13

U. S. ARMY - NAVY JOURNAL OF
RECOGNITION

OCTOBER, 1943

PUBLISHED BY THE DEPUTY CHIEF OF NAVAL OPERATIONS (AIR)
COPYRIGHT 1943 BY LT. GEORGE H. FORSYTH JR.

NUMBER 2

FROM THE GROUND UP

By PETER G. MASEFIELD

"We ask only one question, 'Is it in range?'"—such is a true quotation and was a fair definition of the mental attitude of many air and ground gunners towards any aircraft they might see, at least during the early days of the war. The result of such an attitude has been, on the one hand the loss of many aircraft shot down by their technical "friends" and, even

Youngest and brightest of England's aeronautical experts, Peter Masefield has the advantage of a top-drawer English education (Westminster, Switzerland, Cambridge), plus much practical experience as a pilot, designer, technical editor, war correspondent. A pioneer in recognition work, he is now devoting all his time to the problem as chairman of the editorial committee of our British counterpart, Aircraft Recognition.

more important, the loss of many lives which could be ill-spared and, on the other hand, the escape of many enemy aircraft which, for want of exact knowledge on their type and characteristics, were not even shot at, still less "shot up" or shot down.

In fact this business of aircraft recognition—call it an art or a science, or more properly a combination of both—is a good deal more important to the united war effort than appears at first sight or has hitherto been generally appreciated. Aircraft recognition is a subject which can be deadly dull—or fascinatingly interesting, depending on the mental approach.

In Great Britain we have had to learn our aircraft recognition the hard way—from bitter experience. Official records now show that almost without exception every type of combat or training airplane in the R. A. F. has been shot at, up or down by British gunners.

Civilians Began Britain's Program

Silhouettes and photographs of the various aircraft hardly existed in those early days. Somewhat naturally the aeronautical technical press of Great Britain was in a position to understand the problems and produce the material more rapidly and comprehensively than any other means at that time. Thus most of the early work on aircraft recognition was done privately, standards set and problems of presentation and training hammered out by a band of aircraft enthusiasts who sought nothing from it but the satisfaction of an important job well done.

During the Battle of Britain and the night bombing which followed it, the Observer Corps, a civilian volunteer group working in co-operation with the radar system, did magnificent work in plotting raids so that the comparatively small fighter force of the R. A. F. could be used to the maximum effect.

In the beginning enough R. A. F. planes were shot down over England to pose a serious problem. The loss of airplanes in these circumstances from a none-too-plentiful production, combined with the tragically heavy loss of life, especially impressed Lord Beaverbrook, then Minister of Aircraft Production, with the need for improved training in Aircraft Recognition. Accordingly, the Director General of Aircraft Distribution, Mr. Eric Bowater, was instructed to set up a department within the Ministry to prepare all the necessary training and reference material on an official basis and to co-operate closely with the Services in meeting the needs. At the same time an Inter-Services Aircraft Recognition Committee was formed to discuss training methods and requirements and an advisory panel, including members of the technical aeronautical press, was set up.

And so things progressed, at first slowly and with great difficulty but later with increasing efficiency as the Aircraft Recognition Branch at M. A. P. got under way under Commander H. B. Wyn-Evans. Draftsmen were enrolled to prepare silhouettes and a Hampden and a photographer were obtained to provide adequate photographs of such British, American and captured enemy aircraft as were available. Added to this an Army film unit began to specialize in training films on the subject and in September 1942 there appeared the first issue of the British *Aircraft Recognition (Inter-Services Journal)*.

So much for the generalized story of the build-up of aircraft recognition in Great Britain. Much has been done. Much more remains to be done. Aircraft recognition is not a subject that can be drilled into students unless they are anxious to learn. In the past there has been much too much emphasis on such provedly unsatisfactory methods of training as the "WEFT" (Wings, Engines, Fuselage, Tail) and "WETFUR" (Wings, Engines, Tail, Fuselage, Undercarriage, Radiator) systems. There is only one way of attaining proficiency and that is by knowing each airplane as a conglomerate whole and not as a number of bits and pieces added together. In knowing the characteristic whole the bits and pieces must be assimilated. But piecemeal recognition is not only unsatisfactory but dangerous as well.

Teaching Must Have "Glamor"

In fact there is no short cut to recognition. But there is one golden rule in either teaching or learning the subject—"Make It Interesting." Background data is most important in building up for each airplane a living character and personality and removing from it the stigma of a dead silhouette or a featureless photograph with no past, present or future. In fact "glamor" is half the battle in getting it across. In practice each airplane has more vitality and personality in sight, sound, smell and handling qualities than any other man-made machine. Told in detail these features stamp themselves in the memory as a logical sequence instead of a series of unconnected and uninteresting facts, unwoven in the "WEFT."

Having absorbed the background which brings each type to life, with the silhouette as the skeleton, as many photographs as possible as the flesh on the bones and the detailed interest as the breath of living personality, flash training provides an excellent background for co-ordination of mind and memory, provided new and unfamiliar photographs are used each time.

Let us not forget that aircraft recognition is not just another subject to be swotted up and forgotten. It is a matter of life and death—yours and the other man's. In action prompt, precise and accurate recognition in a fraction of a second is the only sort that counts. Absolute familiarity with both hostile and friendly aircraft is the only standard. Fortunately acquiring the knowledge to reach that standard can be a process of absorbing interest when it is approached the right way.

CASABLANCA

NEWEST ESCORT CARRIERS
HAVE NEAR CRUISER LINES

IN HEAD-ON VIEW, Casablanca Class carriers are readily identified as American escort vessels by broad hull, small cantilever island on starboard.

TRANSOM STERN distinguishes the Casablanca from similar Bogue Class. Casablanca has single stern gun sponson, flight deck extended length of hull.

Since the beginning of the war the U. S. Navy has substantially increased its strength by the addition of several "baby" carriers for convoy escort duty and ferrying planes to the fronts (*See Journal, Sept. issue*). These ships were built on merchant or converted oiler hulls. Now a new baby carrier has been added to the list, a ship designed and laid down as a carrier and having the many advantages of integrated plans. This class, known as the Casablanca, is illustrated on these pages.

Being designed specifically as a carrier, the Casablanca has numerous improvements over the Bogue and Long Island classes. Because of her "baby" cruiser hull lines, the Casablanca lies lower in the water. She looks planned for her job, not adapted to it. Notice, for example, the uniform arrangement of her gun platforms. Her performance also reflects her purpose in somewhat increased speed and maneuverability.

RECOGNITION: The Casablanca is very similar to the Bogue Class carriers. Both of the flight decks are symmetrical, tapering slightly forward of the island, abruptly at the stern. The Casablanca's deck is somewhat longer than the Bogue's, extending the full length of the hull. On both, the island is built out over the sea on the starboard side. The Casablanca has a square "bobtail" cruiser, or transom, stern; the Bogue a rounded merchant-cruiser stern. The Casablanca has a single gun sponson on the stern, the Bogue has twin gun blisters. The hull lines on the Casablanca are perfectly straight; the Bogue follows merchant lines.

THE NEW CASABLANCA CLASS CARRIERS LIE LOW IN THE WATER, HAVE SLIM STRAIGHT LINES. WHEN SEEN AT A DISTANCE, SHE IS A LOW

SEEN FROM ABOVE, Casablanca has a symmetrical deck tapering forward and aft, with a fringe of gun mounts along either edge. Twin stacks project flush with deck on both sides amidships. Elevators (*down in above picture*) are inconspicuous when flush, are uncertain recognition features.

OLID MASS, SHOWING LIGHT FOR ONLY A SHORT DISTANCE UNDER HER FLIGHT DECK. GUN MOUNTS AND STACKS BLEND INTO THE HULL

GENERAL IMPRESSION OF THE HELLCAT IS STUBBY FUSELAGE, BOXY, SQUARED-OFF WINGS. THE PLANE'S ARMAMENT, ARMOR ARE STILL SECRET

HELLCAT

NEWEST DEADLY

NAVY FIGHTER IS

THE GRUMMAN F6F

Newest Navy fighter is Grumman's F6F, the Hellcat. Reported in its first action in the recent raid on Marcus Island in the Pacific, the F6F is said to have accounted for itself handily.

A descendant of the famed Wildcat F4F, the Hellcat was originally intended as a more powerful version of the earlier plane. However it became, through lessons learned in actual combat, a totally different aircraft. As it now stands the F6F is bigger, faster, heavier and in every way a better fighting weapon than the Wildcat.

RECOGNITION: F6F has a radial engine, is low mid-wing monoplane. Wing has equal taper and square tips. Inboard wing panels are horizontal, outboard panels have pronounced dihedral. Head-on the fuselage is egg-shaped; lower rim of cowling has prominent "mouth" which is intake for cooling and carburetor air. Cockpit is high, narrow, provides excellent visibility. Fin and rudder have bluntly rounded top, steep leading and trailing edges.

F6F'S WIDE TAILPLANE TAPERS ON LEADING EDGE, HAS ROUNDED TIPS

F6F'S "MOUTH" is visible in head-on view (*above*). The Hellcat is known as a "pilot's" plane because it flies easily and has great maneuverability.

The Hellcat is a land- and carrier-based plane. It is first U. S.-built aircraft ever to go into mass production before it was completely test-flown.

EMILY IS A HUGE NEW JAP SEAPLANE

A recent photographic reconnaissance flight over an enemy-held island in the South Pacific brought back pictures of a new Japanese plane. This huge, four-engine flying boat (*see below*) is known by the code name of Emily and is one of the largest planes in the Japanese air forces.

Mavis, the parasol-wing flying boat (*see Journal, Sept. issue*) has long been the standard Japanese long distance patrol plane; Emily may be a further development of this widely used type. Though reports indicate that it is only in operational use in limited numbers, it has already been seen by U. S. planes on reconnaissance over enemy territory. However, even though it appears that Emily has been mainly used well inside Jap-held areas, there are indications that it has made reconnaissance flights.

RECOGNITION: Complete identification characteristics of Emily are not yet available. From the plan view it is apparent that both edges of Emily's wings are tapered with the stronger taper on the trailing edge. Emily has a gull wing on which the four engines are set on two levels, extremely high single fin tail. The plane has a long nose which projects markedly beyond the leading edge of the wing. The hull has a sharp taper on the after end.

SIDE-VIEW shows bottom of the deep hull is stepped for hydroplaning. Silhouette below shows the Emily somewhat resembles U.S. Navy's PBM.

EMILY IS A HUGE AIRPLANE, HAS WING SPAN OF 118 FT., IS 91 FT. LONG

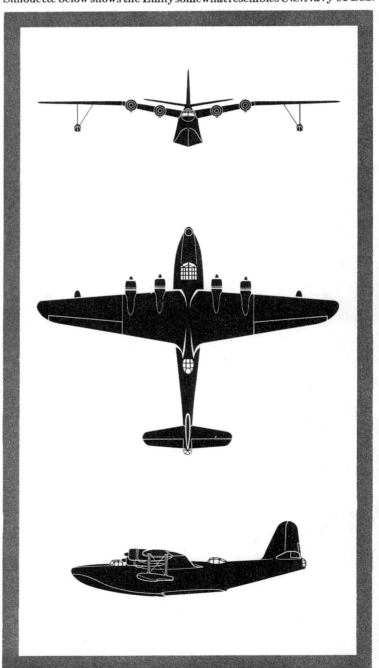

RECOGNITION TRAINING LIST

OCTOBER 1943

The following training list is basically the same as the U. S. Navy Recognition Training Operational List published by the Bureau of Personnel, Sept. 1. Changes effective since the Navy list was issued have been incorporated in this list, which has been verified by U. S. Army Air Forces and by the British R.A.F.

The aircraft in Class A are generally the most important. Those in Class B are important only in limited areas, are less important numerically than Class A or, though important numerically, are being gradually replaced. No attempt has been made to include those training planes not found in combat areas nor aircraft which are not numerically important.

Each plane is listed under the category of its widest use. For example, the Army's A-29 is called the PBO by the Navy, but since the A-29 is seen more frequently than the PBO, it is listed as the A-29. Instructors should make themselves acquainted with all the designations of each plane.

It is recommended that emphasis in training be placed on Class A and that all planes which do not appear in list A or B be eliminated from Recognition Training as no longer in use.

U. S. NAVY

CLASS "A"

Designation	Common Name
F4F	Wildcat
F6F	Hellcat
F4U	Corsair
SOC	
SO3C	Seagull
OS2U	Kingfisher
SBD	Dauntless
SB2C	Helldiver
TBF	Avenger
PBY-5 & 5A	Catalina
PV	Ventura

CLASS "B"

SNJ	Texan
J2F	Duck
PB2Y	Coronado
PBM-3C	Mariner

U. S. ARMY

CLASS "A"

Designation	Common Name
P-38	Lightning
P-39	Airacobra
P-40	Warhawk
P-47	Thunderbolt
P-51	Mustang
A-20	Boston (Havoc)
A-29	Hudson
A-30	Baltimore
A-31 (A-35)	Vengeance
B-17	Fortress
B-24	Liberator
B-25	Mitchell
B-26	Marauder
C-46	Commando
C-47	Skytrain
C-54	Skymaster
C-60	Lodestar

CLASS "B"

L-1	Vigilant
L-2	Taylorcraft Grasshopper
L-3	Aeronca Grasshopper
L-4	Piper Grasshopper
L-5	Sentinel
L-6	
CG4-A	

BRITISH—R.A.F.

CLASS "A"

Common Name

Spitfire
Hurricane
Typhoon
Mosquito
Beaufighter
Wellington
Lancaster
Halifax
Stirling
Sunderland
Beaufort
Blenheim

CLASS "B"

Whitley
Hampden
Whirlwind
Oxford
Master

AMERICAN AIRCRAFT USED BY R.A.F.

P-51	Mustang
A-20	Havoc (Boston)

A-29	Hudson
A-30	Baltimore
B-25	Mitchell
PV	Ventura
B-17	Fortress
B-24	Liberator
PBY-5	Catalina
B-26	Marauder

BRITISH FLEET AIR ARM

CLASS "A"

Common Name

Seafire
Swordfish
Barracuda

CLASS "B"

Fulmar
Albacore
Walrus
Seafox

OTHER AIRCRAFT USED BY FLEET AIR ARM

(ON U.S. NAVY AND R.A.F. LISTS)

F4F	Sea Hurricane
TBF	Martlet
F6F	Tarpon
F4U	Gannet (Hellcat)
SB2C	Corsair
	Helldiver

RUSSIAN

CLASS "A"

Designation	Common Name
Lagg 3	
IL-4	Stormovik
PE-2	
SB-3	
PE-2B (PE-3)	
DB-3F	
TB-7	
Yak-4 (BB-22)	

CLASS "B"

Yak-1 (I-26)
Mig 3 (I-18)
Su-2
ER-2
AR-2 (improved SB)
DB-3
GST (Catalina)
PS-84 (C-47)
I-16

AMERICAN AIRCRAFT USED BY RUSSIANS

(ON U.S. ARMY LIST)

P-39	Airacobra
P-40	Warhawk
A-20	Boston (Havoc)
B-25	Mitchell
P-51	Mustang

GERMAN

CLASS "A"

Designation	Common Name
Me-109F & G	
Me-110C, E & F	
Me-210 (410)	
FW-190A	
Ju-87B & D	Stuka
Ju-88A & C	
He-111H & K	
Do-217E (Do-217M)	
He-177	
Ju-52	

CLASS "B"

Ar-196	
BV-138	
BV-222	
Hs-129	
He-115	
FW-189	
Hs-126	
Fi-156	
Ju-90	
Ju-290	
Me-323	
Ju-86P	
FW-200K	Kurier
D.F.S. 230	
Go-244	

JAPANESE

CLASS "A"

Designation	Common Name
T-0 Mark 1	Zeke
T-0 Mark 1	Rufe
T-0 Mark 2	Hap
T-3	Tony
T-1	Oscar
T-100	Dinah
T-0	Pete
T-97	Kate
T-99	Val
T-99	Val, Mark 2
T-0	Jake
T-96	Nell
T-97	Sally
T-97	Sally, Mark 2
T-99	Lily
T-1	Betty
T-97	Mavis
Mc-20	Topsy

CLASS "B"

T-97	Nate
T-95	Dave
T-96	Slim
T-0	Glen
T-0	Helen
T-99	Cherry
T-2	Emily
T-97	Thora
T-1 (TK-3)	Teresa

ITALIAN

CLASS "A"

Designation	Common Name
Cr-42	Freccia (Arrow)
Mc-200	Saetta I (Lightning)
Mc-202 (205)	Saetta II (Lightning)
Re-2001	Falco II (Falcon)
Cant-Z1007 bis	Alcione (Kingfisher)
SM-79	Sparviero (Hawk)
SM-82	Canguru (Kangaroo)
SM-84	
Cant-Z506B	

CLASS "B"

G-50	Falco (Falcon)
Re-2000	Falco I (Falcon)
Ro-37 bis	
Ca-311 and Ca-312 bis	
P-108	
Br-20M	Cicogna (Stork)
Cant-Z501B	
Rs-14	

SUB PROCEEDING AT 20

KNOTS LEAVES A WIDE

HERRINGBONE PATTERN

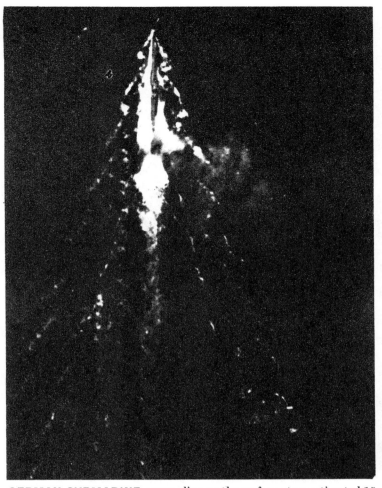

GERMAN SUBMARINE, proceeding on the surface at an estimated 15 knots, churns up white water and leaves a long track trailing behind.

U. S. SUB at ten knots creates less hull and propeller turbulence, shows how speed of vessel (*see German sub*) changes appearance of the wake.

WAKES VESSELS LEAVE IDENTIFYING TRACKS ON OCEAN'S SURFACE

Like every moving thing ships leave telltale tracks behind them as they cut across the surface of the seas. From these tracks it is possible to recognize with considerable accuracy the type of ship below from a plane flying high above the water. Despite this, however, it has been a common mistake for patrol plane pilots to report small surface craft as submarines. Such mistakes, which can be fatal, have been frequent enough to prompt the District Intelligence Office of the 15th Naval District, Balboa, Canal Zone, to make a detailed study of this recognition problem. Although photographs sharpen the effect of the designs, the pattern is usually clear enough for the human eye to differentiate between types. Herewith, the *Journal* presents the pictorial results of that study.

The characteristic wake can be broken down into three distinct parts. This wake pattern varies according to the design and speed of each vessel to a marked enough degree to be valuable in recognition.

In the wake pattern the three parts are: 1) The bow wave which is formed by the bow of the vessel pushing through the water. This wave leads away from the hull in the form of an inverted "V," stretches aft in a widening, herringbone scheme.

2) The hull and propeller turbulence. This turbulence, which is caused by the rush of water along the skin of the vessel and by the churning action of the propeller, streams out behind in a white line. Its length depends on the vessel's speed.

3) The stern wave which sets up a pattern of swells at right angles to the vessel's course.

Vessels with broad bows and with wide or transom sterns create a heavy wake while vessels with fine, trim lines create considerably less wake. In fact, a trimlined vessel creates a smaller wake than a less trim vessel even when operating at higher speeds. The sharpness of definition of a wake pattern increases with altitude and all wakes are distinguishable in up to moderate seas. Heavy weather destroys most wake patterns.

The submarine, with which most small craft are confused, is fully streamlined. Proceeding on the surface a sub creates a wake which even at high altitudes and at considerable distances have certain features which distinguish it easily from surface craft. The angle of its bow wave is more acute than that of a YP or PT boat operating at a comparative speed. Surface craft, by their hull construction and "sit" in the water, turn over a prominent bow wave.

The wake of the submarine, in addition, has finer vibrations on the inside of the "V" and the skin turbulence clings closely to the hull, outlining it in white water. At ten knots or less the hull turbulence blends with the propeller turbulence with little or no demarkation (*see top p. 13*), tapers off astern until it subsides. At ten knots or better, the propeller turbulence fans out astern, widening as the speed increases (*see bottom, p. 13*).

Spotting a submarine periscope and keeping it in sight is a remarkable feat under the best conditions. However, the periscope's wake is distinctive, has two recognizable features: the inverted "V" wake and churning white water (*see p. 12*). In the case of a submerged sub even seeing it is impossible except under the most favorable light and water conditions. Submerged, the sub appears only as a dark, shapeless mass; at the beginning or end of a dive, when the tanks are being blown, swirls of greenish water will disclose the submarine's position.

By studying the patterns of surfaced and diving submarines on this and the following pages and comparing them to the patterns made by various types of small craft (*see p. 15*) it will be possible to work out a yardstick of recognition.

PERISCOPE AT 4 KNOTS LEAVES A THIN WHITE INVERTED "V"

AT 6 KNOTS PERISCOPE TRACK IS MORE MARKED, HAS LONGER TRACK

LOW SIDE VIEW SHOWS WHITE WATER, FAINT HERRINGBONE

DECK AWASH, SUB MAKES UNUSUAL BOW AND BOILING PROPELLER WAKE

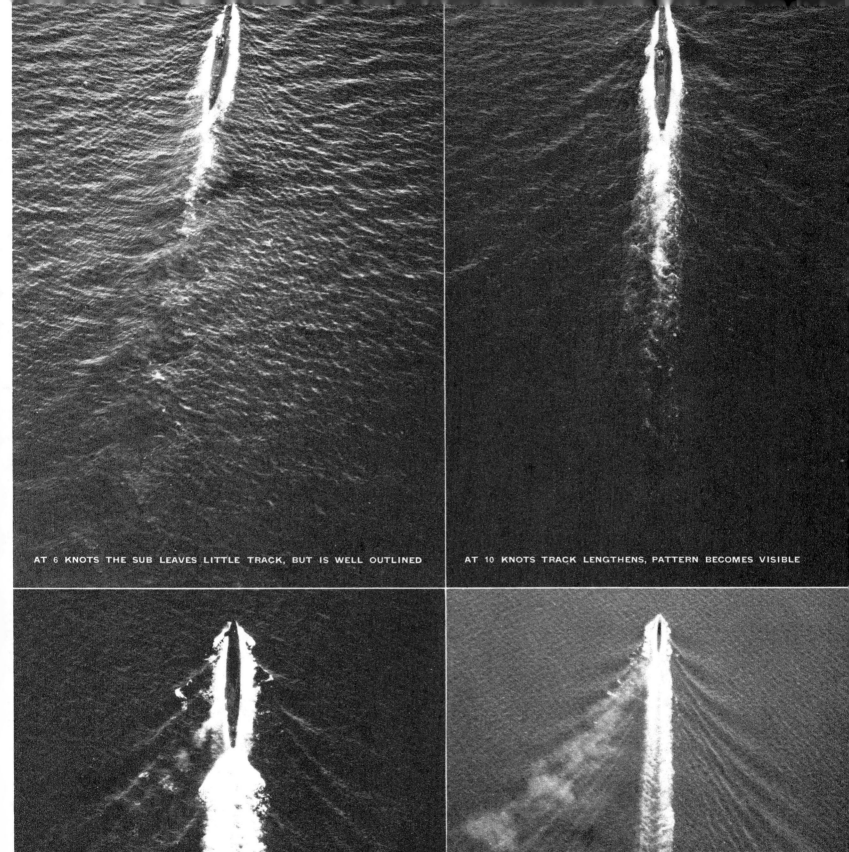

AT 6 KNOTS THE SUB LEAVES LITTLE TRACK, BUT IS WELL OUTLINED

AT 10 KNOTS TRACK LENGTHENS, PATTERN BECOMES VISIBLE

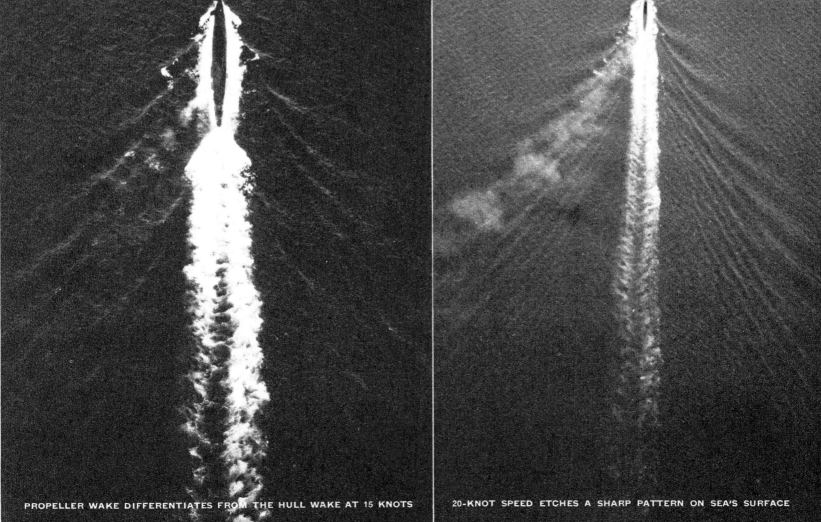

PROPELLER WAKE DIFFERENTIATES FROM THE HULL WAKE AT 15 KNOTS

20-KNOT SPEED ETCHES A SHARP PATTERN ON SEA'S SURFACE

CRASH DIVES

MAKE A SWIRLING PATTERN

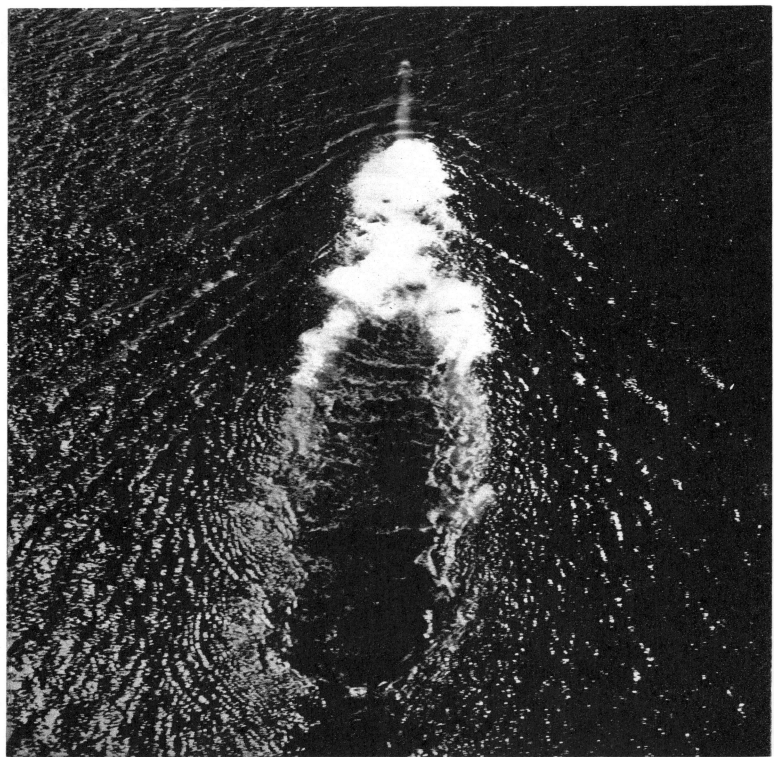

CONNING TOWER of crash-diving submarine is visible in the froth. Note the faint herringbone design leading up to patch of white water.

Swirls sighted at sea and reported as crash-diving subs are often nothing more than sportive whales or blackfish which are sometimes bombed for their indiscretion (*see Journal, Sept. issue*). In an actual crash dive of a submarine the swirl created is large and turbulent, especially at the moment the conning tower goes under the surface (*see below*). Since crash dives are made at speeds up to six or eight knots, there is always a wake leading up to the point of the dive, as shown in the picture at left.

The sub chasers opposite show the wake pattern set up by small surface craft which have wide sterns. Note that the wake pattern is broad and fans out sharply from the vessel's stern.

IMMEDIATELY AFTER SUBMARINE HAS SUBMERGED IN CRASH DIVE, THE WATER SETS UP A BUBBLING, BOILING APPEARANCE ON THE SURFACE

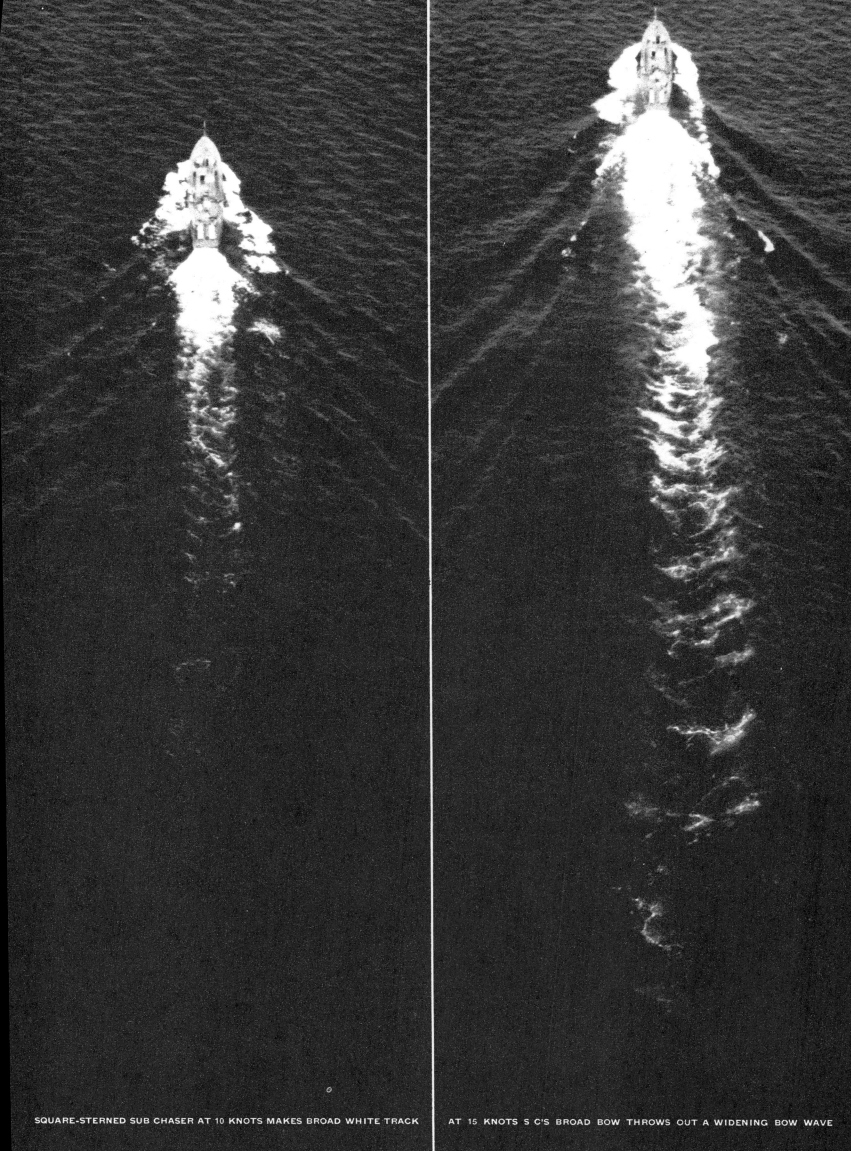

SQUARE-STERNED SUB CHASER AT 10 KNOTS MAKES BROAD WHITE TRACK   AT 15 KNOTS S C'S BROAD BOW THROWS OUT A WIDENING BOW WAVE

A U. S. DESTROYER, knifing through the water at 20 knots, cuts a well-defined design on the sea. From the destroyers squared-off stern the churning wake of the propeller streams out in a broad, flat band. Since the destroyer's bow is sharply edged and thin, there is little bow wave except the herringbone which flows out diagonally to the ship's course. Notice how the hull, unlike the sub's, is not too clearly surrounded by white water.

FAST PT BOAT makes an unusual pattern as it cruises along at 25 knots. Because of the high position of the boat's hull in the water as it hydroplanes, the bow wave starts out at abrupt right angles to the hull, then cuts back to stream parallel to the propeller wake. Since the bow itself does not cut through the water, the herringbone pattern is set up well aft of stern of PT boat, is considerably looser and less sharp than the DD's.

THE MOTORIZED MIGHT OF ALLIED FORCES MOVES INTO ACTION IN THIS FINE PANORAMA OF AFRICAN BATTLEFRONT. IN CENTER, U. S. HALFTRAC

ARMORED CAR M-8 has low silhouette, angular surfaces to deflect projectiles. As command car it has unarmored turret, mount for machine gun.

FROM ABOVE, M-8 is a rectangular mass with 360-degree turret in center from which long thin 37-mm. gun protrudes beyond the end of the hull.

ARMORED VEHICLES

When the Germans put this war on wheels, they played right into our hands. To meet this German challenge, the combined forces of American industry and American ordnance experts have developed a motorized army which in every way equals or surpasses that of our enemies.

Our newest weapon on wheels is the M-8 armored car. It was designed to replace armored halftrack and light scout car for reconnaissance work. M-8 is as fast as the scout car, can be used as command car. It carries superior armor to old armored halftrack and its six wheels, all of which are powered, give it almost as much flotation on bad terrain.

RECOGNITION: The M-8 is as American as the Sherman tank. The straight clean lines of its hull, into which the angular mudguards fair smoothly, distinguish it completely from the cumbersome German cars. The turret from which the 37-mm. gun protrudes is almost circular and is located only slightly forward of the hull's center. Though M-8's are sent out in groups of two or more accompanied by jeeps and tanks, they will usually be seen alone because of their rapid scouting duties.

Though some of the uses of the halftrack are being taken over by the armored car, the halftrack remains the war's most versatile vehicle. It is made in a variety of models to perform a great many jobs. They are used to carry troops and supplies, as prime movers and self-propelling mounts for guns up to 105-mm., as command and scout cars.

RECOGNITION: Long tapered angular hood and rectangular box body mark most U. S. halftracks. Tracks are very distinctive. Track support has four bogie wheels and one central support roller. Large drive sprocket at forward end and idler sprocket at rear look about the same. When a large gun is carried, the muzzle projects out over the hood and a large beveled shield is erected behind the driver's seat. From the rear, it is a rectangular box.

HALFTRACK IN FOREGROUND mounts two machine guns and carries crew of six. In background, halftrack hauls 13 men and one machine gun.

NEWEST HALFTRACK has mount for machine gun over the seat beside driver. All models will be so equipped. Roller in front helps cross ravines.

HALFTRACK MOUNTED ARTILLERY, now being replaced by the M-7 mounts, is still active. Gun and shield make prominent addition to hull.

MOVABLE COMMAND POST is carried on halftrack. Radio and protective AA machine gun are mounted in body, gear is lashed to all sides of car.

EIGHT-WHEELED German armored car is ungainly but effective motorized vehicle. Double driving trucks give it good flotation, make it serviceable car for desert warfare. Above, 20-mm. gun is pointed to rear from standard German light turret. No. 1 driver sits in cab ahead of front truck.

HIGH PROFILE of eight-wheeled car is extended by parasol-type antenna, is more apparent in head-on view than when seen from the side.

NAZI ARMOR

SIX- AND EIGHT-WHEELED ARMORED VEHICLES MAY BE SEEN BY ALLIED INVADERS

STUBBY 75-MM. GUN makes the eight-wheeled car a potent weapon against supply columns. High speed, fair fordability make it handy vehicle in most terrain. From above, hull has short taper to front, long taper to rear. Turret is an angular mass located over rear wheels of front truck.

GERMAN ARMORED COLUMN moves along behind lines. In action, the six-wheel cars would be dispersed over the countryside, usually seen alone or with tanks. From rear, turret fairs smoothly into hull, giving car more streamlined appearance. Taper on hull is particularly noticeable from rear.

As new allied troops pour into the continent, many of them will be meeting German motorized equipment for the first time. To better acquaint these inexperienced fighters with the armored cars and halftracks which their fellows have already met in Africa, these pages are devoted to German rolling equipment.

Since the war began, the Germans have used three armored cars. The four-wheeled model proved unsatisfactory and has almost passed out of use. The eight-wheeled version is now their standard armored car, but the six-wheeler is still seen in large numbers.

For such an awkward-looking conveyance, the eight-wheeler is a very agile car. It has a driver at both ends and can move equally fast in either direction. Since all wheels steer, it can turn in a very small radius for its size. It mounts either a 20-mm. or a 75-mm. gun as well as machine guns. The car's engine is extremely quiet.

The six-wheel car was the standard German armored car through 1941. Both it and the eight-wheel car have a streamlined, 360-degree traverse turret adapted from the PzKw II tank. Like the eight-wheeler, it has dual control but can not move as swiftly backwards as forwards. All six wheels are powered.

RECOGNITION: The eight-wheeled car is about a foot larger in each dimension than the six, being about 19 ft. long, 7 ft. wide, and 8 ft. high. Both slope to a peak at the top of the hull, but the eight is longer in the rear half, the six longer in front. On the sides, both of the hulls slope up toward the turret, in toward the chassis. Both cars sometimes carry parasol antenna. Motor is forward in six, aft in eight. Mudguards on both are heavy and angular.

SLOPING HULL and angular cutaway on side of the vehicle make German six-wheeler easily distinguishable from U. S. armored car. Though deadly, the six-wheeler looks not unlike float in a baby parade. This model carries a crew of four: driver-commander, two gunners and radioman.

GERMANY'S VERSATILE HALFTRACK

ARMORED HALFTRACK captured in Africa shows essential characteristics of Nazi vehicles.

Compare track assembly with those on facing page, design of hull with that of armored cars.

COMING AT YOU, German armored halftrack looks somewhat like American equipment. Chief

differences are in sloping sides of hull and hood, lack of ventilators on front of engine housing.

AGILITY OF HALFTRACK is shown by this vehicle mounting a heavy machine gun. German

halftracks are slower than comparable American vehicles, having an estimated speed of 30 m.p.h.

Long before we entered the war, the German army had proved the value of halftrack vehicles for modern mobile war. Their basic chassis is still their most adaptable and widely used conveyance. In both armored and unarmored versions, it is doing a superb job of moving men and matériel.

The chief use of the unarmored halftrack is carrying personnel. In this form, it looks like a huge sightseeing bus. It serves as the standard prime mover for the famous 88-mm. antitank-antiaircraft gun which temporarily set back our African forces. It tows or mounts all varieties of field artillery, pulls supply trailers of various sorts, serves as command cars, decontamination units and smoke producers. Practically no job requiring the movement of men or equipment is too much for it.

The armored halftracks do all that the unarmored versions do and then some. Though they carry less personnel, small squads can be sent out in sorties. Being protected, these halftracks are better for frontline action, can serve as mobile machine gun and antiaircraft emplacements. They have even been used as substitutes for tanks in running down infantry.

The family of halftracks is a good example of the way in which Germany planned for the war. As in so many fields, a few models were designed to do a great variety of jobs. All halftracks are built on a single basic chassis design. The range of sizes covered by this single design may be seen by comparing the two large vehicles on the right-hand page with the small armored command car in the upper left. The size of the power plant varies with the application; the track is lengthened and widened depending on the load to be moved.

RECOGNITION: The immediate identifying feature of any German tracked vehicle is the design of the propelling equipment. Large bogie wheels are used not only to support the weight of the car but as return rollers for the track. There is always an even number of them and they are staggered so that the first one behind the drive sprocket is on the inside of the track, the second outside, and so forth. The rear bogie is on the inside and serves as the track idler.

National characteristics of German equipment are seen in both classes of halftrack. In general, they look lumbering and awkward. The nose and mudguards of the unarmored forms look like commercial trucks. Angular faces of the armored vehicles are ugly but practical, make for simple assembly by mass production methods.

PERSONNEL-CARRYING HALFTRACK looks like cumbersome char-abanc. In this, German troops paraded through Warsaw, Paris, but it is more than a show vehicle. It carries large bodies of troops, moves big guns.

STANDARD HALFTRACK CHASSIS (*below*) is a mount for all sizes of guns. Light box shield protects gun crew for 75-mm. gun in this model. In earlier types, light anti-tank guns were mounted on unshielded platforms.

QUIZ NO. 2: FIGHTERS OVER EUROPE

For answers, see p. 50

BATTERED MOGAMI CLASS CRUISER SYMBOLIZES MODERN JAP NAVY. THOUGH HIT HARD SHE IS STILL AFLOAT AND POTENTIALLY DANGEROUS

JAPANESE NAVY
BULWARK OF JAPANESE IMPERIALISM

In 200 A. D., Jingo Kogo, militant Empress of Japan, sent a fleet to Korea to conquer it and return with 80 spoil-laden ships and the Korean King's promise of tribute to Japan "until the sun rose in the west, till the rivers flowed backwards, and the stones of earth became stars in heaven." Since then the Japanese have not changed a bit. They are still an aggressive, imperialistic people, sea-wise and proud of their Navy.

The modern Japanese Navy must still be rated as a first-class power. Almost completely a product of the last 50 years, it has made the best of western practice while adding to it the centuries of experience of a seagoing people. This is apparent in all the ships of the fleet from the BB's to the powerful new destroyer Terutsuki. It is also apparent in the men who man them. They are fine gunners, able ship handlers and good tacticians quite adept at improvisation. The officers are men of good education, bred to the sea, and thoroughly trained; the enlisted personnel are tough men schooled on blue water.

The ships of the Jap Navy are good ships. Though the foundations of Japan's modern Navy were laid in British and European yards, most of the ships used in this war have been built by the Japs themselves. They still have some British lines, but have been adapted to the demands of Japan's naval war. Hence their appearance, as will be seen from the pictures, has definite Japanese characteristics. And since we shall have to fight the Japs in their waters, it is important that we know what their ships look like, how they fight.

25

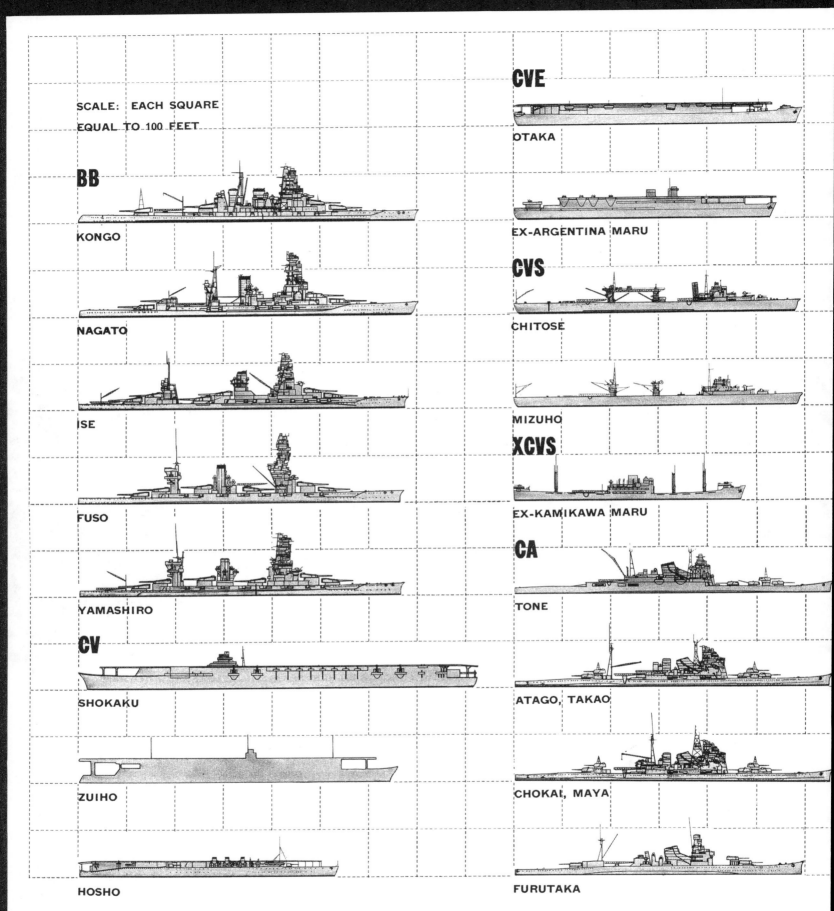

SCALE: EACH SQUARE
EQUAL TO 100 FEET

BB

KONGO

NAGATO

ISE

FUSO

YAMASHIRO

CV

SHOKAKU

ZUIHO

HOSHO

CVE

OTAKA

EX-ARGENTINA MARU

CVS

CHITOSE

MIZUHO

XCVS

EX-KAMIKAWA MARU

CA

TONE

ATAGO, TAKAO

CHOKAI, MAYA

FURUTAKA

This month the *Journal* presents on these pages in silhouette the most formidable Axis naval power, the Imperial Japanese Navy. The Japanese Navy is a potent and dangerous foe. Although it has suffered severe setbacks at Midway, Santa Cruz and in the Battle of the Solomons, many of its best ships remain afloat and constitute a constant threat to our lifelines in the Pacific. In addition since Japan has always been highly secretive about the exact status of her naval arm, there is a large possibility that there are Japanese fighting ships about which nothing is yet known.

It will be noted that not every ship heads in the same direction. The

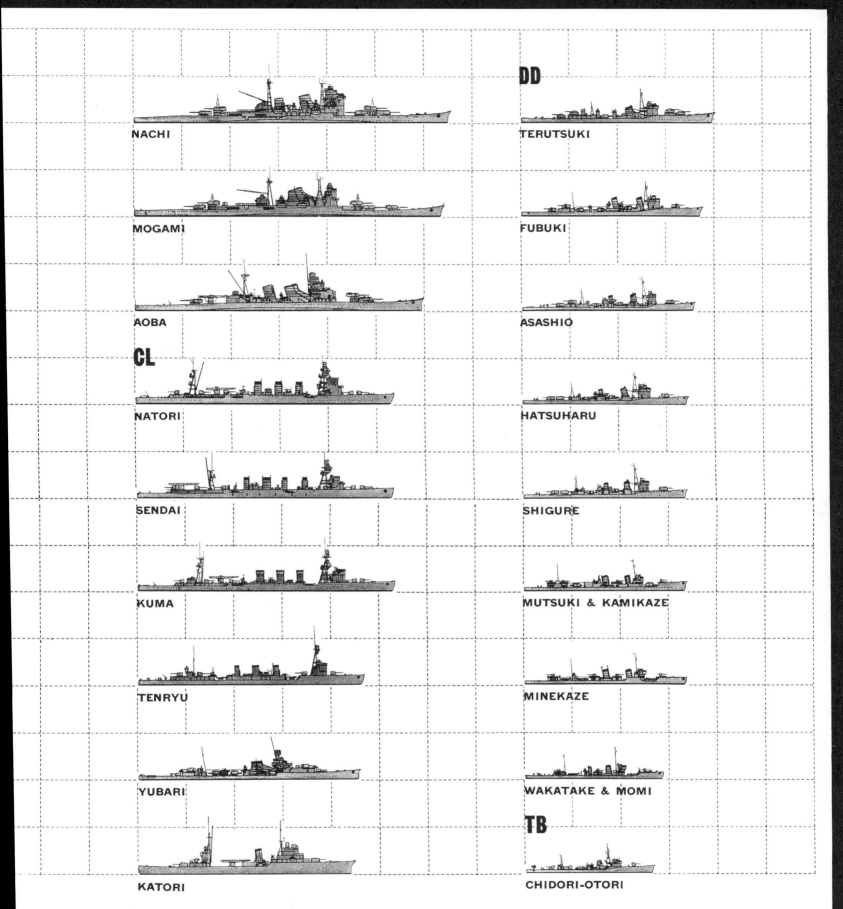

DD

NACHI	TERUTSUKI
MOGAMI	FUBUKI
AOBA	ASASHIO

CL

NATORI	HATSUHARU
SENDAI	SHIGURE
KUMA	MUTSUKI & KAMIKAZE
TENRYU	MINEKAZE
YUBARI	WAKATAKE & MOMI

TB

KATORI	CHIDORI-OTORI

reason for this is simply that, in a few cases, there are only limited views in our possession. To switch the direction of the silhouette would present port features as starboard features. In the case of new aircraft carriers the available views were taken from the air.

An important addition to the Japanese Navy is the new destroyer

class known as the Terutsuki (see *last column of silhouettes, see also pp. 38–39*). The Terutsuki, which is the newest of Japan's destroyer classes since Pearl Harbor, is well-armed and fast. It apparently was inspired by the British Tribal Class and the U. S. Porter and Somers classes. Its simplified design should make for all the qualities desirable in a heavy DD.

FUSO LEADS TWO KONGO CLASS SHIPS IN PARADE OF BATTLE POWER. FUSO'S TOWERING FOREMAST IS STEPPED BACK IN LOWER HALF, FORWARD

ISE CLASS SHIPS like the Hyuga are identified by searchlight platforms on stack, twin main batteries between blunt stack and low tripod mainmast, broken hull line.

BIG SHIPS ARE

The exact strength of the main Jap battleline on Dec. 7, 1941, is a question which will not be answered until the war is over. Known ships included six older battleships and four reconstructed battle-cruisers and possibly one new battleship. Two pocket battleships were reported building. This seems a light force with which to engage the two greatest naval powers in the world, but the Japs had planned well and undoubtedly have reserves which we have not yet encountered.

Most of the Japanese battleships of which we know are built to British designs, some of them in British yards. But the design has been supervised by Japanese naval experts so that, in some cases, the ships built for Japan have been better than those which the British built for themselves. Other designs were allotted to German and French yards so that the Japanese might acquire the best points of all navies. Since the 1920's, however, Jap Navy and commercial yards have grown until they now rival our own.

Though the ships illustrated on these pages are old in

NAGATO CLASS is newer. Pagoda mainmast is built on tripod structure. Searchlight platforms on fore edge of the stack give more solidified appearance to island.

IN UPPER, GIVES TOP-HEAVY, UNBALANCED APPEARANCE

YAMASHIRO, unlike her sister ship Fuso, has straight pagoda foremast. Heavier searchlight platforms about shorter stack and heavier mainmast also distinguish her.

OLD BUT GOOD

years they are not to be written off as outdated. Throughout the years Japan has maintained a careful modernization program. What we have done since Pearl Harbor is what the Japs have been doing all along. Nearly every capital ship in the Jap Navy was converted to oil and repowered, additional protection was worked into the designs, the number of stacks was reduced and the anti-aircraft armament increased.

RECOGNITION: The most prominent feature in Japanese battleship design is the towering pagoda foremast. Control, gun and searchlight platforms are built up the mast to a great height, which gives the foremast a top-heavy and vulnerable appearance. Another recognition feature is the split-up island, the stub mainmast and the single stack (the Kongo Class has two stacks). In the older single-stack types, one or more main batteries are mounted between the stack and the masts. In the Nagato Class, the eight 16-in. guns are fitted fore and aft of the island in twin mounts, while the secondary casemate guns are mounted abreast of each mast.

OLD KONGO CLASS ships have low foremast, two stacks. Tall tripod mainmast rises forward of aft stack while a stack-high tower is between stack and No. 3 turret.

LONG NARROW SHOKAKU SWERVES TO AVOID AMERICAN BOMBS IN CORAL SEA BATTLE. BIG JAP CARRIER HAS VERY SMALL ISLAND STRUCTURE

JAP FLEET BET ON ITS CARRIERS

If the pre-war Japanese Navy seemed weak in battleships, it was largely because they were convinced that fast striking fleet aircraft, launched from carriers, could carry their fight. Their announced carrier list was long—it outnumbered ours by two but flew fewer planes—and it is believed that several battleships reported building were really carrier hulls. Moreover, the Japanese undoubtedly are increasing their carrier strength by the addition of conversions and new hulls.

Jap CV's have distinctive lines, but are easily confused with our CVE's (See Journal, Sept. issue). However, small Jap carriers have no island structure and the flight deck has more rounded lines. The big Shokaku Class ships have a small rectangular island like our CVE's but the contrast between the island size and deck length of the Shokaku should identify her immediately

SEAPLANE TENDERS are a vital part of Japanese reconnaissance system, carry float planes to strategic areas. Mizuho Class (*above*) has no apparent stack; control tower, two twin 5-in. dual-purpose guns, plane-handling booms are amidships, catapults astern and amidships.

RYUJO IS SMALL carrier by pre-war standards, only slightly larger than U. S. "baby" carriers (CVE's). In plan view, flight deck and bow have general outlines of rifle cartridge with stacks and gun sponsons extending from sides. In beam view, the hull line is low, sides cluttered with sponsons.

HOSHO WAS FIRST carrier laid down by Japs. From above, the flight deck has gracefully curved outline, widest at quarterdeck and tapering forward. In beam view, hull line is broken with low stern and high bow. Three stacks rise forward of amidships, are lowered to horizontal during action.

CHITOSE CLASS tenders have raked pipe stack behind island. Plane-handling equipment is decked over amidships. Two catapults are abaft the stack, two behind plane-handling structure. Head-on, Chiyoda (*above*) and Chitose look like cruisers except for the square masses of their islands.

BIG CRUISERS PROTECT THE JAP CARRIERS

To naval men cruisers have glamor but they have never caught the imagination of the public as other ships have. Their striking force is much less than that of the giant battleships and fast carriers nor do they have the dash of the scurrying destroyers. As a result the general public has tended to ignore them. To partially correct this impression we are devoting the following four pages to the Japanese heavy and light cruisers.

In no navy is the cruiser more important than in the Japanese. The main Japanese naval attack group is the carrier task force. Since the carrier is lightly armed it has no defense against surface craft except its planes and its speed. To overcome this weakness, it is accompanied by fast cruisers and destroyers designed to out-gun everything the carrier cannot out-run.

The cruiser also serves the Japanese as a potent defensive weapon. The long sea lanes which tie the Japanese Empire together are exposed to raider attacks. Swift cruisers, most of which make over 30 knots, can be called into action when reconnaissance planes have spotted suspicious surface craft, rush to the spot and, if possible, destroy the invader.

Japanese naval characteristics are clearly seen in the design of their cruisers. The pagoda foremast so typical of the Jap battleships (*see pp. 28–29*) is also found in a shorter version in the cruiser. The control tower is cluttered with an array of control, gun and searchlight platforms. The forward stack is usually broad, raked and with a heavy trunk connecting with the forward uptake. The deck line usually undulates from high clipper bow to low stern.

GREAT SPEED of Tone Class cruiser is revealed by turbulence of the wake (*see pp. 10–17*). Air view also reveals four main batteries on foredeck, each equipped with two guns.

KUMANO is sister ship of battered Mogami shown on page 25. Pagoda foremast, raked stack and undulating deckline mark her as Japanese. Twin dual-purpose mounts on island give good anti-aircraft protection. Three triple 8-in. turrets forward and two aft give the cruiser heavy firepower.

ATAGO CLASS Chokai has typical features of Jap cruisers including general cluttered appearance. The main batteries are distributed three forward, two aft; Nos. 2 and 4 raised on high barbettes above turrets 1, 3 and 5. Deckline curves gracefully from high clipper bow to the low stern.

NACHI CLASS Ashigara has distinctive dual-purpose secondaries on high sponsons abreast stacks. In end-on view, secondaries are particularly prominent. Like most Jap heavies, two catapults are mounted between after stack and turrets, plane boom is suspended from tripod mainmast.

CHOKAI in this beam view clearly shows its characteristics. Older Atago class CA, the Takao, differs in having tripod mainmast just forward of after turrets, plane catapults between it and the island structure. In end on view of Atago class cruisers, full width pyramidal tower is conspicuous.

YUBARI is frequently mistaken for Mogami and Tone CA's and Katori CL's as well as all types of destroyers. Chief individual features are prominent trunked stack, special torpedo-control platform amidships and blast shields on Nos. 2 and 3 turrets. Destroyer-type hull is broken amidships.

JAPAN'S CL'S WON BATTLE OF JAVA SEA

Though Japanese light cruisers have been criticized as being too slow, too lightly armored and gunned, their effectiveness was bitterly demonstrated to us in the Java campaign. In the battle which took place off Surabaya on Feb. 27–28, 1942, a force built around seven Jap CL's (light cruisers) and two CA's (heavy cruisers) effectively destroyed our last naval defenses of the Malay Barrier. To be sure, our forces consisted of an old and battered conglomeration of Dutch, British and American ships, but the Jap victory made clear that the general public's prewar belittling of Jap ships and seamanship was particularly short-sighted.

Since every naval officer serves one year in a training cruiser after his three academic years at the Naval College, the Japanese command is particularly well acquainted with vessels of this size. Hence, they use them well. Their training emphasizes ma-

NATORI CLASS, like most other Jap CL's, is sometimes used for mine-laying; ships carry 80 mines and 24 depth charges. Though broken, deckline appears straight because of decked-over section aft. Single gun turrets are mounted two forward and two abreast of tower, three in line on afterdeck.

OLD TENRYU CLASS has three different sized stacks, a broad one in the center, an oval one forward, a round one aft. The two aft turrets are mounted on circular platforms on the raised quarterdeck structure. The cruiser hull is broken aft of tower to allow firing of forward torpedo tubes.

SENDAI CLASS are only Japanese four-stack light cruisers. Third stack is broad and oval, others round. Cruiser hull appears long and unbroken, but torpedo wells can be seen behind fore, aft stacks; stern has little freeboard. Main guns and torpedo tubes follow same pattern as on Natori Class.

neuvers under severe battle conditions. The personnel lives at all times under rigorous conditions, quarters are barren and recreational facilities nonexistent. Constant maneuvers are held under difficult weather conditions and ships have been worn out and ammunition depleted in their severe practice cruises.

In general, there has been a distinct alteration in the design of the newest Japanese light cruisers. This change roughly parallels the change in American destroyers. The older Natoris, Kumas (and to a certain extent the Tenryus) look flush-decked; all have three stacks, appear fragile and slow. The Yubari and Katori Classes are high bowed, with single raked stacks and a powerful, racy appearance. The chief exception is the Sendai Class which has retained the multiple stacks and the long deckline. Moreover, the Sendai represents a return to the heavier armament of some of the early CL's, having, as she does, seven 5.5-in. guns and eight torpedo tubes. The designed speed of the Sendai is the same as that of all Japanese fighting cruiser types, 33 knots.

Though the Katori is the newest of the illustrated ships, she is somewhat smaller and much slower (18 knots) than other light cruisers. She is officially classed as a training cruiser, but has undoubtedly been converted into a faster fighting ship.

KUMA CLASS cruisers closely resemble the Natoris. Chief distinctions are the flared stacks and the slight separation between bridge and tripod foremast on Kuma. In both classes, plane catapult is forward of mainmast, between Nos. 5 and 6 turrets. Kuma has very good underwater protection.

KATORI training cruisers are similar to fighting Yubari, but have single straight-raked stack. Cruiser hull is broken amidships but has extreme freeboard for full length. Both island structures are heavier than those of other CL's; main armament is limited to twin turrets fore and aft of island.

ASASHIO CLASS DD'S like Arashio (*above*) have one turret forward, two aft, banks of four torpedo tubes between stacks. Single turret forward is typical of Jap DD armament.

WE HAVE SUNK MANY JAP DD'S

More Japanese destroyers have been sent to the bottom than any other type of Jap fighting ships. American attacks in the Coral Sea and off Midway and the East Solomons may have seriously reduced their number. However, those that are still afloat are good ships and we may expect those that are building to be among the best in the world (*see following page*).

The many tasks which fall to the destroyers make them vital to all navies. They are used in battle to launch torpedo attacks on enemy battle lines or to lay tactical minefields. When a task force is moving up, squadrons of destroyers steam ahead and on all sides to search for the enemy, and until the development of escort vessels and carriers, they supplied the chief protection for merchant convoys. On detached service, the destroyer's chief task is the destruction of submarines.

The national characteristics of destroyers are probably less apparent than those of any other type of ship. At a cursory glance, most modern destroyers look alike. However, Jap DD's have a lower silhouette than ours and the newer ones have sharply raked stacks. With the exception of the Terutsuki, they are neither as fast nor as heavily armed as American destroyers. Older Japanese types have a maximum top speed of about 34 knots and mount only four to six guns and six to nine torpedo tubes.

SAMIDARE DIFFERS from Arashio in having one twin and one single turret aft, both mounted on deckline, no fantail anti-aircraft guns. The Samidare belongs to Shigure Class.

HATSUHARU CLASS Yugure has torpedo tubes in banks of three. Forward bank is on raised structure between stacks, surmounted by AA guns.

INAZUMA, a DD of Hibiki group, Fubuki Class, has small forestack, broad aft stack, both raked. Torpedo tubes are in three banks of three.

ASAGIRI (Amagiri group, Fubuki Class) has two stacks. In this class the No. 3 turret is mounted on low deckhouse. Shields ring base of each stack.

SHINONOME GROUP of Fubuki Class's chief features are ventilators abreast of forestack and just forward of second stack, twin AA forward.

MUTSUKI CLASS destroyers are lightly armed, having only four single 4.7-in. guns mounted one forward, one between the stacks, and two raised above the quarterdeck on circular platforms. From above, stern is broad and hull straightsided. One set of torpedo tubes is in well-deck forward.

KAMIKAZES resemble Mutsukis but have three pairs of torpedo tubes, one in well-deck forward of bridge, two on deck forward of aft gun mounts.

AKIKAZE, a DD of Minekaze Class has two 4.7-in. guns. The stacks are straight pipes just bridge high. The forestack is close up to the foremast.

YUGAO (Wakatake Class) has one broad, one pipe stack. Some Wakatakes have been converted to minelayers with stern broken down for ramp.

MOMI CLASS DD'S like Tsuga (*above*) are small, lightly armed, have three main guns and two pairs of torpedo tubes, one in well-deck, one aft.

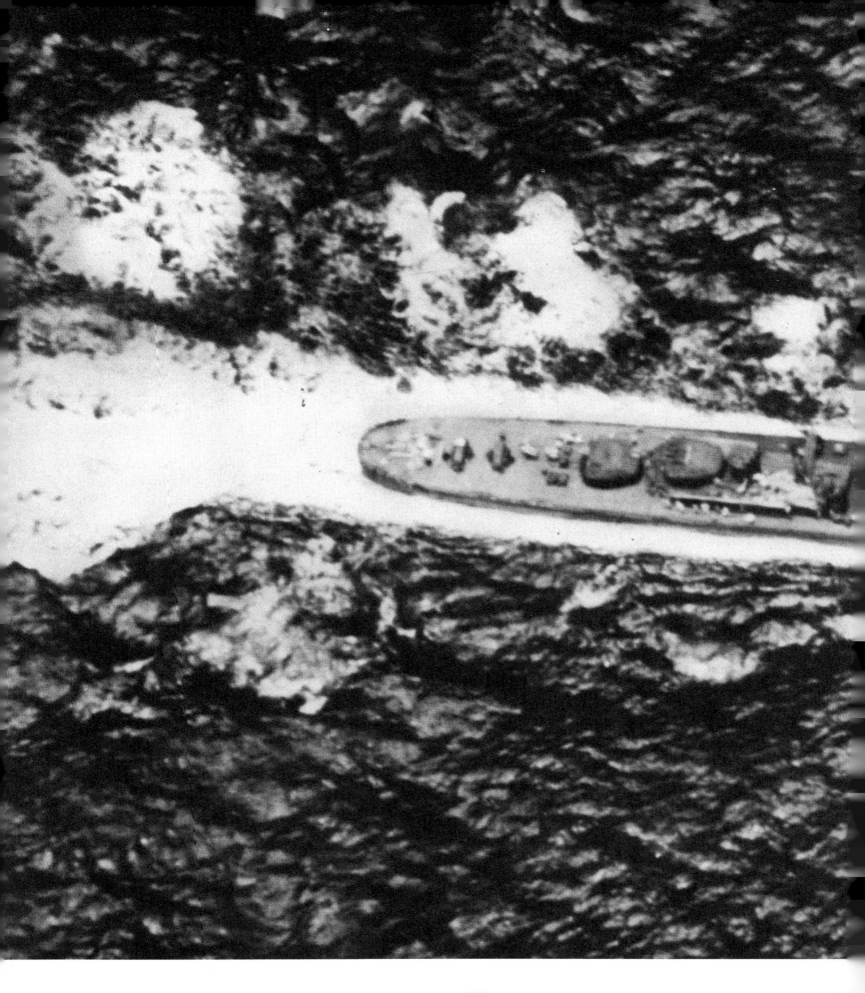

TERUTSUKI, JAPS'
FINEST DESTROYER

The new Jap destroyer, Terutsuki, appears to be one of the finest DD's afloat. Capable of great speeds (estimated at over 40 knots), she is nonetheless highly maneuverable. Her hull is 405 ft. overall, and she carries eight dual-purpose 5-in. guns, a heavier armament than some light cruisers. In fact these ships are sometimes identified as cruisers.

Though completely Japanese, it is probable that her design was inspired by the British Tribal and our Porter and Somers Classes of DD's. The torpedo battery has been sacrificed for heavier gun-

power which can be turned against both ships and aircraft. The Terutsuki can substitute for slower light cruisers in screening operations and can serve as an AA ship in protecting carriers.

RECOGNITION: The Terutsuki has particularly clean lines for a Japanese ship, but she is definitely Jap in her high bow and curving foredeck. She has the broad raked stack typical of the newer Japanese cruisers and destroyers. Distinctive features include four turtleback turrets which house her main gun batteries. A single raked stack and single bank of torpedo tubes are amidships.

TERUTSUKI IN PROFILE differs from the somewhat similar Mogami and Yubari in having pairs of twin turrets forward and aft, torpedo tubes amidships, and a tall tripod foremast separated from the bridge structure.

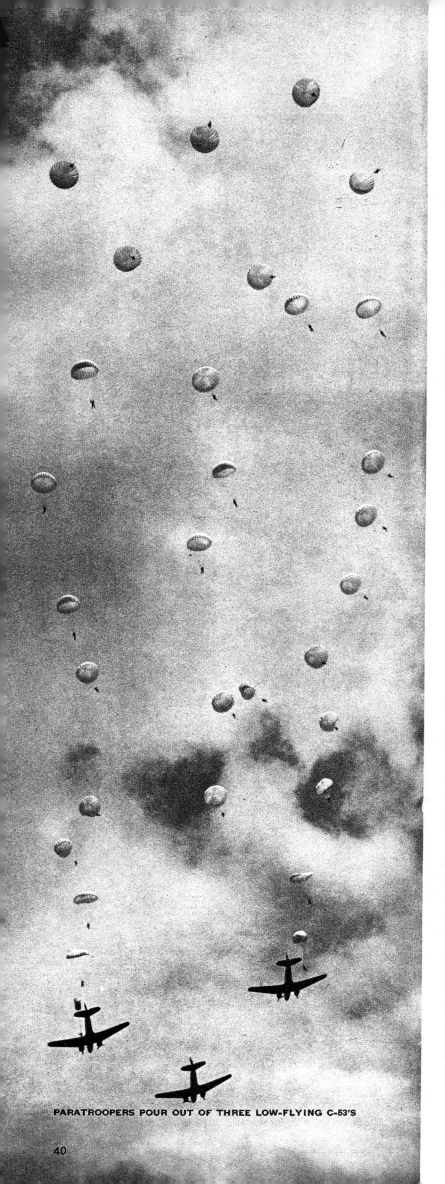

PARATROOPERS POUR OUT OF THREE LOW-FLYING C-53'S

HEAD-ON the C-47 shows its oval fuselage and low wing. The twin engines are mid-wing and the tail fin projects well above plane's fuselage.

TRANSPORTS

U.S. TRANSPORT PLANES

ARE MAJOR LINK IN ALL

ALLIED INVASION PLANS

C-47 FLIES OVERLAND towing a CG-4A glider. Towing plane hauls either loaded cargo gliders or the 15-place troop glider. In the recent in-

C-47 HAS TOP SPEED of 230 m.p.h. It is powered by two Pratt & Whitney, 14-cylinder radial, air-cooled engines. The plane has a range of 1,205 miles carrying 27 fully-equipped troops at 170 m.p.h. For cargo-carrying the plane's cabin floor is reinforced to hold the extra weight.

Flying routes which a few years ago were undreamed of and carrying cargoes farther and faster than man had ever hoped, the transport planes of the Allies are today spanning the world, reducing it almost to the limits of a commercial airline run. They are tying the battlefronts of the world into the pattern of victory.

Carrying paratroopers, airborne infantry, light artillery, jeeps, food, blood plasma and ammunition to the fronts from Sicily to Munda and ferrying out the sick and the wounded these transports are making aviation history.

The DC-3 has two war listings. As the C-47, the Skytrain, the plane has carried airborne infantry, cargo freight, and has hauled troop gliders. As the C-53, fitted with special jumping hatches, it has flown deep into enemy territory to discharge paratroopers.

The DC-3 flies for the RAF as the Douglas Dakota, and also for the Chinese. It is also used as a standard transport by the Soviet Air Force.

This work horse of the Allies flies without armor or armament. In the hot days of the Solomons battle last fall the C-47's came into Henderson Field armed only with a tommy gun and Springfield rifles, to be fired out the windows in case of attack. They can get in and out of unbelievably small, rough fields. They often fly as bellwether for single engine planes on long over-water hops.

RECOGNITION: Twin-engine, low-wing monoplane. Leading edge has sharp taper from engines, the trailing edge is straight. The wing tips are sharply rounded. Tail fin is faired forward one-third the length of the fuselage; the tailplane has sharply tapered leading edge. Plane's span is 95 ft., length is 64 ft. 6 in.

vasion of Sicily the RAF used Dakotas (C-47's) to haul their Hamilcar gliders. The USAAF also used C-47's and Commandos for the same job.

CG-4A GLIDER has squarish, roomy fuselage with good space for cargo or passengers. Nose of glider is hinged, opens up for cargo unloading.

41

THE IMMENSE SIZE AND PECULIAR WHALE-LIKE SHAPE OF THE C-46 TRANSPORT IS EMPHASIZED BY THE P-40 FIGHTER PLANE FLYING WING ON IT

THIS HEAD-ON VIEW OF THE C-46 SHOWS WELL-ROUNDED FUSELAGE

LARGE TRANSPORTS HAUL BIG CARGOES

The AAF's largest twin-engined transport is the C-46 which somewhat resembles a whale both because of its size and shape and because of the amount of cargo it can carry, a maximum load of 14,900 lb. Originally designed as a 36-passenger plane, the C-46, now carries 40 fully equipped troops 1,500 miles or a small tank or jeeps. It is also used as a glider tug. It is operative on all war fronts.

RECOGNITION: C-46 is a low, mid-wing monoplane. Wings taper outboard of engines with most of taper on leading edge. Fuselage is oval with pointed nose perfectly streamlined, flowing back without a step for the cockpit. Rounded single fin and rudder sweep into fuselage.

The C-54 (*opposite page*) is the largest transport in operational service for the AAF. It carries aircraft engines, construction machinery, large, bulky freight. As a troop transport it can carry under certain circumstances as many as 50 troops; it has a range of more than 2,000 miles; it can also carry a tank and crew.

RECOGNITION: Four-engine, low-wing monoplane. Narrow, equally tapered wings with rounded tips. Thick fuselage with long nose. Tall fin and rudder faired into fuselage. Straight trailing edge on rudder.

THE HIGH ROUND TAIL OF THE C-46 IS PROMINENT RECOGNITION FEATURE.   ITS FUSELAGE FAIRS SMOOTHLY INTO THE SHARPLY ROUNDED NOSE

GREAT WEIGHT OF THE C-54 DEMANDS DOUBLE WHEEL ASSEMBLIES AND PLANE IS LIMITED TO LONG, WELL-PREPARED RUNWAYS FOR TAKE-OFFS

NOSE OF THE PLANE EXTENDS WELL BEYOND LEADING EDGE OF THE WING. THE TAPER OF THE TRAILING EDGE IS CLEARLY SHOWN IN THIS VIEW

ONE OF THE C-54'S PROMINENT FEATURES IS ITS TALL TAIL STRUCTURE. THE PLANE'S TOP SPEED IS ABOUT 280 M.P.H., CRUISING SPEED 180-200

THE C-60'S TAILPLANE WHICH IS SET ON TOP OF THE AIRPLANE'S FUSELAGE IS VISIBLE IN THIS HEAD-ON VIEW.   THE FINS ARE SLIGHTLY INBOARD

THE C-60'S FUSELAGE is bulky and deep. The high speed of the airplane makes it an extremely valuable cargo carrier; in peacetime it set several transcontinental speed records.

C-60 CARRIES

FAST FREIGHT

The C-60 is the military version of one of the fastest commercial transports, the Lockheed Lodestar. Popular before the war as a fast, luxurious airliner carrying 14 passengers, the Lodestar was widely used. But when war came the Lodestar was readily adapted to several vital jobs.

In the winter of 1940 the British bought dozens of Lockheed's commercial type 14, modified them by adding a top gun turret, and called them Hudson bombers. For recognition Lockheed's Hudsons, Venturas and Lodestars have a strong family resemblance. They were among the first U. S.-made planes to see heavy war action. The Dutch in the Netherlands East Indies used them as paratroop planes. Now, they have been stripped down for use as cargo carriers.

The C-60 can take off loaded in 17 seconds and can cruise at 230 m.p.h.

RECOGNITION: C-60 is twin-engine, low mid-wing monoplane with pronounced dihedral. The wings have unequal taper to sharply rounded tips, and inner portion of trailing edge is curved. An important recognition detail is the Fowler flap guides, small projections on trailing edge. The fuselage is deep with sharply rounded nose. Twin fins are egg-shaped, rudders set inboard.

PLAN VIEW OF THE C-60 SHOWS ONE OF ITS PROMINENT RECOGNITION FEATURES: FOWLER FLAP GUIDES WHICH PROTRUDE FROM TRAILING EDGE

THE C-60'S SHARP NOSE PROTRUDES WELL BEYOND THE RADIAL ENGINES. THE WING HAS STRONG TAPER ON BOTH EDGES, TAIL WHEEL IS FIXED

MIDWING MONOPLANE S-4 set world's record at 226.752 m.p.h. over Southampton Water in 1925, was wrecked in Schneider trial at Baltimore.

THE SPITFIRE

ENGLAND'S CRACK FIGHTER
BORN IN SCHNEIDER RACES

R. J. MITCHELL, AIRMAN

In 1922, Italy held two legs on the Schneider Trophy. A third successive victory would retire the cup. To prevent this, the directors of the Supermarine Aviation Works turned over to a young ex-railway engineer, Reginald J. Mitchell, the job of designing a racing seaplane capable of beating the Italians. From this beginning, Mitchell went on to plan and build the line of Supermarine racers and their direct descendant, England's wartime ace-in-the-hole, the Spitfire.

The first Mitchell-designed racer was an adaptation of the Supermarine flying boat, a pusher biplane. It broke the Italian string, but the following year it was beaten by a U. S. Navy plane. Mitchell then departed from his old ideas of design. The S-4, which came to Baltimore in 1925, was a full cantilever mid-wing monoplane with its engine streamlined into the fuselage. Though it developed wing flutter and could not compete, the design was used in later low-wing versions, the S-5, S-6 and S-6B, which won in 1927, 1929 and 1931 to retire the trophy.

Reginald Mitchell's experience was put to practical use in 1934, when the Air Ministry accepted his specifications for a single-seater fighter plane, mounting eight guns, with a flight duration of about 1¾ hours at full throttle. Designed around Rolls-Royce's powerful new Merlin engine, with the smallest possible frontal area and cockpit space, the prototype was first demonstrated in June 1936, and after some slight modifications, the Spitfire was born.

NAPIER-POWERED S-5 initiated string of Schneider victories when Flt. Lt. Webster flew it 281.5 m.p.h. to win at Venice. Italians were forced down.

S-6 & S-6B CLINCHED TROPHY by winning at 328.6 m.p.h. in 1929, 340 m.p.h. in 1931. Small frontal area, thin wing section permitted great speed.

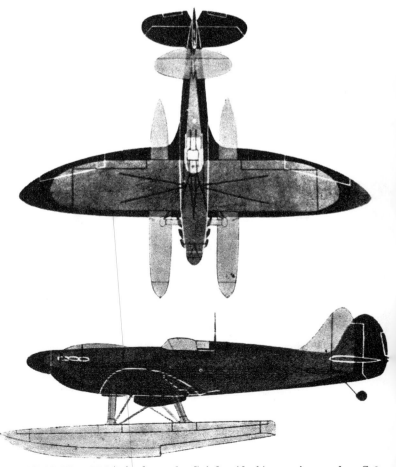

WORLD'S SPEED RECORD for straightline course was set at 407.5 m.p.h. by S-6B piloted by Flt. Lt. G. H. Stainforth, shortly after winning trophy.

FAMILY RELATION is shown by Spitfire (dark) superimposed on S-6. Greater lift, maneuverability required large wing, pronounced dihedral.

FIRST SPITFIRE was designed with all-metal, stressed-skin construction to give smallest outline around the engine, pilot, armament and equipment. Original propeller was broad, two-bladed, fixed pitch; later stages had two-pitch, then constant-speed airscrew with three blades and now four.

LANDING GEAR of the Spitfire folds outward, a distinctive feature. Lines have same cleanness as those of the Mosquito, with few outstanding projections. Though there are fighters which exceed her in individual qualities, her all-round performance makes her the darling of all who fly her.

SPITFIRE SITS IN AIR like an arrow, always seems to be aimed straight at its target. Originally designed to mount eight machine guns, many models now are armed with 20-mm. cannon. The Seafire, a development of the Spitfire, is now the British Fleet Air Arm's most important fighter.

QUIZ NO. 3: AIRCRAFT CARRIERS

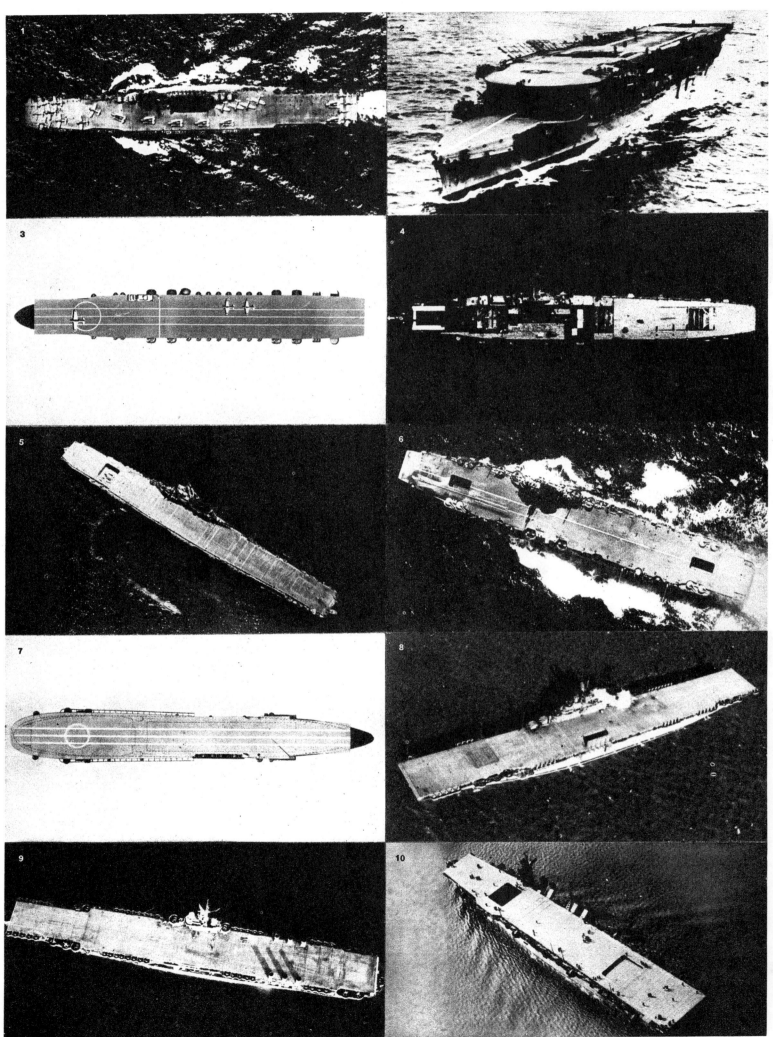

For answers, see p. 50

LONG TRANSPARENT NOSE of B-25 curves evenly into slender fuselage in plan view. Tailplane has straight trailing edge; wings taper evenly.

B-25 & DO-217

HAVE MANY DIFFERENCES

Two outstanding long-range bombers, which are sometimes confused because of their similar features, are now appearing in large numbers in the European Theater. They are Germany's new deadly precision and dive bomber—the Do-217, lately reported operating as a nightfighter, and our B-25 which has seen increasing action over Europe since its first appearance with the RAF in a raid on Ghent Jan. 22, 1943.

Careful study of the pictures shown here will reveal marked differences in their overall appearance as well as particular details. The Do-217 has the crowded-forward heavy-headed look of many Nazi planes (Hs-129, Ju-88, FW-189, Me-210) with the cockpit and gun blisters hunched up on the short stubby nose; fuselage tapering sharply to a shallow aft section. The tailplane is set high, giving the plane an overall sway-backed appearance. A jettisonable diving brake is sometimes fitted to the tail.

The B-25's fuselage is slender and slab-sided with smooth unbroken belly line tapering evenly into high tail section. Long extended nose gives it a racy look. Its motor nacelles project markedly beyond trailing edge of wing whereas Do-217's project only slightly. Head-on the B-25's gull wing clearly shows its inboard dihedral, slight outboard negative dihedral. The Do-217's wing is bar-straight, broken by the usual German type keyhole nose.

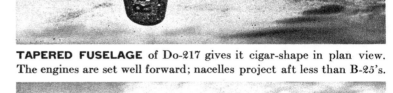

TAPERED FUSELAGE of Do-217 gives it cigar-shape in plan view. The engines are set well forward; nacelles project aft less than B-25's.

GULL WING due to dihedral inboard panel, negative dihedral outer panel, clearly distinguishes B-25 from Dornier. Fuselage is slab-sided.

KEYHOLE NOSE, straight wing denotes Do-217. Wing is 5 ft. shorter than B-25's. Fins bisect underslung motors; B-25 has wider tailplane.

SIDE-VIEW OF B-25 shows clean curve of bellyline, long nose, lopsided rectangular fins and rudders. Dorsal gun turret is set well back.

DO-217 has long shallow fuselage aft, front-heavy look accentuated by underslung nose-gunner's position, giving it a double-chin appearance.

NEWS & MISCELLANY

NEW SILHOUETTE

Germany's bomber and night fighter, Ju-88, has a new nose. Formerly cockpit and nose positions were separate glass-enclosed structures; some new models now combine both in one unbroken, transparent enclosure as shown in the top silhouette.

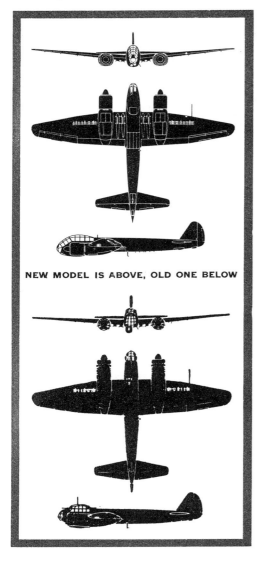

NEW MODEL IS ABOVE, OLD ONE BELOW

NEWS

The new British escort carrier the Unicorn has a strong similarity to the Illustrious Class (Brit. CV). The Unicorn has a high island superstructure with a short stack and light tripod foremast. The flight deck runs the entire length of the ship with a long overhang aft and

COMMUNICATIONS

CHANGE OF ADDRESS: *Communications should now be addressed to the Deputy Chief of Naval Operations (Air), Training Division, Training Literature Section, Navy Department, Washington, D.C.*

from the air has rounded taper and squared-off ends.

•

The P-70 ("Nighthawk") is the modified A-20A adapted to night-fighter work.

•

The Japanese DD Class formerly referred to as either "D-one," "New one stack" or "Unknown one" and subsequently named "Teratsuki" has officially been changed to "Terutsuki."

SOURCE MATERIAL

The Assistant Chief of Air Staff, Intelligence, has recently distributed three Informational Intelligence Summaries which will be of interest to AAF recognition training officers:

    Summary No. 84, Dec. 1942, describes Italian aircraft and armament;
    Summary No. 43-26, Apr. 1943, deals with Japanese aircraft and armament;
    Summary 43-33, June 1943, gives performance data and other information on German aircraft and armament.

It is understood that a sufficient number of copies of each of these three publications has been made available to the Headquarters of the various AAF Commands and Air Forces to supply the needs of recognition training instructors in subordinate units.

•

Recognition aids being distributed to the Army Air Forces activities include the following:

    Projection equipment for AAF Method of Recognition Training
    Pamphlet, AAF Method of Recognition Training and Use of Instructional Equipment
    Joint Army-Navy Pictorial Manual (Aircraft) FM 30-30 (available on requisition through channels to AGO depots)

Slides on aircraft, naval vessels and armored vehicles
Scale models of aircraft, naval vessels and armored vehicles
Silhouette posters of aircraft
Silhouette booklets on aircraft
O.N.I. publications on ship recognition
Information regarding the above recognition material may be obtained upon request, through channels, to:

    Training Aids Division
    Army Air Forces
        One Park Avenue
            New York City 16, N. Y.

TEACHING AIDS

In the Amphibious Forces, much actual spotting practice is given after reviews through the synthetic method of flashmeter projectors and slides. Recognition officers are given a pair of 7 x 50 power binoculars and are sent down to the beach to actually observe ships and planes since there are many Army and Navy activities around Norfolk—both aerial and water borne. Observers at this activity have an unusual opportunity to practice their recognition training under highly favorable outdoor conditions.

DISTRIBUTION

This *Journal* is distributed in substantial quantities to Headquarters of the various Air Forces, Commands and Training Centers of the Army Air Forces for redistribution to activities in the field. Additional copies in limited quantities are available upon request through channels to Army Air Forces, Training Aids Division.

Copies for Ground and Service Forces are automatically distributed by Adjutant General Depots on the basis of five copies per AA or seacoast artillery batteries and two copies to companies or similar units in other arms and services. It also goes to troops in the United States, Hawaii, Caribbean Defense Command and Iceland.

Distribution to all ships and stations of the U. S. Navy and Marine Corps is automatic. Additional copies for Naval activities may be obtained only through regular channels by addressing the Vice Chief of Naval Operations (Air).

"TOPSY" TYPE MC-20

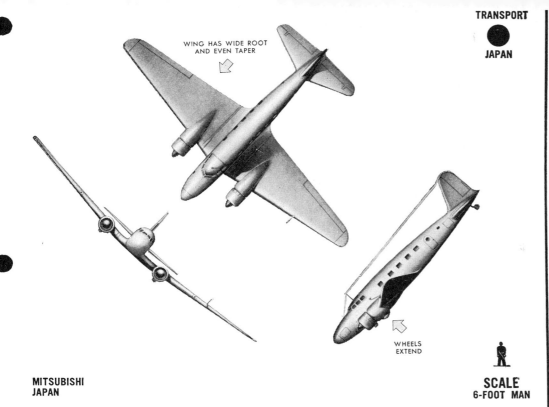

WING HAS WIDE ROOT AND EVEN TAPER

WHEELS EXTEND

SCALE 6-FOOT MAN

MITSUBISHI
JAPAN

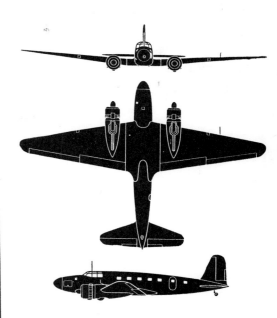

DISTINGUISHING FEATURES: Twin-engine, low-wing monoplane. Wings taper sharply to rounded tips and have pronounced dihedral. Nose is long and sharply rounded. Fuselage smooth except for break at pilot's cockpit and tapers symmetrically to point at tail. Tail surfaces have pronounced taper on leading edge with rounded tips. Fixed tail wheel, retractable landing gear.

INTEREST: This aircraft has been reported used in paratroop operations in the Southwest Pacific. It has a cruising range of 1,170 miles with normal fuel and cargo load at an average speed of 197 m.p.h. and at an altitude of 9,200 ft. It is a transport version of the Mitsubishi commercial transport, type MC-20, for which sales were solicited in South America before the war.

SPAN: 74 ft.
LENGTH: 52 ft. 8 in.
MAX. SPEED: 266 m.p.h. at 10,500 ft.
SERVICE CEILING: 23,000 ft. with normal load

RESTRICTED

NOTE: This page is to be cut along dotted lines (*above* and *below*), added to the proper nation's section in the Recognition Pictorial Manual. The dots indicate perforations.

"PE-2" & "PE-2B"

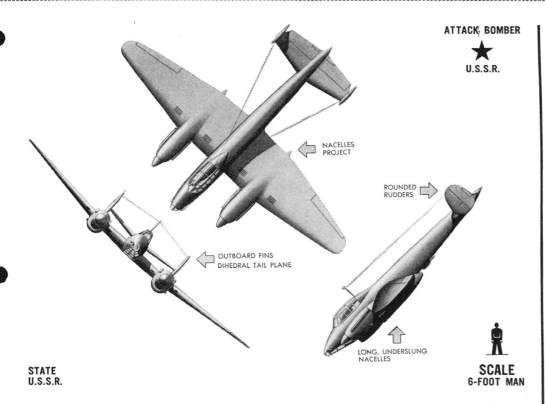

NACELLES PROJECT

ROUNDED RUDDERS

OUTBOARD FINS DIHEDRAL TAIL PLANE

LONG, UNDERSLUNG NACELLES

SCALE 6-FOOT MAN

STATE
U.S.S.R.

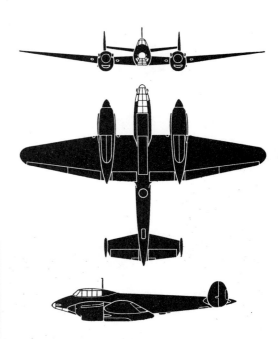

DISTINGUISHING FEATURES: Twin inline engines, low-wing monoplane. Wing has rectangular center section. Leading edge and trailing edge of outer section equally tapered to elliptical tips. Engine nacelles are underslung and project beyond trailing edge of wing. Fuselage has graceful slender taper. Small raised transparent greenhouse is mainly forward of leading edge of wing. Warped oval-shaped twin fins and rudders are mounted outboard on stabilizer which has pronounced dihedral.

INTEREST: The 16th German Army at Staraya Russa will remember this plane which was used to bomb their airfields in the 1942 offensive. The PE-2, a light bomber, has often met German fighters in close combat. Originally designed as a dive bomber, this fast, highly maneuverable "twin-tail" has performed many kinds of offensive and defensive actions. The fighter version of this plane has no bombardier's windows under the nose and is known as the PE-2B or PE-3.

SPAN: 56 ft. 1 in.
LENGTH: 41 ft. 5 in.
APPROX. SPEED: Over 300 m.p.h.
SERVICE CEILING: 32,000 ft.

RESTRICTED

A

B

C

TOPSY, probably Japan's foremost military transport plane, has been reported as being used in paratroop operations in the Southwest Pacific. This is a military version of a commercial transport plane, sale of which was solicited in South America before the war.

PE-2 is one of several Soviet planes designed primarily for army cooperation, working closely with ground forces. Originally equipped with dive brakes for use as a dive bomber, PE-2 has been modified, appears also in a fighter version as the PE-2B or the PE-3.

A

C

B

D

U. S. ARMY-NAVY JOURNAL OF
RECOGNITION

P-38 FIRING

NOVEMBER, 1943
NUMBER 3

QUIZ NO. 1
AIRCRAFT

(For answers, see p. 50)

(For answers, see p. 50)

1

2

3

4

5

6

7

8

9

10

11

12

13

14

15

16

17

U. S. ARMY - NAVY JOURNAL OF
RECOGNITION

NOVEMBER, 1943

COPYRIGHT 1943 BY LT. GEORGE H. FORSYTH JR.

NUMBER 3

SILHOUETTED ON HORIZON THREE SHIPS PASS AT A GREAT DISTANCE. BY "BUMP" METHOD THEY ARE RECOGNIZED AS FLETCHER CLASS DD'S

THE LONG VIEW

At no time in the war has recognition been more important. As each new offensive starts rolling, thousands of fresh troops go into battle for the first time, newly trained seamen help man the escorting naval vessels, pilots make their fledgling combat flights. These men are well-trained, ready and eager to make their fight and to win. They have been crammed full of the latest intelligence on the enemy. They carry the best possible precision tools of modern war. Yet despite this apparent well-rounded background there sometimes is something lacking.

As fighting men they are doing a fine job but many of them have not yet realized that recognizing friend from foe is a talent of war second only to the ability to shoot straight.

Recently, in Sicily, recognition was a major problem. In the first issue of the *Journal* we printed a letter which described a case of mistaken identity during the landing operations. Later, during the fighting in the interior, there were similar incidents. Planes flying cover for our troops were spotted as Axis planes and shot down; Axis planes were identified as friendly and allowed to slip past our defenses.

Such slipshod recognition is hard to excuse. By handing the decision, even though it might only be a temporary one, to the enemy on a silver platter, we are giving him an advantage at a cheap price. It is also putting too cheap a price on our own lives.

This is a serious flaw but it is not one which can be blamed on the men who teach recognition. Working with lectures, slides, peep-boxes and films they transmit available material as rapidly as they can. However, it seems apparent that this teaching should be taken up in even greater detail by each individual unit.

The blame for much of the confusion in recognition can be laid to at least two uncontrollable factors: distance and weather conditions. Both of these are variable and change constantly. On this and the two following pages the *Journal* presents a series of pictures taken in combat. This is what war looks like in the long view in uncertain weather—the recognition view.

An excellent example of distance pictures is the seascape above. Three tiny ships on the horizon can be made out, none of them too clearly defined. It is at this precise moment that rapid, correct identification is necessary since the ships are near enough to do considerable damage with their guns, yet far enough away to make an escape. The same is true of the other pictures of tanks and planes.

In the case of ships several approaches have been made to the problem of recognition at a distance. Interested officers of the Coast Artillery have worked out one such aid in identifying ships (*see pp. 21–25*), which they called the "Bump" method. Planes and tanks have not been reduced to such simple terms. Nor are planes likely to be. The base of all good recognition is long, hard, constant practice since recognition, like tennis, cannot be learned out of a book. But it can be learned. The best method is to study in an organized class under specially trained officers. Then, follow up with practice and practical demonstrations at every opportunity.

Men are expected to die in war, but they must not be allowed to die because we did not know the enemy when we saw him.

BACKGROUNDS MAKE RECOGNITION

CONVOY OF MERCHANT SHIPS ON THE MURMANSK RUN CREEPS OUT OF FOG BANK. UNLESS QUICKLY RECOGNIZED BY PATROLLING SHIPS AND PLAN

FORCE OF U. S. TANKS enroute to raid Sened, Tunisia, during the North African campaign last spring. At this distance and against the dun colors of the background, tanks are especially hard to see.

U. S. TANKS WAIT to join battle at El Guettar with the third wave. Once they

DIFFICULT

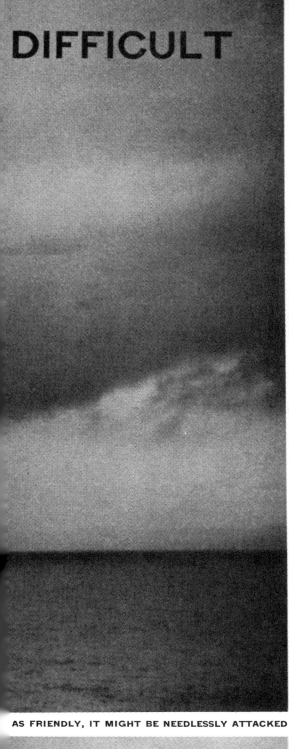

AS FRIENDLY, IT MIGHT BE NEEDLESSLY ATTACKED

are on the move they will raise a huge cloud of dust, be almost impossible to detect as friend or enemy.

NAZI DIVE BOMBERS cluster against a dull morning sky in attack on U. S. ground positions in Africa. Plane in bottom picture is beyond safety mark as far as recognition is concerned.

HUGE AMPHIBIAN FLOATS turn standard C-47 into ideal craft for carrying freight into water-bound areas, cut speed, add 600 gal. to fuel capacity. Though plane has distinctive lines of America's most numerous transport, floats may cause confusion with large enemy floatplanes.

TWO NEW PLANES

Newsworthy additions to two of the world's air forces are these planes. One, the float version of the USAAF's C-47, will increase the chances of survival of Allied aviators forced down in South Pacific waters. It will be able to land at small coral atolls, roll up on the beach and load or discharge survivors and equipment.

The other new plane of the month is a twin-motored Japanese plane of medium size, possibly used as a night fighter, fighter-bomber or photo-reconnaissance plane. Little is known of it except what is shown in the photograph below. However, the *Journal* will print further information as soon as it becomes available.

RAID ON WEWAK disclosed one new Japanese plane, pictured in this remarkable low-angle reconnaissance photograph. This aircraft is unlike any other Japanese design, but it resembles the famous British plywood Mosquito. The gas truck in foreground shows relative size of the plane.

RECOGNITION TRAINING LIST

NOVEMBER, 1943

The following training list is basically the same as that contained in Bureau of Naval Personnel Circular Letter No. 163-43, issued July 16, 1943. No changes of recognitional importance have been necessary since then.

The ships listed under Class A are the most important from a numerical or operational standpoint, and hence from a recognition standpoint. They form the "must" list for all study of surface craft recognition. Class B ships are less important. They should be taken up when the Class A list is known thoroughly, or in areas where the full line-up of a particular navy may be encountered, therefore must be known thoroughly.

In each list where the word "Class" appears after the ship name, it indicates that more than one unit of similar structure and appearance exists. Where only the ship name is given, a single unit is indicated. When two classes are similar, they are marked a—a′, b—b′, etc.

In all navies, older ships are frequently being modernized. Recognition training material covering these ships should be chosen carefully since, in refitting, the appearance, as well as performance, is often greatly changed (*see Journal, Sept. issue*).

U.S.

CLASS A	CLASS B
I. Battleships:	
(BB) (7)	(3)
a. NEW YORK Class	a′. ARKANSAS
b. PENNSYLVANIA	b′. NEVADA
c. NEW MEXICO Class	....
d. TENNESSEE	....
e. NORTH CAROLINA Class	
f. SOUTH DAKOTA Class	
g. IOWA Class	
....	h. COLORADO Class
II. Aircraft Carriers: (CV) (3)	(1)
a. ESSEX Class	....
b. ENTERPRISE	....
c. SARATOGA	
....	d. RANGER
III. Aircraft Carriers, small: (CVL) (1)	(0)
a. INDEPENDENCE Class	....
IV. Aircraft Carriers, Escort: (CVE) (3)	(1)
a. BOGUE-PRINCE WILLIAM Classes	a′. LONG ISLAND-CHARGER
b. SANGAMON Class	....
c. CASABLANCA Class	....
V. Heavy Cruisers: (CA) (4)	(2)
a. PENSACOLA Class*	
b. NORTHAMPTON Class	b′. PORTLAND Class
c. NEW ORLEANS Class	....
d. BALTIMORE Class	....
....	e. WICHITA
VI. Light Cruisers: (CL) (3)	(2)
a. OMAHA Class	
b. BROOKLYN Class	b′. ST. LOUIS
c. CLEVELAND Class	c′. ATLANTA Class
VII. Destroyers: (DD) (6)	(4)
a. "Old Flush Deckers"	....
b. MAHAN-DUNLAP Classes	b′. PORTER Class
c. GRIDLEY-BAGLEY-BENHAM-SIMS Classes**	c′. SOMERS Class
d. BENSON-LIVERMORE Classes	....
e. FLETCHER Class	
f. Destroyer Escorts (DE-51 Class)	f′. Destroyer Escorts (DE-1 Class)
	g. FARRAGUT Class

*Subject to immediate change in appearance.
**The GRIDLEY-BAGLEY Classes have flat-sided stacks. The BENHAM-SIMS Classes have elliptical cross-section stacks; SIMS Class fitted with sloping stack caps—the only one-stackers so fitted.

BRITISH

CLASS A	CLASS B
I. Battleships:	
(BB) (4)	(3)
a. ROYAL SOVEREIGN Class	a′. MALAYA
b. QUEEN ELIZABETH-VALIANT	b′. WARSPITE
c. NELSON Class	....
d. KING GEORGE V Class	d′. RENOWN
II. Aircraft Carriers: (CV) (2)	(0)
a. FURIOUS	....
b. ILLUSTRIOUS Class	....
III. Auxiliary Aircraft Carriers: (CVE) (2)	(3)
a. UNICORN	
b. BATTLER Class	b′. ARCHER Class
....	c. ARGUS
....	d. ACTIVITY
IV. Heavy Cruisers: (CA) (2) (see note)	(2)
a. LONDON	
b. KENT-DEVONSHIRE-NORFOLK Classes	b′. CUMBERLAND-SUFFOLK (KENT Class)
....	c. HAWKINS Class
V. Light Cruisers: (CL) (6)	(5)
a. DRAGON-CARLISLE Classes	a′. CALEDON Class
b. EMERALD Class	
c. LEANDER Class	
d. ARETHUSA Class	d′. HOBART
e. DIDO Class (5 turret)	e′. DIDO Class (4 shield)
f. FIJI Class	f′. SOUTHAMPTON Class
	g. ADVENTURE
VI. Destroyers: (DD) (7) (see note)	(4)
a. "Town" Class	
b. "V-W" Classes	b′. "Wairs"
c. "A" to "I" Classes	c′. WALLACE-DOUGLAS-SAGUENAY Classes
d. CODRINGTON Class	....
e. "J," "K" AND "N" Classes	e′. "L" AND "M" Classes
f. "O" to "T" Classes	....
g. "Hunt Class"	
....	h. "Tribal" Class

NOTE CA: KENT-BERWICK and AUSTRALIA of the KENT Class can be distinguished from DEVONSHIRE-NORFOLK classes by having less space between No. 2 turret and the bridge. CUMBERLAND and SUFFOLK of the KENT Class have the hull cut away at deck level abaft No. 4 turret and are fitted with large box hangar abaft the stacks.
NOTE DD: "Wairs" are "V-W" class destroyers rearmed with anti-aircraft guns.

GERMAN

CLASS A	CLASS B
I. Battleships:	
(BB) (2)	(2)
a. SCHARNHORST	a′. GNEISENAU
b. TIRPITZ	
....	c. SCHLESWIG-HOLSTEIN Class
II. Aircraft Carriers: (CV) (1)	(0)
a. GRAF ZEPPELIN	....
III. Heavy Cruisers: (CA) (2)	(2)
a. ADMIRAL HIPPER	a′. PRINZ EUGEN
b. ADMIRAL SCHEER	b′. LUETZOW
IV. Light Cruisers: (CL) (2)	(2)
a. KOELN	a′. EMDEN
b. NUERNBERG	b′. LEIPZIG
V. Destroyers: (DD) (3)	(3)
a. MAASZ Class	a′. WOLF-MOEWE Classes
b. "NARVIK" Class	b′. ROEDER Class
c. T-1 Class	c′. M-1 Class AM (inserted for great similarity to T-1)

JAPANESE

CLASS A	CLASS B
I. Battleships:	
(BB) (4)	(0)
a. KONGO Class	....
b. FUSO Class*	....
c. ISE Class	
d. NAGATO Class	
II. Aircraft Carriers: (CV) (1) **	(1)
a. SHOKAKU Class	....
....	b. HOSHO
III. Seaplane Carriers: (CVS) (1)	(1)
a. MIZUHO Class	a′. CHITOSE Class
IV. Heavy Cruisers: (CA) (3)	(3)
a. NACHI Class	a′. AOBA Class
b. ATAGO Class	b′. CHOKAI-MAYA
c. MOGAMI Class	c′. TONE Class
V. Light Cruisers: (CL) (2)	(3)
a. SENDAI Class	
b. KUMA-NATORI Classes	b′. TENRYU Class
....	c. KATORI Class
....	d. YUBARI (see DD's)
VI. Destroyers: (DD) (5)	(4)
a. MUTSUKI-KAMIKAZE Classes	a′. MINEKAZE-WAKATAKE-MOMI Classes
b. FUBUKI Class, AMAGIRI Group	b′. FUBUKI Class, SHINONOME & HIBIKI Groups
c. SHIGURE Class	c′. HATSUHARU Class
d. ASASHIO Class	
e. TERUTSUKI Class***	e′. CHIDORI-OTORI Classes YUBARI (CL)

*FUSO and YAMASHIRO differ (catapult, No. 3 turret, after part of bridge)
**There are more Jap CV's in operation on which adequate illustrated coverage is lacking.
***Formerly referred to as either: "D-One," "New one stack," or "Japanese Tribal."

ITALIAN

CLASS A	CLASS B
I. Battleships:	
(BB) (2)	(1)
a. CAVOUR Class	....
b. LITTORIO Class	b′. DORIA Class
II. Heavy Cruisers: (CA) (1)	(1)
a. BOLZANO	a′. GORIZIA
III. Light Cruisers: (CL) (3)	(2)
a. MONTECUCCOLI Class	a′. SAVOIA Class
b. GARIBALDI Class	....
c. REGOLO Class	
....	d. "CADORNA"
IV. Destroyers: (DD) (4)	(1)
a. TURBINE Class	....
b. "Navigatore" Class	....
c. SPICA Class	....
d. AVIERE Class	
....	e. "Generale" Class

NOTE DD: There are many more individual design classes, but those listed above are typical enough to cover all.

Germany spreads its wings in prewar show of Luftwaffe's power

THE LUFTWAFFE

The first great air force of World War II is hard-pressed

When war began four years ago, Germany had in her hand the greatest weapon in history, the Luftwaffe. Conceived, trained and equipped in secrecy and in violation of all international agreements, the German Air Force had been welded into an almost invincible war machine. With 4,300 up-to-the-minute warplanes, a production of 1,100 planes a month, and well-trained men to man and maintain them, the Reich was set to dominate the air over Europe. Yet, despite its world-shaking victories in Poland, The Netherlands and Belgium, the Luftwaffe has failed. When it had the advantage it did not or could not strike the final blow. And now, with British and American production over-reaching the Germans and the pick of the manpower of America and the British Empire pouring into the Allied Air Forces, the Third Reich has lost the initiative.

This is not to say that the Luftwaffe is a pushover. It is, by all means, the toughest enemy we have to beat. It will take many men and many machines to overcome German strength and ingenuity, but every day it grows more clear that it can and will be done.

Nazis' plans run amiss

The essential German failure probably lay in betting on the wrong horse. The Luftwaffe was conceived by Göring, Milch and Udet as an army co-operation force. Its main offensive strength was placed in fast, lightly-armed medium bombers like the Heinkel 111 and Dornier 17, in the terror-striking Stuka, and in fast fighters like the Messerschmitts. When the fighters had driven the weak European opposition from the air, the bombers could fly at will over undefended cities like Rotterdam and Warsaw and blast them to rubble. The screaming Ju-87 (Stuka) could dive on unprotected troops and civilians, destroy their lines of communication unopposed.

But this theory of airpower was based on two premises which are by no means universal: first, that the opponent has little air strength; second, that a fast-moving land army can march in to consolidate the airman's gains before the victim can recover. These conditions held during the lightning wars on Poland, the Low Countries and France, but when the battle came to the edges of England's rugged island neither premise was valid. The German Air Staff did not revise its ideas and the Blitz on England only succeeded in stiffening British backs.

Even though its invincibility has been disproved, the Luftwaffe has been an amazing success. Banned from military aviation by the Versailles Treaty, the Germans prepared for this war underground. They took up sport flying very extensively. The Deutsche Luftsportverband grew to a membership in 1932 of 60,000 enthusiasts. At the same time, the Deutsche Luftverkehrschule estab-

lished branches all over Germany to train pilots. Under the Lufthansa and the financing of Nazi-minded millionaires, commercial aviation in Germany boomed. Thus, on March 10, 1935, when Hermann Göring announced the formation of the Luftwaffe, he could impress French and British military attachés with a dramatic display of a single flight of 400 planes. To be sure, they were Ju-52 transports in war paint, but even so the attachés were impressed.

From 1935 to 1939 the curtains of secrecy were down and behind them German aeronautical experts bent themselves to designing and building the finest warplanes in their power. When they were sure that their basic planes were good enough, designs were frozen, production lines were set up and delivery speeded until the Reich should have numerical superiority in all types over any possible opponent.

Model freezing slowed transition

Just as German war plans were set up for a short war, so too was German production organized for a quick victory. Model freezing made for getting a lot of planes into the air quickly but hindered the rapid adaptation to new planes for specialized purposes. Thus, whenever the Luftwaffe stalled, it was forced to make modifications in existing equipment which prevented the use of production lines for new models. Meanwhile, the more flexible Allied air forces were gaining the initiative.

The destiny of the Luftwaffe is no longer in German hands. The shape it must take from here on out is being forced upon it by the Allied offensive. Within a year's time, the production of defensive fighters has risen by about 50%, while bomber production has fallen off about 10%. Experimental models are being developed, and radically new types may soon appear in combat.

Though now constrained to fight a defensive war, Germany still has the men and equipment for a major offensive. The quality of the planes illustrated on the following pages is high and there is no extreme shortage of pilots. In the Focke-Wulf 190 and Messerschmitt 109 series, the Reich has two of the best fighters in the air—fast, maneuverable and capable of operation at all altitudes. In the Junkers 88—a plane that has been encountered in at least thirty different adaptations—the Nazis have the world's most versatile aircraft. Their medium bombers are still among the finest of the war for tactical bombing.

Finally, it must be remembered that, regardless of all known defects, the Luftwaffe will increase in effectiveness as its lines of supply and the distances between fronts decrease. When Germany withdraws from Italy and begins to fight from the heart of Europe, it will be fighting for its life. The Fortress of Europe will not crack overnight.

GÖRING beats the drum for Nazi air power at early Brown Shirt jamboree.

8-M.M. ARMOR PLATE BEHIND PILOT'S SEAT

PILOT'S HEAD ARMOR (10-M.

BULLET-RESISTING GLASS

REFLECTOR SIGHT

TWO SYNCHRONIZED M.G. 17 GUNS (7.9-M.M.), FIRING THROUGH AIRSCREW 500 ROUNDS PER GUN

BELT FEED FOR M.G. 151 200 ROUNDS

OIL COOLER

COOLANT TANK

OIL TANK

M.G. 151 (20-M.M.), FIRING BETWEEN CYLINDER BANKS AND THROUGH AIRSCREW HUB

ME-109, LUFTWAFFE STAND-BY

Oldest fighter plane still in service with the Luftwaffe, the Me-109 has been in constant use since 1939. The models now serving in the high-altitude fighting over Europe are the Me-109F and Me-109G which are practically identical for recognition purposes. They represent a definite change from the Me-109E which was soundly trounced by the Spitfire in the Battle of Britain.

Models F and G are shown on these pages. The latter has a power rating 350 h.p. higher than its predecessor's 1,150 h.p. It is also more heavily armed, carrying a 20-mm. cannon mounted under each wing in addition to the armament shown in this exploded diagram of the F. Defensive fighters, the Me-109's are capable of better performance at high altitudes than the famed Focke-Wulf

190. Fast and maneuverable, with a high service ceiling (almost 40,000 ft. for the G), the Messerschmitts are excellent planes but do not quite equal the best Allied fighters at substratosphere levels: Lightning, Thunderbolt, Spitfire.

RECOGNITION: Me-109F and G are single-seat, low-wing monoplanes with inline engines. Unlike most British and U. S. fighters, there is no break in the symmetry of the nose where the spinner begins. The nose is thick, looks like a high-explosive shell extending from the fuselage. Slight dihedral from the roots, rounded tips and a taper of the trailing edge mark the wing. Low cockpit fairs into long fuselage neatly, giving little impression of bump. Markedly high is the position of the stabilizer on the small fin and rudder.

FUEL TANK EXTENDS
UNDER PILOT'S SEAT

OXYGEN BOTTLES

ACCUMULATOR

COMPRESSED AIR BOTTLES

WIRELESS EQUIPMENT

LAMINATED DURAL PLATE
MASTER COMPASS

COOLANT RADIATOR

WING FLAP

AUTOMATIC SLOT

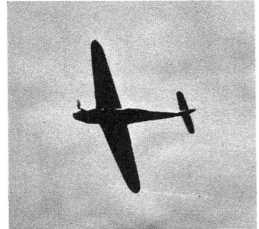

FUSELAGE OF ME-109 IS LONG AND TAPERING

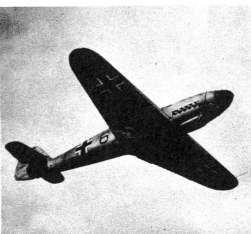

AIRSCOOP GIVES DEPTH TO ME'S BULLET NOSE

STABILIZER IS SET HIGH ON THE TAIL ASSEMBLY

FW-190

It serves as a fighter and bomber in new Nazi defensive air strategy

When the Focke-Wulf 190 was first introduced in the summer of 1941, it was the finest fighter in the world. Not until the Spitfire IX was there a fighter in Europe to equal it. Though Allied fighters now equal or better it, it is still one of the top planes of the war.

In the FW-190A model, this aircraft has been used on hit-and-run bombing attacks on England. Its usual bomb load is one 550-lb. bomb but it can carry up to 1,100 lb. As a fighter-bomber, it is difficult to intercept, since after it drops its load and jettisons its extra fuel tanks, it can perform as a fighter. As a fighter it mounts two or four 20-mm. and two 7.9-mm. weapons. Carrying a full bomb load and extra fuel tanks, the FW-190 has a speed of 320 m.p.h. at 19,000 ft. After dropping its load, its speed increases to 370 m.p.h. The fighter version is in 400 m.p.h. class.

Like the Spitfire and Mustang in our forces, the FW-190 is a great favorite with pilots. The controls are extremely simple, light to handle. Wing flaps and propeller pitch are automatically controlled. **RECOGNITION:** FW-190's fuselage tapers from blunt radial engine to thin tail. Prop spinner is especially large. Wing and tailplane have square tips. Wing tapers slightly on both edges; tailplane is straight. Cuts below show plane with bomb and extra fuel tanks. Span: 34 ft., 6 in.; length: 29 ft., 1 in.

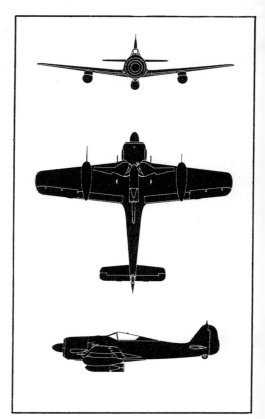

FUSELAGE TAPER, straight tailplane are distinctive points of the FW-190's plan form, even when seen from an angle. Fuselage aft contrasts sharply with heavy nose. From head-on, the FW-190 has been confused with our P-47, but FW's propeller is centered and cowling is a true circle.

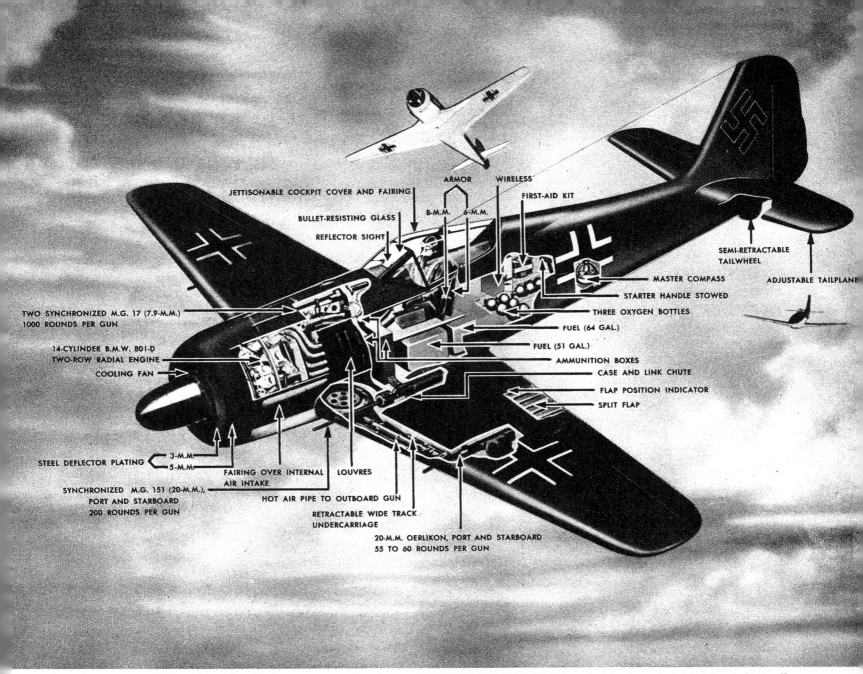

CUTAWAY DRAWING of FW-190 shows details of armament and equipment. Landing gear folds inward to improve roll: tailwheel retracts part way. Four guns fire through propeller arc: two outboard guns are also mounted.

JETTISONABLE CANOPY has electrically exploded holding bolts to allow speedy exit of pilot when plane is shot down. Canopy has straight fairing into deep, slim fuselage. Vertical tail surfaces are tall, broad for fast fighter.

JU-88

Dive-bombing and night-fighting are but two of the plane's many uses

Most versatile plane of the war to date has unquestionably been the Ju-88. Horizontal and dive bomber, night fighter, reconnaissance plane and torpedo plane, occasionally equipped with floats, it outdoes even the Havoc and Mosquito in the number of uses to which it has been put by the German Air Force.

The Nazis have been mass-producing this plane ever since the outbreak of the war. Modified frequently to incorporate necessary changes for its varied missions, it has, nevertheless, retained its original airframe. An expected new model will have radial rather than inline engines, but this is not expected to change the appearance of the nacelles, as the Ju-88's nacelles look as if they housed a radial engine.

RECOGNITION: Ju-88 is a twin-engine, low-wing monoplane. Its heavy radial-type nacelles protrude considerably and are in line with the plane's nose. The appearance of the nose itself will vary considerably. A glassed-in tip features the bomber's nose while the fighter has a solid one carrying as many as three cannon and three machine guns. The bombardier's position under the nose is off center. Extreme forward position of the cockpit and single fin and rudder projecting well beyond the elevators are additional features worth noting. Span: 66 ft.; length, 47 ft.

GUNNER'S OR BOMBARDIER'S position is below cockpit on starboard of fuselage. Like many Nazi planes, it has engines and humped cockpit bunched forward, appears nose-heavy.

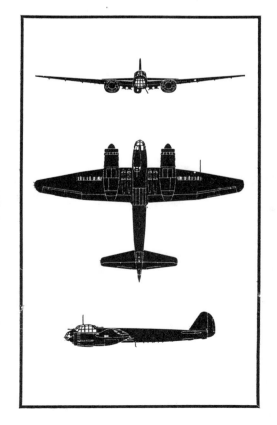

PRONOUNCED SWEEP-BACK of wing identifies Ju-88. Outboard section tapers to rounded tips; dihedral is conspicuous. Large round radial-type nacelles house twin inline engines.

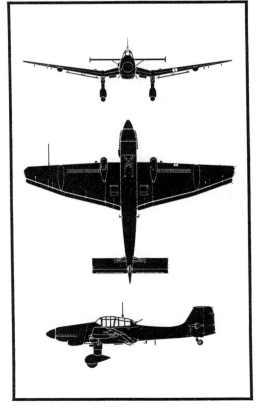

PROMINENT RADIATOR visible under nose is smaller in the latest models of the Stuka.

Two-man cockpit has also been more streamlined, now mounts twin free guns in the rear.

WHEELS AND WING are distinctive features. Angular fuselage, wing and tail are also typical.

JU-87

Now outdated, the Stuka once terrorized Europe

Equipped with sirens in its fixed landing gear, the Stuka ran its own interference by frightening first and bombing afterward. With the air cleared of Allied fighters in the weeks when the big ground campaigns were under way, the Stukas dive-bombed their way over inexperienced anti-aircraft gunners in Poland, France and the Low Countries. Over England, however, their lack of speed and firepower made them defenseless against fighters, while gun crews soon learned not to shoot too early.

The model now in use is the Ju-87D. It has a smaller radiator and cockpit than earlier models, but these changes should not affect recognition at combat range. Recently 15 Stukas were intercepted by a flight of Lightnings over the Strait of Scarpanto near Rhodes. The USAAF batted 1.000 on this trip, shooting down all 15. Because of debacles such as this, the Ju-87 is being used very little against Anglo-American forces at the present time. However, it is still seeing considerable service in the free-for-all fight on the Russian front.

RECOGNITION: The Stuka is a low-wing monoplane with a single inline engine. Its inverted gull wing, nonretractable landing gear, square rudder and humped cockpit combine to make it one of the leading contenders for the title "The World's Ugliest Plane." Rectangular tailplane is braced by struts. Span of Ju-87: 45 ft., 4 in.; length: 36 ft., 5 in.

ME-110

Twin-engine fighter proved a failure as an escort plane for daylight raiders

ARMAMENT OF ME-110 is concentrated in plane's nose. One or two machine guns can be brought to bear against fighter attacks from rear.

ME-110'S UNDERSLUNG NACELLES are broad at the base to hold inverted-V inline engines. The plane's nose protrudes well in front of nacelles.

ME-410

Successor to Me-210 sees action as a fighter-bomber, long-range fighter

LARGE FIN seems out of proportion to the Me-210's slender fuselage. Side guns swing 35° above or below center and 45° laterally, protect rear.

POSITION OF THE NOSE, clearly behind propeller spinners, marks the plan view of the Me-210. From this angle the side guns are barely visible.

Brought into the Battle of Britain as a plane able to outrange the Luftwaffe's standard 1940 fighter, the Me-109E, the Me-110 was not a serious threat to the British fighters despite its high speed and impressive armament. Used to provide fighter cover for the Heinkel and Dornier daylight raiders, it showed several structural weaknesses and a lack of maneuverability.

Its other functions as ground strafer and hit-and-run bomber have been taken over by later Messerschmitt models, the 210 and 410 (*see below*). The Me-110 can definitely be classed as an obsolescent plane, but the Luftwaffe's strained condition has forced the Nazis to keep it in operation as a trainer and defensive fighter.

Most spectacular contribution to the war made by the Me-110 so far was the delivery of Rudolf Hess to the British. The No. 3 Nazi took off from Augsburg in Bavaria and bailed out over the countryside near Glasgow.

RECOGNITION: The Me-110's most noteworthy feature is its twin tail assembly, the only one ever attempted by the Messerschmitt engineers. It is a low-wing, two-place monoplane powered by two inline engines housed in heavy nacelles. The tailplane is set above the thin, tapering fuselage. Span: 53 ft., 11 in.; length: 40 ft., 4 in.

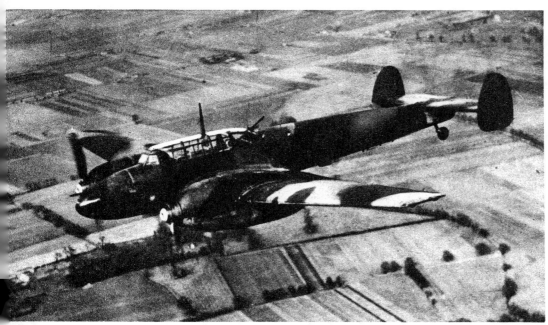

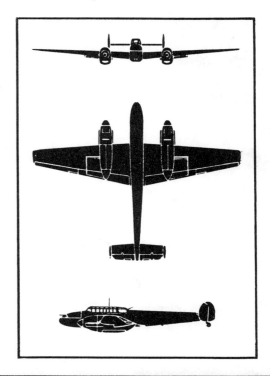

SQUARE WING TIPS, like those on obsolete Me-109E, have been retained on Me-110. Fins and rudders are set outboard of the elevator and stabilizer. Fuselage is unusually long and thin.

Third plane of the twin-engine Messerschmitt series, the Me-410 has been designed to replace the Me-110 and Me-210. Pictures of this newest model are not available as yet. However, it closely resembles the Me-210 shown in these pictures. The *Journal* will print photographs of the new plane as soon as they are obtained.

The Me-410, like the Me-210, can be used for several purposes. As a hit-and-run bomber it carries an estimated maximum bomb load of 3,300 lb.; because of its speed it can be used on fighter missions against ground forces or landing craft.

Novel feature of the Messerschmitt 210 and 410 are the side blisters which mount single 13-mm. machine guns, fired by the radio operator by means of a reflector sight and a remote-control mechanism. The wide cone of fire gives considerable protection.

RECOGNITION: Like the Me-210, the Me-410 is a low-wing, two-place monoplane powered by two inline engines. Unlike the Me-110, it has a single fin and rudder, rounded wing tips and a pushed-in nose. The cockpit is very markedly humped, breaking the contour of an otherwise slender fuselage. This hump and the taper of the wing's edge distinguish the Me-410 from the Mosquito which it somewhat resembles. Span: 53 ft., 9 in.; length: 40 ft., 3 in.

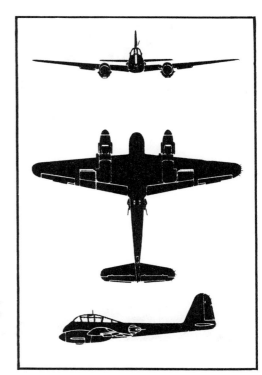

NOSE ARMAMENT in Me-210 consists of two fixed 20-mm. cannon and two fixed 7.92-mm. machine guns. While impressive, it does not equal the firepower packed by comparable Allied aircraft.

THREE TORPEDO-CARRYING HE-111'S SWOOP LOW ATTACKING SMALL ALLIED FREIGHTER BOUND FOR MURMANSK. SHARPLY SWEPTBACK WING, BROAD

TWO TORPEDOES can be carried by the He-111 in place of bomb load. Fuselage tapers to a sharp point behind the gracefully elliptical tailplane.

HE-111

Nazi medium bomber paid heavily for day and night assaults over England

The He-111 has been the Luftwaffe's standard medium bomber ever since the beginning of the war. During the mass raids on Britain, He-111's often made up two-thirds of the attacking bomber formations. Deficient in armament and armor, they were shot down in such numbers that the British were able to supply spare parts for He-111's which Turkey had bought from the Reich.

Continual improvements in design have added armor, cannon, and machine guns. Carrying torpedoes for attacks on Allied convoys, the He-111 has operated from France, Norway, Italy. Although still widely used, it is becoming obsolete by present standards.

RECOGNITION: The He-111 is a twin-engine, low-wing monoplane. The wing's leading edge tapers outboard of the nacelles, while the trailing edge has a deep "bite" on either side of the fuselage. The lopsided nose, belly gun positions, and the hump of the top turret are also noteworthy. Span: 74 ft., 3 in.; length: 54 ft., 5 in.

DAMAGED HENSCHEL 129 with desert camouflage for the North African campaign being examined by soldier. Engines in underslung nacelles have typical German huge spinners.

HS-129

Underpowered engines are said to handicap

Henschel 129, tank-busting attack-bomber

Heavily armored and carrying a 30-mm. cannon in its belly, the Hs-129 is Germany's entry in the tank-buster class of warplanes. Its fixed armament in the nose consists of two 7.92-mm. machine guns, two cannon of either 15- or 20-mm. In the Tunisian campaign a single 550-lb. bomb sometimes replaced the 30-mm. cannon for dive-bombing missions.

Used mostly on the Russian front, the Henschel 129 apparently has failed as a threat to hostile armored units. It is a relatively slow plane, doing but 240 m.p.h. at sea level, and Allied experts are of the opinion that it is underpowered.

RECOGNITION: A low-wing, single-seat monoplane, the Hs-129 is powered by two radial air-cooled Gnôme-Rhône engines. The armored nose is round and on a line with tips of the spinners. Span of the Hs-129: 44 ft., 6 in.; length: 33 ft., 3 in.

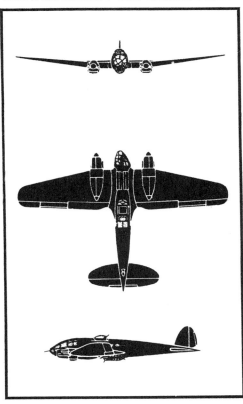

SOLID NOSE between radial engines provides housing for Henschel's guns, gives it protruding chinned appearance. Leading edge of the wing is straight while trailing edge tapers.

TAILPLANE IDENTIFY THIS GERMAN BOMBER

DORNIER 217 HAS A LONG THIN FUSELAGE, LARGE BULBOUS NOSE. TAPERED FINS AND RUDDERS RISE HIGH AT OUTBOARD END OF TAILPLANE

DO-217

Shows Nazis' fondness for multi-purpose planes

The current representative of the Dornier line of bombers is used for all varieties of bombing tasks. Flown chiefly in western Europe, it has appeared as level bomber, dive bomber, torpedo plane, minelayer and night fighter. The night bombers used over England recently have been mostly Do-217's. Armament varies but a typical pattern might be one 20-mm. or 13-mm. gun forward, one 13-mm. in the bottom, two twin 7.92-mm. guns in the sides, and one 13-mm. gun in an electrically controlled top turret. The night-fighter version undoubtedly is still heavier armed. As a bomber, the Do-217 can carry a nor-

mal load of over two tons, a maximum of almost three and a half tons. Top speed of the older models is about 300 m. p. h.; of the newer M series, 350 m. p. h.

RECOGNITION: The Do-217 is a lineal descendant of the old Do-17, the "Flying Pencil," and like it the Do-217 has a rather long thin fuselage. The straight wing is set high on the fuselage and the two radial engines are underslung from it. The cockpit canopy projects above the fuselage, has a gun turret in aft end. Twin tail assembly has high tapered fins and rudders at outboard end of horizontal stabilizer. Span: 62 ft., 5 in.; length: 56 ft., 6 in.

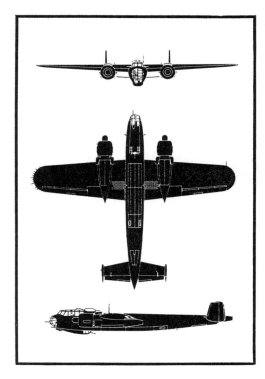

RESEMBLANCE TO B-25 is pronounced head-on. Bumpy contours of nose and belly turret far forward distinguish Do-217 from the Mitchell.

WIDE ROUNDED WINGTIPS minimize slight taper on edges of main plane. In rear angle views, pointed projection of the fuselage stands out.

20

DETAILS SUCH AS GUNS, CRANES, PLANE BOOMS ARE ABSORBED IN MAJOR MASSES. COMPARE BUMP AND PHOTO OF NORTHAMPTON CLASS ABOVE

BUMPS Warships are quickly recognized by new Coast Artillery Bump silhouettes

Equally as difficult as recognizing a plane at great heights is spotting and recognizing a ship hull down over the horizon. In order to overcome this problem a new aid to recognition teaching, the "bump" method, has been devised. First developed by the Coast Artillery School for shore-based observation posts, the basis of this method is the presentation of the total form of a ship as a rough outline which emphasizes the characteristic upper portions of the ship's superstructure, reduced to a simplified silhouette. The observer can thus study the overall shape of the ship as it appears at a great distance.

These silhouettes have three primary purposes: recognition of ship types, classes and nationalities. Basically a training aid, they may be used as an actual means of identifying warships. The Bump technique is applied to a ship from the top down, and the top third of the superstructure

which appears first over the horizon is therefore the most important. The uppermost bumps should give a clue as to the type of ship in view—i.e., whether it has the towering foremast of a Jap battleship, three high close-set stacks of most British cruisers, or the long low squat silhouette of an Italian vessel.

On this and the following pages the *Journal* presents in Bumps all classes of heavy cruisers—Allied and Axis—listed in the current training list (*see p. 7*), and a companion photographic quiz on pp 26–27. The Northampton Class shown above in both photograph and bump has a very high foremast, two short widely separated stacks, a light tripod aft. Pensacola and Portland Classes are similar.

Careful study of the bumps of Allied cruisers on the following spread and those of the Axis cruisers on pages 24–25 will reveal very distinct national character-

istics. The Jap Navy is an excellent example of strongly marked national naval architecture. Like the Japs, the larger units of the German Navy are easy to identify by nationality, although difficult to distinguish individually. They have pronounced heavy lines, thick stacks which contrast sharply with the typical Jap raked stack and the close-set tall thin stacks of most British and American cruisers. Newest addition to the list of Allied cruisers is the Italian Bolzano (*see p. 23*) which has widely spaced superstructure elements and extremely clean lines with lower foremast than appears in cruisers of other nations.

Bump charts of the Navies of the major warring nations are to be included in the *Recognition Pictorial Manual of Naval Vessels* (FM 30–50; NavAer 00—80V—57), which will soon be issued following the similar FM 30–30; BuAer 3.

HEAVY CRUISERS OF ALLIED NAVIES

TOWERING FOREMAST, WIDELY-SPACED STACKS OF PENSACOLA CLASS RESEMBLE NORTHAMPTON

CLOSE-SET STACKS, STUBBY CONTROL TOWER, PLANE CATAPULT AFT IDENTIFY NEW ORLEANS

BUMP OUTLINE OF NEW BALTIMORE CLASS SHOWS MIDSHIP CONCENTRATION OF SUPER-STRUCTURE ELEMENTS

STACKS OF PORTLAND CLASS HUNCH INTO THE SHIP'S BULK, ARE SEPARATED BY PLANE CATAPULTS

WICHITA CLASS SHOWS TRENDS IN U. S. CRUISER DESIGN: STACKS, CONTROL TOWER CENTERED

SHOWN IN SIMPLE "BUMP" OUTLINE

LONDON CLASS DIFFERS FROM MOST BRITISH HEAVIES; HAVING WIDELY SPACED STRAIGHT STACKS

SLENDER SLANTING STACKS OF BRITISH COUNTY GROUP MAKE DEVONSHIRE CLASS UNMISTAKABLE

CUMBERLAND GREATLY RESEMBLES DEVONSHIRE, CAN BE DISTINGUISHED BY REAR PLANE HANGAR

BUMP OF WORLD WAR I HAWKINS CLASS SHOWS MANY SMALL SCATTERED SUPERSTRUCTURE PARTS

HEAVY CRUISERS OF AXIS NAVIES

SINGLE SQUAT COWLED SMOKE STACK CROWDS UP TO CLUTTERED FOREMAST OF ADMIRAL HIPPER CLASS

LONG BULKY CENTER SECTION OF NAZI CRUISERS LOOMS HIGH AS ON THE ADMIRAL SCHEER ABOVE

PRINZ EUGEN CLASS HAS CLOSE-SET STACK, FOREMAST LIKE THE HIPPER, BUT A MORE BROKEN AFT SECTION

LUETZOW CLASS OUTLINE RESEMBLES SCHEER, HAS CLUTTERED FOREMAST OF MOST NAZI HEAVIES

REVEAL DEFINITE NATIONAL TRAITS

ATAGO, TAKAO CLASS HAS HEAVIER BULKED CONTROL TOWER THAN NACHI; AFT TRIPOD SET WELL BACK

MOGAMI CLASS CRUISERS HAVE LONGEST FORWARD SWEEP OF RAKED STACK, SMALLEST CONTROL TOWER

BOTH STACKS OF THE AOBA CLASS HAVE MARKED BACKWARD SLANT; JAGGED CONTROL TOWER

EXCEPT FOR THE POSITION OF THE AFT TRIPOD, CHOKAI-MAYA CLASS SOMEWHAT RESEMBLES ATAGO CLASS

VALUE OF THE "BUMPS" IS DEMONSTRATED IN THIS VIEW OF ASSEMBLED UNITS OF THE U.S. FLEET. WARSHIPS AND MERCHANT VESSELS CAN BE

RECOGNIZED FROM BULK SILHOUETTE OF THEIR SUPERSTRUCTURES. SEE HOW MANY YOU CAN SPOT BEFORE TURNING TO PAGE 50 FOR ANSWERS

27

Germany's huge bulky Mark VI is largest tank in world. Admiring Nazis show its tremendous size

SQUARE HULL RISES HIGHER ABOVE TRACKS AT REAR. MAMMOTH TURRET, MOUNTING MUZZLE-BRAKED 88-MM. GUN, IS FORWARD OF CENTER

HEAVY TANKS

They are difficult to maneuver on all terrain, but they have terrific firepower

Late in the African campaign, Allied tanks were lured into attacking formations of lighter German tanks, only to have them fan out, exposing the Allied force to the heavy guns of Germany's newest motorized weapon, the PzKw VI, or Tiger, tank. This massive 60-ton weapon mounts an electrically fired 88-mm. gun and has frontal armor 102-mm. thick, making it a formidable opponent when properly used. It is so heavy, however, that it can only travel on hard smooth terrain, cross stoutly reinforced bridges.

An attempt has been made, reports indicate, to increase its mobility by installing gaskets on all ports so that it can be sealed watertight and driven through streams up to 16 ft. deep. Air is sucked in through a tall demountable pipe which sticks up from the stern. Gaskets must be specially installed for every crossing.

RECOGNITION: The Tiger's prime recognition feature is its great size. It is 27 ft. long, about 12 ft. wide and 9½ ft. high. The 360° flat-topped turret is long and deep to absorb the recoil of the pole-like gun, the sides are almost vertical. The hull is rectangular but rises slightly to the rear in the side view. Two widths of tracks are used. With the narrower one, two overlapping rows of eight Christie-type bogie wheels are used; with the wide ones, three rows of eight. Tracks extend well beyond hull.

EXHAUST STACKS project from the square back of the Tiger's low profiled hull. From all angles, the PzKw VI looks massive and powerful.

LONG 88-MM. GUN overhangs the Tiger's bow by almost 7 ft. Small tubes on the turret sides are smoke ejectors used to obscure slow tank.

CHURCHILL

Britain's biggest tank does finest work as an infantry support weapon

Current backbone of the British Army Tank Brigades is the 40-ton Churchill. It played a most important role in the Tunisian campaign where it was used to support infantry advances over all types of terrain. Mounting variously a 6-pounder, 2-pounder or 3-in. howitzer, it was effective against machine-gun or light artillery emplacements, personnel, or other tanks. The 3-in. howitzer is mounted in the hull, used for close support work. In special adaptations, the Churchill may be used for bridge laying or as a recovery vehicle to salvage disabled equipment.

The Churchill is slow, having a top speed of only 17 m.p.h. It is powered by a 12-cylinder Bedford pancake-type engine with a rated horsepower of 325. Its cruising range is slightly more than a hundred miles.

RECOGNITION: The Churchill is the only operational tank with overall tracks. These extend as high as the hull and protrude beyond the end to form two horns. A vertical shield extends along top of track to protect return rollers, support rear drive sprocket and front idler. Air louvres protrude from skirt back of center. The tank rides on nine evenly spaced bogies and one slightly raised at each end. Overall, the tank is 24 ft. long, 10½ ft. wide, and 8 ft. high. The turret is in the center of the high, flat-topped hull and may be of either cast or welded construction. The sides of the turret are rounded in the cast version and angular when welded. The face from which the gun protrudes is square. A rectangular storage bin is fitted at the right rear. Both turret hatches are flush with the flat top surface. The combination of shallow turret, overall tracks, and half skirting makes the Churchill easily distinguishable from any other tank.

LUMBERING CHURCHILL climbs out of a depression. Note how hull extends to rear end of tracks, is short in front. This model has cast turret.

CREW OF FIVE MEN look out of turret and hull hatches. Driver and machine gunner occupy seats in front of hull, commander in the turret. Gap between tracks is best recognition feature from air.

NUMEROUS SMALL BOGIES mark the tank's track suspension; height between

CHURCHILL HAS LOWER PROFILE than any other large tank, a distinct advantage in desert fighting. In silhouette, long low hull, centrally mounted turret makes tank easy to recognize even when details are obscured. Coaxial machine gun may be seen mounted above 6-pounder gun.

tracks makes for quick recognition. Protruding air louvres can be seen in almost all views.

ANGULAR TURRET marks the welded model. Opening in front of turret allows higher elevation of main armament. British tank design starts with turret; Churchill has ideal fighting chamber.

KLEMENTY VOROSHILOV, MARK I, SERVES AS ARTILLERY EMPLACEMENT IN RUINED RUSSIAN CITY. TURRET ATHWART HULL PROJECTS OVER TRACK

KV-I & KV-II

Formidable Soviet heavy tanks mount biggest guns, heaviest armor of war

The two Klementy Voroshilov tanks illustrated on these pages are the Soviet Republic's entries in the race for heavier motorized armor and guns. Like all heavy tanks, they are bulky, slow and difficult to maneuver across country. The KV's make up for these weaknesses, however, by their heavy armor and large guns. Even when halted, the KV's have been able to maintain strong fire to hold off the Nazis until reinforcements could come up.

The KV-I and KV-II are built on the same chassis. Their only

EXTRA FUEL DRUMS ARE OFTEN STRAPPED TO SIDES OF KV-I WHEN MOVING INTO ACTION.   TANK MAY ALSO BE USED TO TRANSPORT INFANTRY

STILLS TAKEN FROM SOVIET MOTION PICTURE "ONE DAY OF WAR" SHOW TWO KV-I TANKS IN OPERATION ON FLAT TERRAIN OF THE RUSSIAN STEPPES

differences are in their turrets and armament. The KV-I has a large flat-topped turret in which a 76.2-mm. gun is mounted. The KV-II's turret is a huge cube-like mass from which protrudes either a 122-mm. gun or a 152-mm. howitzer. The chassis, derived from the World War I Vickers Mark VI, is powered by a 12-cylinder Diesel engine of 600 h.p. Maximum speed is about 20 m.p.h.

RECOGNITION: The hull of both tanks is long and low, set between massive tracks. It is 22 ft. overall and 11 ft. wide. Tracks are supported on six medium sized bogies and return on three small rollers. Large rear drive sprocket and front idler are set high. Turret of KV-I is large and flat with inclined sides joining a rounded, undercut elongation in the rear. The flat sloping front mounts a large rounded gun mantlet from which the slender 76.2-mm. gun extends to the end of the hull. The KV-II turret is a massive box with vertical, slightly rounded sides. The top is perfectly flat, while the front is largely obscured by an immense gun mantlet.

KV-II

HUGE MANTLET & GUN COVER FRONT OF KV-II'S TURRET   KV-II'S BOX-SQUARE TURRET WILL TRAVERSE ONLY WHEN THE TANK IS LEVEL

DUMMY PLANES

Reconnaissance photos of landing strips reveal many enemy "planes" are fakes

DUMMY PLANES shown above were scattered around airfields in Libya to draw bombs and strafing fire. The dummy in lower picture was tough to spot because of markings, raised position which cast correct shadow.

Peculiar to all wars is the art of camouflage. Every war brings with it new developments in deception, new methods of hiding the tools of warfare from the enemy.

Until World War I deception had been limited to the comparatively simple task of fooling the human eye; its role was later extended to circumventing the camera. Now, in World War II the strides that have taken place in aerial photographic reconnaissance have dictated a concurrent intensive development in ground camouflage, notably in the faking of airfields and dispersal areas.

On these pages the *Journal* presents the results of a study of enemy planes made by the Army Air Forces. This type of camouflage is not so much to hide matériel as to fake worthless objectives to draw fire.

To combat this, aerial gunners and bombardiers should watch particularly for the following: first, color of the plane—if it is so light as to stand out against its background, it is a fair bet that it is a phoney. Then, check as carefully as possible whether it casts a normal shadow, whether or not it is symmetrical (dummies are often thrown together hastily of junked material), whether it conforms to the known types of aircraft in the area, whether the position remains the same on successive sorties (*see the opposite page*).

Seaplanes moored in unprotected areas should also be studied critically, since moorings are ordinarily placed where water is quiet. Any plane spotted on the edge of a beach is sure to be suspect, since an operational plane is liable to serious damage from surf and tide unless well moored; if it is on the water the relation of the plane to direction of the wind should be carefully checked.

LIGHTER PLANES (RIGHT) SITTING AT MERCY OF KISKA SURF AND TIDE ARE FAKES. NOTE HOW THEY HAVE FAILED TO SWING INTO WIND

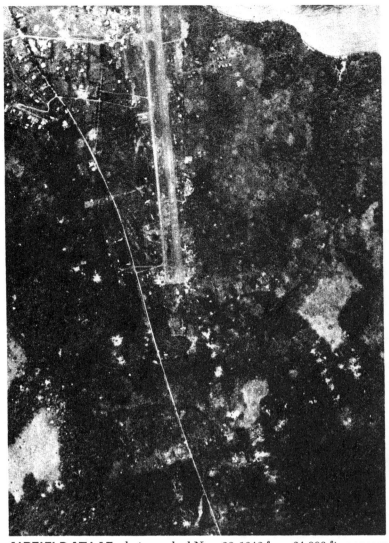

AIRFIELD AT LAE, photographed Nov. 26, 1942 from 24,000 ft., appears to have several dozen planes carelessly scattered along runway. Cautious bombardier, however, will wonder why these "planes" are so obvious.

TWO WEEKS LATER this photograph of same field from 20,000 ft. reveals most of these dummy planes still in identical positions. The few that have moved appear to be dummies that have been knocked aside by bomb hits.

THESE "PLANES" AT KISKA ARE UNMISTAKABLY DUMMIES. NOTE HOW THEY STAND OUT UNNATURALLY, ARE TOO BRIGHT, CAST NO SHADOW

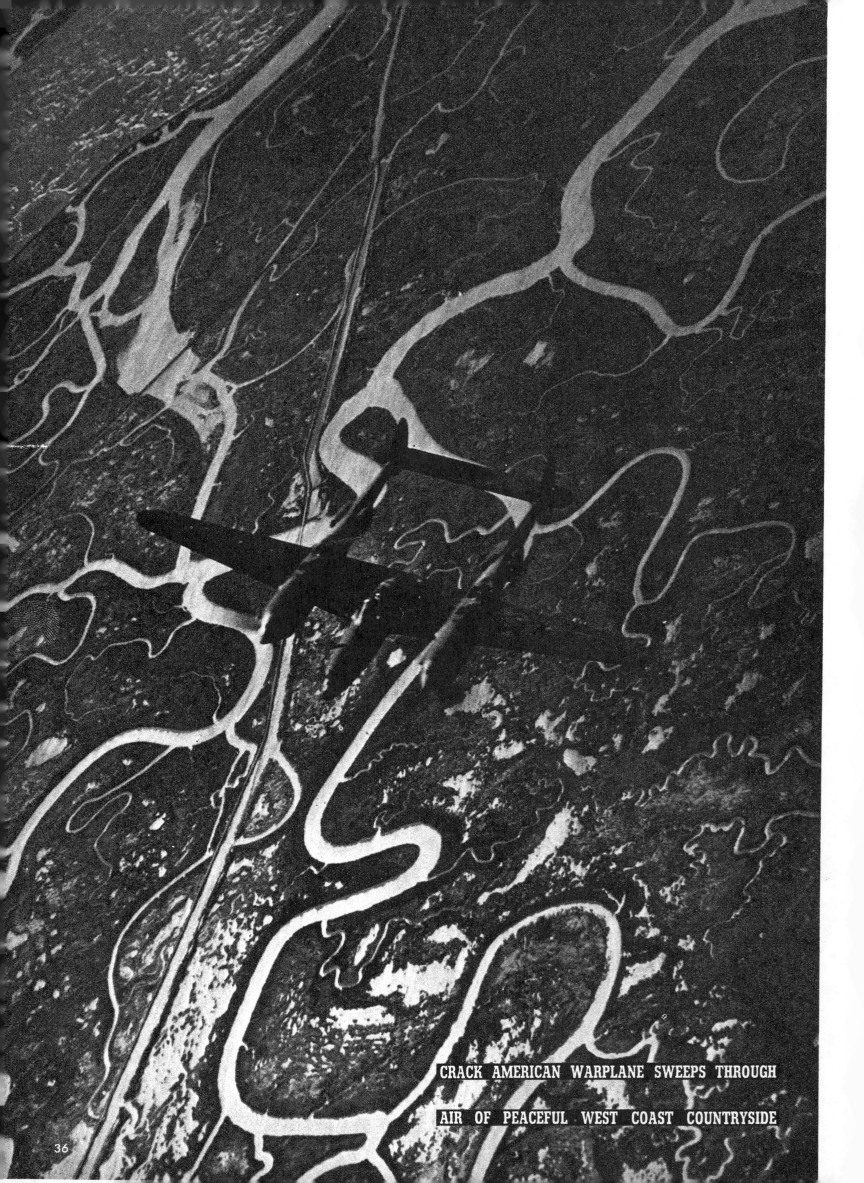

CRACK AMERICAN WARPLANE SWEEPS THROUGH

AIR OF PEACEFUL WEST COAST COUNTRYSIDE

THE FIRST AMERICAN PLANE TO GO INTO BATTLE, THE P-40 HAS SEEN SERVICE ON ALL FRONTS UNDER SEVEREST FIGHTING CONDITIONS

ARMY FIGHTERS

USAAF HAS BALANCED ARRAY OF FIGHTING PLANES

When in 1939 war once again broke out in Europe, our air force consisted of only 20,000 men. Only one Army fighter capable of meeting the Nazis was in extensive production. Two others were abuilding. And by European standards, all our planes were poorly armed and armored.

But though our preparations were meager, our plans were good. No longer merely an adjunct to a small Army, the AAF is now the largest and most powerful air force in the world. By the end of this year, 2,500,000 men will be enlisted in this branch of the service (a four-year growth of 12,400%). In some categories, the planes they fly and service are the best in the world, in all classes, they can hold their own with anything the enemy has in the air. In six months (Jan. 1 to June 30) they shot down 763 enemy planes to a loss of 375.

Most of our current fighters were designed before the war with very specific purposes in mind. The job each was expected to perform was clearly outlined. But war has a way of upsetting preconceived notions. When the fighting was confined to western Europe, planes could work on a limited operation basis. But as the war spread out over the world, it became obvious that airplane designs had to be adaptable. At outposts where service facilities were limited, available aircraft had to do all sorts of jobs with a minimum of adaptation. Range, speed, firepower, maneuverability and altitude had to be juggled to get the best combination for the widest possible field of service. Planes had to be able to get up high enough fast enough to stop enemy bombers, to carry a fair sized bomb load for ground attack, to maintain enough low level speed to protect themselves from ground AA.

Our P-38, P-40, and P-51 are fine examples of the versatile fighter. The P-40, the sixty-minute man of the American combat team, has never had the high-performance rating of the best British and German fighters, yet it has one of the finest battle records of the war. The P-38 has been even more versatile, adding bombing and photo-reconnaissance to its duties. The P-51, our newest plane, is the fastest low altitude fighter in the world. In its high altitude and fighter-bomber versions, its potentialities are just being explored.

With the P-47 to fly high cover for our bombers and the flying cannon of the P-39 to smash enemy ground forces, we have a well-balanced line-up. And with the new planes now in American factories, we shall maintain our air superiority.

LONG TAIL BOOMS OF LIGHTNING SEEM TO STREAM OUT BEHIND NOSE AND NACELLES AS FLIGHT RACES ACROSS THE AFRICAN DESERT. TEAR-

Long tapering wing of P-38 is broken by underslung engine nacelles and mid-wing pilot's nacelle. Cockpit enclosure rises prominently above the nacelle.

Peeling off, Lightning displays graceful plan form. Though wing trailing edge has greater taper, foreshortening makes it appear straight.

38

P-38

HOMESICK ANGEL IS AAF'S MOST VERSATILE FIGHTER

Since Feb. 11, 1939, when Lt. Ben Kelsey flew the XP-38 across the continent at an average speed of 350 m. p. h., the Lightning has been one of the fastest, hardest hitting, and most versatile of our fighters. Originally, the P-38 was designed with a high rate of climb to perform as an interceptor-fighter. In its present operational models, however, it fights at all altitudes, strafes and bombs, and is used for high-speed photographic reconnaissance. New models will have stepped-up horsepower and improved intercooling systems for higher altitude work; better pilot vision for low altitudes.

The two propellers turn in opposite directions. This arrangement counteracts engine torque and gives the plane increased maneuverability over other twin-engine planes. It also allows the P-38 to turn in either direction with equal facility, a tactical advantage over single-engine fighters which turn easiest in the direction of torque.

The guns of the P-38 are concentrated in the nose and fire directly ahead. The firepower is thus more effective at long range than that of planes having wing-mounted guns which converge and disperse at a point several hundred yards in front. In the photo-recon version, the F-5A, the nose guns are removed and five aerial cameras installed in their place. This plane is used for high, fast strip filming and low oblique "dicer" shots.

As an attack bomber, the P-38 carries two 1,000-lb. bombs on external racks inboard of the motor nacelles. Racks can also be used to mount jettisonable fuel tanks which add to already lengthy range. With added tanks, Lightning has flown Atlantic.

RECOGNITION: The P-38 is almost unmistakable. Narrow twin tail booms, with air scoops humping out on either side, pilot's nacelle projecting well beyond engines, beautifully tapered wing set it apart from all other operational types. The only possible confusion is with the FW-189, now in only limited operation.

DROP-SHAPED FINS, RUDDERS ARE PROMINENT RECOGNITION FEATURES

Aerodynamically clean though P-38 is, in flight it seems to project in all directions. Conspicuous bumps are air scoops on the tail booms, cockpit upward, downward extending fins and rudders.

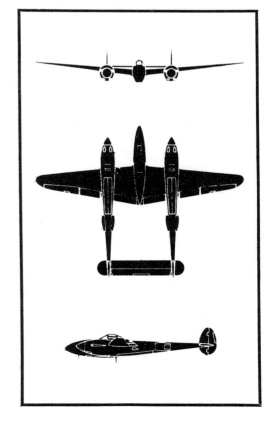

P-39

CANNON-CARRYING FIGHTER BLASTS ARMORED VEHICLES

The performance of the P-39 since the start of the war has amply justified its unorthodox design. From the beginning it has been a good medium and low altitude fighter and an excellent ground attack plane. The 37-mm. hub-firing cannon, one of the heaviest guns carried by a plane, is a powerful weapon against troops, supply trucks, trains and armored vehicles. When a faster firing 20-mm. cannon is substituted and wing guns mounted, the P-39 becomes a formidable aerial combatant. The tricycle landing gear permits the plane to get in and out of small fields, while placing the cockpit forward of the wing gives the pilot a wider field of view than is possible in other fighters.

RECOGNITION: The Airacobra has a number of distinctive features. Its long nose, short tail and rocking-chair sit in the air are unique. The cockpit canopy is highest forward and fairs down into the fuselage just ahead of a prominent air scoop. The wings, which have rounded tips, are stubby, taper from a thick root into slender wing tip. The fin and rudder are fully rounded, extending well beyond trailing edge of elevators.

Pointed nose of the P-39 Airacobra is chief recognition feature in most views, is made possible by mounting engine behind the pilot's enclosure.

EXCEPTIONAL VISIBILITY IS A FEATURE OF THE AIRACOBRA. PILOT SITS IN COCKPIT SLIGHTLY FORWARD OF THE LEADING EDGE OF THE WING

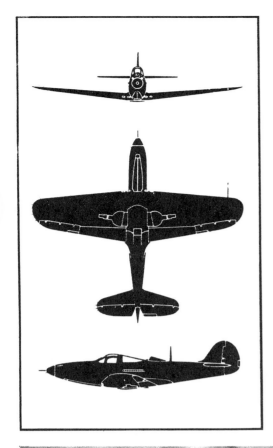

P-39 fuselage appears long in contrast to the stubby wing, though actually the span is greater than the length. In the plan view the smooth lines of plane are unbroken by protuberances.

TALL NARROW FUSELAGE SITS HIGH ON THE AIRACOBRA'S THICK STUBBY WING, WITH THE HORIZONTAL STABILIZER CLEARLY VISIBLE BEHIND

Deep radiator under the plane's long nose distinguishes P-40 from other single-seat fighters equipped with liquid-cooled, inline engines. Originally powered by a 12-cylinder Allison, the P-40 now uses a powerful Packard-built Merlin engine, which substantially raises speed and service ceiling.

P-40

IS A VERSATILE ALL-PURPOSE FIGHTER

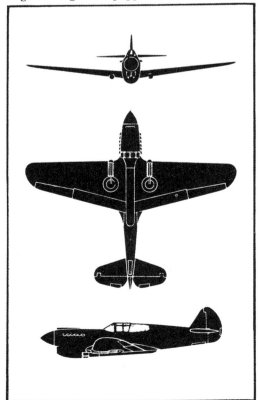

The first U. S. fighter plane to be manufactured on a mass production basis, the P-40 has been used in every theater of operations. Rugged, maneuverable and easy to service, it has piled up an excellent all-round combat score. Besides its record as a fighter (losing 204 to the enemy's 560 in a 17-month period) the P-40 has been used effectively for light bombing and strafing.

The P-40 first came into prominence when it was used in China and Burma by the American Volunteer Group in one of the most amazingly one-sided aerial campaigns of the war. As Kittyhawks (P-40-D&E) they were a headache to

SHARK MOUTH WAS A.V.G. TRADEMARK

Rommel in Africa, strafing and breaking up his supply columns.

The P-40F (*see above*), called the Warhawk, is the latest and best in the series. It is first to feature the Packard-built Merlin engine which has added to its speed and ability to perform at higher altitudes.

RECOGNITION: P-40 is a low-wing monoplane with the long nose typical of liquid-cooled fighter. The wings have a full dihedral. The leading edge is nearly straight, but the taper of the trailing edge is pronounced. Deep radiator below engine is most unique feature. Aft edge of rudder is well rounded.

Tapering wings, bump formed by the cockpit canopy, together with the very prominent landing gear knuckles are all visible in this formation.

Heavy nose, outline of fin and rudder make differentiation from the Hurricane difficult. The dihedral of P-40's wings is, however, more pronounced.

Trailing edges of wing taper prominently in this view from below. Auxiliary fuel tank, six wing-mounted guns give Warhawk range and punch.

Cockpit's bump helps distinguish P-40 from German Me-109. This, with greater dihedral of the P-40's wings, is important clue at certain angles.

P-47

GREAT NEW FIGHTER PLANE HAS FINE COMBAT RECORD

The most frequently heard criticism of American fighter planes in the months immediately following our entry into the war was perhaps their inability to perform at high altitudes. However, the Army Air Forces' new fighter, the P-47, leaves nothing to be desired as a high-altitude plane. The only limit on the height it can reach, as a matter of fact, is said to be the ability of the pilot to keep functioning.

With a speed in level flight of over 400 m.p.h., a terrific diving rate, and extremely heavy armament, the P-47 fully deserves its name of Thunderbolt. Extreme range for a fighter can now be added to these attributes, for Thunderbolts with auxiliary fuel tanks have provided our heavy bombers with fighter escort as far as the Ruhr Valley and Emden on Germany's northwest coast.

One of the most publicized planes of the War before seeing operational service, the P-47 is now fully living up to its advance notices. The Thunderbolt squadrons have shot down 3.2 enemy planes to every one they have lost, a very strong indication of superior quality, considering the fact that most of their fighting has taken place over the Nazis' home grounds.

The basis of the P-47's performance is its 2,000 hp. Pratt & Whitney Double Wasp radial engine, and it is this engine which provides the plane with one of its main recognition points. It is the only land-based Allied fighter in the European theater to have the stub nose which indicates a radial, air-cooled power plant. Unfortunately, one of the Luftwaffe's crack fighters the FW-190 (see pp. 12-13) is also equipped with a radial engine. Because of this superficial similarity serious recognition problems have arisen in the fighting over northwestern Europe.

RECOGNITION: The P-47 is a low mid-wing monoplane with a single radial engine. The wing is straight on the leading edge and semi-elliptical on the trailing. From head-on, oval-shaped engine cowling with the propeller hub set above center is distinctive. Short, stubby fuselage with ridge down the back extends beyond the elevators.

Wing's trailing edge curves sharply in contrast to the straight leading edge. The fuselage tapers to sharp cone beyond the plane's elevators.

Head-on the Thunderbolt resembles an egg with wings. Because of the airscoop on the underside of the fuselage, the propeller hub is placed above center. Tail fin projects well above the cockpit.

P-47's guns pack a wallop which has been estimated to equal that of a fully loaded 13-ton truck hitting a solid brick wall at speed of 60 m.p.h. The plane's ability to carry such heavy armament and still be capable of high speed and great maneuverability gives it a high performance rating.

Extremely small cockpit which fairs into the plane's fuselage preserves the smooth streamlining provided by the P-47's tear-drop shape. The general impression given by the airplane's high tail is roughly that of a triangle with the trailing edge slightly curved and the leading edge straight.

LARGE SCOOP ON MUSTANG'S BELLY ADDS DEPTH TO NARROW FUSELAGE. IN HEAD-ON VIEW WING APPEARS THICK, TAIL FORMS SQUARE CROSS

P-51

IN MUSTANG ALLIES HAVE BEST LOW ALTITUDE PLANE

Our enemies in Europe are daily being harried by a new type of aerial warfare. Strikes of fast low altitude fighters are sweeping across the country treetop-high, reconnoitering for ground concentrations and troop movements before the defenders are aware of the attack. Such approaches are almost inaudible until overhead. Trains, trucks, AA emplacements and enemy shipping have all proved victims of their cannon and bombs.

AAF planes which are accomplishing this are P-51 Mustangs and their fighter-bomber counterpart, the A-36 Invader, the American versions of a plane originally developed by the North American Aviation Corp. to meet British demands for a good ground-attack

LONG NOSE, SLIM FUSELAGE AND SQUARE-CUT PLANE SURFACES IDENTIFY MUSTANG FROM ABOVE

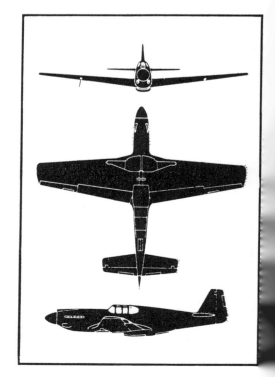

ON RECONNAISSANCE, MUSTANGS WORK TOGETHER, THE PHOTO PLANE FOLLOWING THE ASSIGNED FLIGHT LINE WHILE "WEAVERS" FLIES COVER

plane. Having been designed with the background of RAF combat experience, the resulting craft is clean and powerful, with plenty of speed, high firepower, and considerably greater range than Britain's fine defensive fighters. It saw its first operation in force in the Dieppe raid when it successfully swept in below the enemy radar screen to smash the locator installations.

One of the chief reasons for the P-51's high speed at low altitudes is the unique design of the wing. The airfoil has its thickest section halfway back from the leading edge so that it virtually slices through the heavy ground-level air. When used at higher altitudes, (it has been reported that improved Mustang models will reach 40,000 ft.), this laminar flow wing permits very high diving speeds.

RECOGNITION: In its first appearances, a number of Mustangs were mistakenly shot down through confusion with the Me-109, which is illustrated on pages 10–11. However, the P-51 has distinctive lines and when you are well acquainted with it, you should not confuse it with any other airplane. Its outlines are sharp and strong. The large airscoop just aft of wing gives the plane greater depth through the belly, forms definite break in bottom line of fuselage. In plan form, the design is balanced, with long nose and short tail. Both the wing and tail surfaces have neatly squared tips. Cockpit enclosure fairs smoothly into the narrow fuselage.

DESPITE ITS HIGH TAILPLANE AND LOW WING, THE P-51 HAS VERY LEVEL SIT IN THE AIR, FORMING A STRAIGHT LINE FROM NOSE TO RUDDER

For answers, see p. 50

STUBBY F6F HELLCAT HAS DEEP FUSELAGE AND SQUARE-CUT RUDDER | HAP HAS A SLENDER FUSELAGE TAPERING NEATLY TO SHARP POINT

RADIATOR BELOW ENGINE GIVES HELLCAT AN OVAL-SHAPED COWLING | HAP'S FUSELAGE, RUDDER RISE HIGH ABOVE FULL DIHEDRAL WING

F6F & HAP DIFFER

Don't mistake Hellcat for clip-winged Japanese fighter

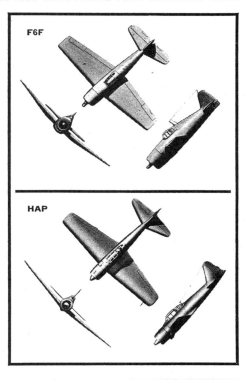

F6F

HAP

With the appearance in the Pacific of the Navy's new F6F Hellcat, fliers, ground and naval forces will have to know how it differs from the Japanese fighter Hap. Both are single-seat fighters with radial engines and square wing tips. But the resemblance of Hap to the Hellcat ends right there.

Rugged and fast, F6F follows the new American trend to larger, more powerful fighters. Hap, on the other hand, is more nearly the size of a typical single-engine pursuit. Its span is 36 ft., and length, 28 ft.

The Hellcat's fuselage is deep and egg-shaped, its cockpit enclosure flows into the general fuselage lines. Hap's fuselage is more slender and tapering, but its canopy stands out much like the greenhouse on a two-seater. Though the wing plans are very similar, Hap has less taper on the leading edge, and Hap's dihedral stems from the root; dihedral on F6F wing starts one fifth of the way out, giving a slight inverted gull-wing effect.

On the Hellcat, tailplane is high and cut out to give play to the rudder. Hap's tailplane is lower, clearly below and forward of the rudder. The fuselage of the F6F ends flush with the rudder, while Hap's tapers to a sharp point behind the tail assembly.

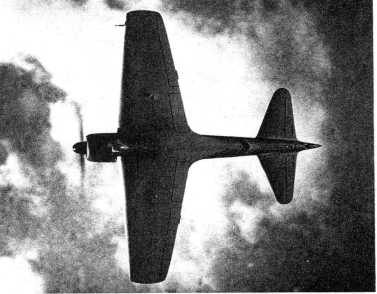

TAILPLANE FLUSH TO REAR, THICK BODY HELP IDENTIFY THE F6F | HAP HAS A BIG SPINNER AND SHARPLY ROUNDED TAILPLANE TIPS

NEWS & MISCELLANY

NEWS

An Me 110-G has been examined for the first time. Although practically similar to the standard Me-110, the aircraft was fitted with D.B. 605A engines instead of D.B. 601's which will have the effect of improving the performance somewhat. In addition, this G sub-type was equipped with faster firing MG 151/20 20-mm. guns instead of Oerlikon MGFF 20-mm. guns.

•

The Do-217M, from a recognition standpoint, differs slightly from the Do-217E. It has an airframe similar to the Do-217K, an experimental model which did not go into mass production. The "M" submodel has a larger cockpit than the "E." It also has a modified bomb stowage, and the nose has been redesigned so that it resembles that of the He-111.

LETTER

Subject: Flight of Zeke from San Diego to the East

Reference is made to statement at bottom of page 33 of the September issue of the *Journal* which is in error.

Volunteer observers of the Aircraft Warning Service are not permitted to report aircraft by name except for certain types in designated areas. All reports on aircraft other than specified types merely call for the number of motors, direction and altitude.

Undoubtedly the Zeke referred to in the article was the one that was captured in the Aleutians, and rebuilt. This plane was flown near San Diego during December and several reports were received from volunteer observers that it was a Zero.

PASS IT AROUND

Though this Journal *is restricted and may not be shown to any unauthorized person without making yourself liable to imprisonment, it should receive as wide a circulation as possible within the armed forces. Do not hide your copy away. Pass it around among the members of your battery, flight unit, or ship.*

When your group has finished reading the Journal, *do not throw it away. Much of the information contained in each issue has a permanent value for recognition. A file of the* Journal *should be part of your recognition library.*

On Dec. 30, 1942 a flight plan was filed by the Navy calling for departure of the Zeke accompanied by a Navy GB-2 from San Diego to the East. These aircraft were tracked and reported in the regular manner across the Wing Area, although naturally the observers had no advance notice of the proposed flight. In spite of not being required to identify any aircraft at that time several observers added that one of these aircraft was a Zero.

Correction is requested so the Ground Observer Corps can be given proper credit.

Army Air Forces
Headquarters San Diego Fighter
    Wing
Office of the Commanding Officer

SOURCE MATERIAL

Recognition aids available to Army Ground and Service Forces activities include the following:

Joint Army-Navy Pictorial Manual (Aircraft) FM 30-30; available on request to AGO depots

Joint Army-Navy Pictorial Manual (Armored Vehicles) FM 30-40 (now being printed. Distribution to begin about Dec. 1943)

Slides on aircraft, naval vessels and armored vehicles (under procurement, will be distributed automatically to film libraries when available)

Scale models of aircraft (under procurement; will be distributed automatically when available)

Silhouette posters of aircraft (available on requisition to AGO depots)

Silhouette posters of armored vehicles (now being printed, will be automatically distributed by AGO depots)

Silhouette posters of naval vessels (now being printed, will be automatically distributed to Seacoast Artillery only)

Training films (see FM 21-7)

Film strips (see FM 21-7)

These aids are available to organizations, not individuals. Requests for AAF and Navy material will be forwarded through channels, not direct.

DISTRIBUTION

The U. S. Army-Navy Journal of Recognition is published by the U. S. War and Navy Departments. It is distributed in substantial quantities to particular activities in all the armed services. Limited numbers of additional copies may be requested through channels from Training Aids Division of the Army Air Forces, Adjutant General Depots, and the Deputy Chief of Naval Operations (Air).

QUIZ ANSWERS

QUIZ No. 1

1. Val	14. Mosquito	(captured, in use by U. S.)
2. He-115	15. PBY	
3. Nate	16. B-24	
4. Rufe	17. Zeke	5. Russian KV-1
5. Ju-88	18. PBY	6. U. S. M-3
6. C-60		7. U. S. M-4; British Crusader
7. York	**QUIZ No. 2**	
8. Val	1. U. S. M-4's	8. German Mark IV
9. He-111	2. German Mark VI	
10. SBD	3. Russian T-34's	9. British Churchill
11. Wellington		10. Russian T-34
12. P-51	4. German Mark II	
13. Sally		

THESE ARE SHIPS OF A U. S. INVASION FLEET

1 EC-2 Liberty	10 EC-2 Liberty	18 Northampton Class CA	26 Pennsylvania BB
2 EC-2 Liberty	11 City Type Transport	19 AM Raven	27 APD
3 Flushdeck Class DD/DMS	12 EC-2 Liberty	20 North Pacific	28 Farragut Class DD
4 Alaska	13 448 Type Transport	21 Farragut Class DD	29 LST
5 Flushdeck Class DD/DMS	14 World War I Freighter	22 Aleutian	30 Farragut Class DD
6 EC-2 Liberty	15 535 Type (formerly President)	23 EC-2 Liberty	31 Flushdeck Class DD/DMS
7&8 C-2	16 Farragut Class DD	24 535 Type (formerly President)	32 Flushdeck Class DD/DMS
9 Fokmer (Danish Maersk Line)	17 Tennessee BB (Tennessee Class)	25 535 Type (formerly President)	33 Fletcher Class DD

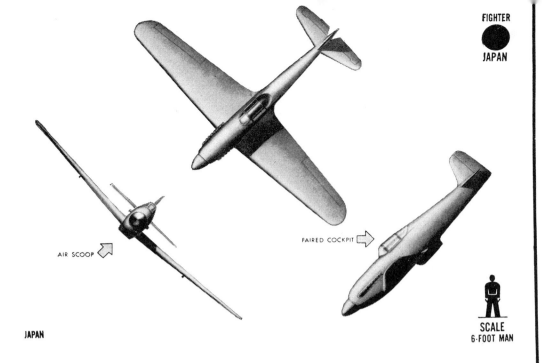

JAPAN

AIR SCOOP →

FAIRED COCKPIT →

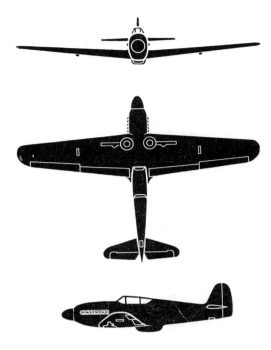

SCALE
6-FOOT MAN

"TONY," TYPE 3SSF

SPAN: approx. 38 ft.
LENGTH: approx. 28 ft.
APPROX. SPEED: 330 to 350 m.p.h.

RESTRICTED

DISTINGUISHING FEATURES: Single inline-engine monoplane. Wings have dihedral from roots and moderate taper on both edges. Long nose. Small cockpit faired into the fuselage. Large airscoop extends beyond trailing edge. Bell-shaped fin and rudder. Tailplane has rounded tips, tapered leading edge and V-cutout in the elevator.

INTEREST: The fuselage and tail assembly of this new single-seat jap fighter are very similar to the He-113. The wings, however, are much longer and narrower. For the first time armor plate placed behind pilot was found in a Jap fighter. Power plant is a 12-cylinder 60° V-type liquid-cooled engine. Fuel tanks may be leakproof. Armament: two 12.7-mm. machine guns firing through the propeller and two 7.7-mm. machine guns in the wings. Provision for cannon installation is present, but no cannon have been found to date.

NOTE: This page is to be cut along dotted lines (*above* and *below*), added to the proper nation's section in the Recognition Pictorial Manual. The dots indicate perforations.

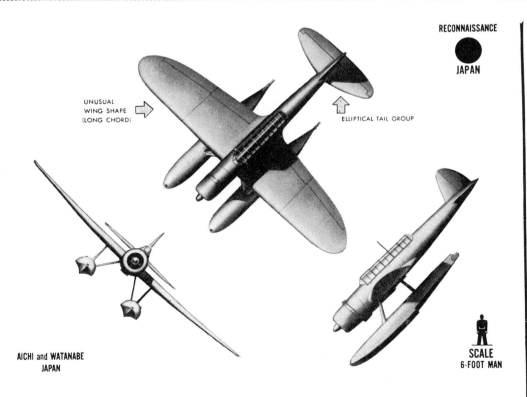

UNUSUAL
WING SHAPE
(LONG CHORD) →

← ELLIPTICAL TAIL GROUP

AICHI and WATANABE
JAPAN

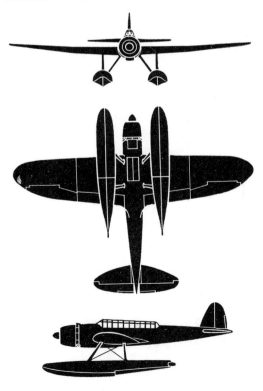

SCALE
6-FOOT MAN

"JAKE" TYPE 0 RF/P

SPAN: 47 ft. 6 in.
LENGTH: 35 ft. 4 in.
APPROX. SPEED: 216 m.p.h. at 7,500 ft.
SERVICE CEILING: 24,400 ft.

RESTRICTED

DISTINGUISHING FEATURES: Single radial-engine, low-wing, three-place monoplane. Stubby wing with tip curves beginning well inboard. Long unfaired greenhouse. Large twin floats. High semi-elliptical fin and rudder. Tailplane has curved leading and trailing edges.

INTEREST: This plane when first reported was thought to be Type 99 dive bomber Val equipped with floats. Recent evidence, however, proves this supposition to have been incorrect. The leading edge of the wing is almost straight and the trailing edge is elliptical. Reports state that Allied shipping has been attacked by this float plane. Its principal use is for observation and patrol missions. It can carry four 132-lb. bombs, two in a small bomb bay and two externally on racks just outboard of the bomb bay. Armament consists of one 7.7-mm. machine gun in rear cockpit.

A

C

B

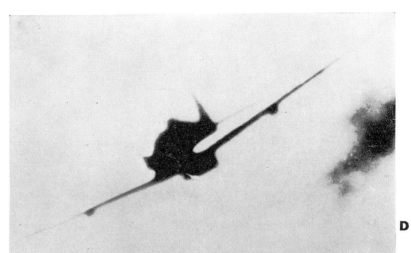

D

TONY, the first fighter in which the Japanese have used an inline engine, resembles both the Hurricane and the HE-113. Less heavily armed than the Zeros, it is at least their equal in speed. Note large airscrew spinner and bulges under wings almost to wingtips.

JAKE, shown below, has been used principally for observation and patrol. Found to be an original design and not the dive bomber Val equipped with floats, it is reported to have attacked Allied shipping in the Pacific. The plane has a load of four 132-lb. bombs.

A

C

B

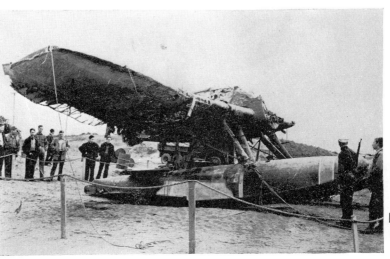

D

U. S. ARMY-NAVY JOURNAL OF
RECOGNITION

ROYAL NAVY

DECEMBER, 1943

NUMBER 4

RESTRICTED

SHARE
THIS
COPY

QUIZ NO. 1
GUNNERY

The puzzle pictures on this page form a double-barreled quiz. Servicemen in all activities should be able to recognize each plane. Free gunners who have been trained in the use of the Mark IX sight can make use of the superimposed red rings to judge whether the plane is in or out of range, and just how far away it is. The answers to the quiz (*see p. 50*) contain three parts: 1) the name of the plane; 2) whether it is in or out of range; and 3) its estimated distance from the gunner.

Other than the recognition of the aircraft type and the estimation of its range, these pictures do not contain any elements of sighting theory. They must not, for example, be assumed to show the proper lead. You have only to settle the first two questions in the gunnery problem: what it is and where it is.

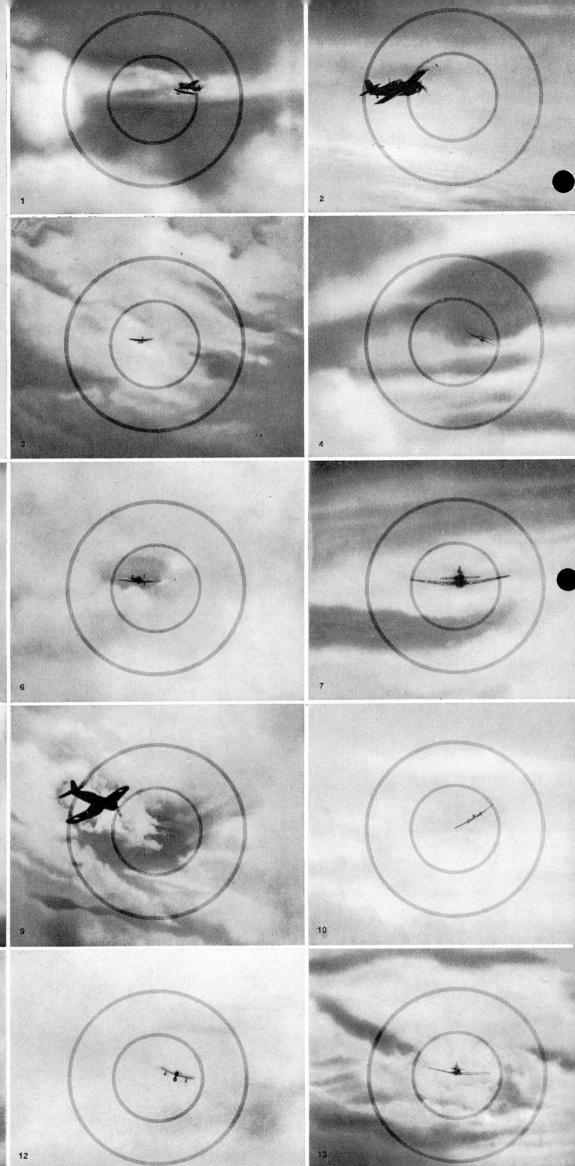

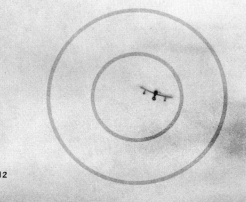

1

2

3

4

5

6

7

8

9

10

11

12

13

U. S. ARMY-NAVY JOURNAL OF
RECOGNITION

DECEMBER, 1943

COPYRIGHT 1943 BY LT. GEORGE H. FORSYTH JR.

NUMBER 4

IT PAYS OFF

This is a success story for trainees on the home front. It begins in the spring of 1942 when a handful of instructors emerged from the Navy Recognition School at Ohio State University to preach the gospel of recognition to the Army and Navy. Theirs was a mammoth task. The problem was brand new with World War II and the advent of the radically different combat conditions of an air war. Recognition teaching methods and procedure were still very experimental. The subject itself was dull and seemingly academic. Students dozed off during lectures and complained of having to spend valuable flying hours in a classroom. WEFT, Renshaw, slides, silhouettes—what did they have to do with winning the war?

But with the spread of the Allied offensive to all fronts, recognition training met its test. Wherever there was a battlefront or an advanced air base, U. S. Armed Forces sent recognition officers to keep dinning into the boys the need for knowing friend from foe.

One by one recognition officers have returned home from combat to report the progress of training in their area, to tell the story of a real achievement. On Guadalcanal a Marine pilot went straight to the recognition officer after his first brush with the enemy. "Got a Jap," he announced proudly. "There was a plane way up ahead of me. All of a sudden it turned, kind of, and right then it looked exactly like Hap on one of your slides. Boy, I let him have it!"

The same officer was in charge of teaching recognition to an Air Group of U. S. Army, Navy and Marine fliers, and some New Zealanders. Early in May a squadron of Marines flying F4U's, returning home from battling Zeros over the Russell Islands, ran into a squadron of P-40's flown by the New Zealanders. The F4U's thought they were seeing more Zeros and opened fire. Meanwhile the poor guys in the P-40's had to break radio silence and holler to the Americans to "Lay off." The next day a P-40 was delivered to the F4U squadron base for study.

After a big air battle in which four U. S. squadrons shot down 77 Jap aircraft, our fliers reported that they couldn't have singled out enemy planes from their own without the drill they'd been getting. "In a dogfight," said one pilot, "you really don't see anything. You just get a sudden impression and squeeze the gun. It seems as if you have to make up your mind in a tenth of a second."

But recognition is more than just knowing when to shoot. It is a vital tool of intelligence. Lack of recognition training in the Pacific was often responsible for upsetting tactical plans. The accuracy with which reconnaissance aircraft reported enemy shipping could and did affect the progress of a whole campaign. A Navy officer in the Aleutians found himself having to start from scratch in teaching Army and Navy patrol squadrons to recognize surface craft. On one occasion reconnaissance planes reported the presence of two Jap destroyers off Attu. Immediately two of our destroyers went out to meet them. It was a costly engagement. The Jap "destroyers" proved to be heavy cruisers, and one of our destroyers never got back.

Revenge came one day when a plane returned with news of a nearby Jap force of two heavy cruisers, two light cruisers, two destroyers and two merchant ships. Our only available warships were two destroyers. But this time we were going to make the most of our firepower and so placed the weight of the two destroyers that they damaged a Jap heavy cruiser, sank a destroyer and chased the rest of the warships home while the two merchant vessels scurried rapidly into the cover of the fog.

We prepared for Sicily

Perhaps the greatest tribute paid to recognition came from the Navy just before our amphibious operations against Sicily. Anticipating the spotting difficulties, Naval Aviation authorities handpicked 22 recognition instructors and made them recognition officers on the biggest ships in the invasion convoy. Some spotted from the bridge, others took charge of lookout stations and range-finders. On the flagship of the convoy, a recognition officer correctly spotted a squadron of Spitfires overhead. Already smaller ships on the outer edge of the convoy had opened fire. The recognition officer called out the identity of the planes and immediately orders went out to the entire convoy to cease firing on friendly planes. Here was recognition in real, live action.

In the Mediterranean, the South Pacific, the Aleutians, Burma, China, and Europe, our pilots and gunners now swear by recognition training. Combat records have proved that it works. The time when you boys now on the home front find yourselves in battle is the time when you too are going to be glad for all the recognition you have learned. It is the best kind of life insurance.

FRENCH SHIPS

Reconditioned units are back at sea with Allies

Back at sea and throwing its weight against the Axis is a sizable unit of the French Navy. Recently reconditioned in the U. S., the battleship Richelieu, pride of the French Fleet and one of the most powerful battleships in the world, was brought from Dakar where it had time and again been battered by the British Navy as a potential enemy. With it in the United Nations' battleline are the light cruisers Montcalm and Georges Leygues, several crack French destroyers which remained outside French home waters in the unsettled months after the Fall of France. They are significant additions to the growing strength of the Allied fleets.

The 35,000-ton battleship Richelieu, completed just before the start of the war in 1939, was the French answer to the Vittorio Veneto and the Tirpitz, compact, speedy battleships designed to combine the mobility of cruisers with the firepower and protection of capital ships. Typical of French naval architecture in its beautiful grace and simplicity of line, the Richelieu possesses the sturdiness and practicality of Britain's Nelson. Designed as a powerful offensive fighter, it has proved its ability to withstand extremely heavy blows. Newly reconditioned, it should more than prove the equal of a Tirpitz Class battleship.

Of the ten capital ships in the French Navy in 1940, not one fell into German hands at the time of the invasion of France. While one was demilitarized at Alexandria, and two surrendered in British ports to become the nucleus of the Fighting French Navy, others, including the four

most powerful units of the Fleet—Richelieu, Jean Bart, Strasbourg and Dunkerque—escaped to North Africa. All were subsequently damaged by the British in a fast-hitting series of attacks at Mers-el-Kebir and Dakar that at a crucial time paralyzed this powerful unit as a potential pawn of the Axis. Two years later the Dunkerque was still under repair at Toulon where it was scuttled in drydock. The Richelieu, alone at Dakar, was crippled by depth charges dropped from a British motor launch in an exploit to rival the sinking of the Royal Oak at Scapa Flow, and torpedoed by seaplanes. Two months later, immobilized, but a floating fort, it turned its guns on the British and Free French naval force under General Charles de Gaulle, sustained further damage in the superstructure. It finally fell into Allied hands with the surrender of French West Africa to Darlan in December 1942.

RECOGNITION: Most prominent feature of this French battleship is the complex stack, peculiar to Richelieu and Jean Bart, which fairs forward to make a single unit with the mainmast. Richelieu has an extremely high narrow tower square amidships and an exceptionally high freeboard. Like the British Nelson, its chief firepower is forward, concentrated in eight 15-in. guns in superimposed quadruple turrets. It carries nine dual-purpose guns in triple turrets aft, is heavily armed with anti-aircraft guns. The ship has graceful, sharply tapering clipper bow, long uncluttered decks and almost vertical cruiser stern. The two catapults formerly at stern have been removed in the process of reconditioning.

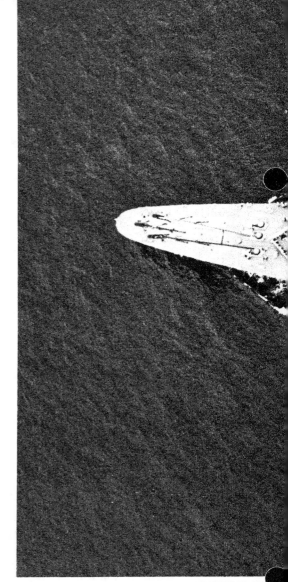

RICHELIEU (ABOVE AND BELOW) RESEMBLES U.S.

RICHELIEU, 35,000-ton pride of the French Fleet, has re-entered service with the Fighting French. Sister ship Jean Bart was put out of action at Casablanca in North African invasion.

NORTH CAROLINA IN BROAD BEAM AND TAPERING HULL. SHE HAS EIGHT 15-IN. GUNS FORWARD, NINE 6-IN. DP GUNS AFT, PACKS HEAVY AA FIRE

THE FRENCH CRUISER MONTCALM HAS TRANSOM STERN, A BROKEN HULL, ODDLY SHAPED TRIPOD FOREMAST. OVERALL LENGTH IS 588 FT., 11 IN.

CRUISERS

Modern French light cruisers are fast, sturdy and carry heavy armament

Into Allied hands at Dakar fell three of France's most modern light cruisers—the 7,600-ton Montcalm, Georges Leygues and Gloire of La Galissonnière Class. Georges Leygues, back in service with the Fighting French, was recently joined by the reconditioned Montcalm. Outstanding examples of modern light cruisers, these ships were designed to combine the maximum of firepower, armament, speed and seaworthiness for their size. Of three sister ships at Toulon—La Galissonnière, Jean-de-Vienne and Marseillaise—two were intact after scuttling, may be used by Germans.

LONG GRACEFUL LINES, flared clipper bow are typical of the newer French warships. In accord with modern trends in naval design, superstructure has been heavily concentrated. Long run of sheer line towards stern has been utilized for installation of heavier anti-aircraft guns.

SPEEDY AND MANEUVERABLE, The Montcalm does not sacrifice armament or firepower. At outbreak of war she had nine 6-in. guns in triple turrets, two superimposed forward, one aft, eight 3.5-in. guns in four turrets amidships. Two catapults were removed in reconditioning.

LE FANTASQUE HAS OVERALL LENGTH OF 435 FT., 5 IN., DISPLACES 2,500 TONS. TOP SPEED IS 37 KNOTS IT HAS NINE 21.7-IN. TORPEDO TUBES

DESTROYERS

Le Fantasque, Le Terrible and Leopard

are three large French super-destroyers

Larger than any U. S. or British destroyers, Le Fantasque, Le Terrible and Leopard are examples of a French specialty, the super-destroyer, designed to answer the challenge of the Italian destroyer. Laid down as offensive warships to be pitted primarily against smaller vessels, the French destroyers are strong in range and seaworthiness, comparatively weak in defensive armament for their size. In appearance they may be mistaken for cruisers (*see Montcalm, opposite*) although their main battery shield mounts in place of turrets should distinguish them quite easily.

LE FANTASQUE shows class resemblance in size and design to light cruiser. Her main battery consists of five 5.5-in. guns mounted in centerline shields, two forward and three aft. Note conspicuously high bow, broad funnels and transom stern. Sister ship, Le Terrible, is identical.

LEOPARD, older and smaller than Le Fantasque Class, was extensively rebuilt, until it now is more akin to Le Fantasque than Chacal Class to which it belonged. Leopard lost a funnel in reconditioning, acquired transom stern. Two sister ships fell undamaged to Germans at Toulon.

FIRST BLAST OF GUN AND CAMERA CAUGHT EMILY TO STARBOARD

EMILY DOWNED

New Navy fighters knock Japan's new four-motored patrol bomber into se●

Early in September the Navy's fast new Hellcat made its initial appearance in the South Pacific. In less than a week two of them brought home the pictures shown here—photographic proof of the superior firepower and fighting ability of the F6F.

Guarding a carrier task force operating east of the Gilbert Islands, they had spotted one of the new four-motored Jap flying boats known as Emily (*see Journal, Oct. issue*). In the ensuing 5-minute tussle they knocked the huge plane into the sea.

While the Hellcats relentlessly whammed away at Emily with their six .50-cal. machine guns, their synchronized gun cameras recorded the battle in these excellent pictures.

Far more important than the recording of a sure kill, these pictures reveal many new recognition features of Emily hitherto unknown to U.S. pilots, resulting in the corrected silhouettes shown in the inset (*above, left*). Whereas Emily was previously believed to have a gull wing, it is now evident that she has a straight slim wing resembling the Liberator's Davis wing. From head-on view, her fuselage is similar to the Navy's PB2Y, or Coronado, but she can be easily distinguished from any four-motored U.S. flying boat by her unusually high single fin and rudder, her long pointed nose.

HELLCATS HIT STARBOARD ENGINES WITH THEIR SIX .50-CAL. GUNS

GASOLINE STREAMING FROM HER TWO ENGINES EMILY APPEARS DOOMED

F6F COMES IN CLOSE TO RAKE EMILY, SETS INBOARD MOTOR AFIRE

WITH CABIN A BLAZING INFERNO, EMILY PLUNGES TOWARD THE WATER

F6F DIVES DIRECTLY UPON PREY; CAMERA SHUDDERS FROM VIBRATION

EMILY HITS WITH VIOLENT EXPLOSION. CREW HAD NO TIME TO BAIL OUT

NAZI GUNS

Self-propelled gun is prime anti-tank weapon

Since the bloody proving ground of Spain, Nazi strategy has consistently strengthened its anti-tank units with captured equipment as well as with guns of their own design. As Allied tanks added thicker armor plate, Nazi tank-destroyers mounted heavier, armor-piercing weapons. As Allied guns grew more deadly, Nazi tank-busters were forced to shield themselves behind re-enforced hulls and improvised armored side-skirting (see below).

The tank-destroyer is still no match for the tank in the open. With high silhouette and light armor it has to exploit its light-tank mobility and its rapid fire-power. Germans use the self-propelled gun as a sort of mobile reserve following the first wave of attacking tanks and frequently moving into prepared positions from which it can ambush infiltrating enemy tanks.

Three big guns stand out in the lineup of Nazi self-propelled artillery, the 75-mm., the 88-mm. and the 150-mm. howitzer. On these two pages are pictures of the 75-mm. cannon mounted on a PzKw III medium tank chassis. Used in several gun lengths, the long-barreled version 75 is newest and best. Its flatter trajectory affords greater more destructive hitting power. Speedy and low-slung, easy to camouflage and furnishing a stable gun platform, the Mark III tank chassis ranks as one of the best German self-propelled gun mounts.

SHORT-BARRELED 75-mm. gun appeared in Germany during 1936. This prewar picture shows two of crew of four, demonstrates vulnerability to air attack because of flat, lightly armored top.

DUG-IN short-barreled 75 is hull-down in Russian wheatfield. All armored equipment is dug in to cover the silhouette whenever tactically possible.

AT OREL Nazis hung slabs of armored skirting on gun chassis to shield hull and suspension system. Periscope and 7.9-mm. AA gun are on top.

CAPTURED GUN is ridden triumphantly near Faibano, Italy, by members of Montgomery's Eighth Army. Gun has the typically German double-baffle muzzle brake. Compare newly re-enforced box-like gun mantlet and bow of chassis, now heavily armor-bolted, to the short-barreled version.

LONG-BARRELED self-propelled 75 crawls across a battlefield in Russia in support of an infantry attack. Note inch-thick emergency armor skirting. Commander's cupola on gun in foreground is recent addition. Six evenly spaced bogies and three return rollers make up suspension system.

MUZZLE BRAKE AT END OF LONG GUN BARREL IS COVERED TO PROTECT IT FROM DUST. YOKE-LIKE RODS ON BOW SUPPORT GUN WHEN NOT FIRING

LIGHT CHASSIS

75's are also mounted on French Lorraine and German PzKw II Tanks

Two more self-propelled 75-mm. guns are pictured here mounted on a German and a captured French chassis. Obsolescent as a light tank, the PzKw II (*top and lower left*) went into action late in the Tunisian campaign as a highly mobile mount for cannon. Gun turret slopes sharply at the rear. Suspension system consists of five evenly spaced bogies with four return rollers.

The Lorraine (*lower right*) is an obsolescent chassis of French design, captured in quantity by the Germans and converted to a gun carrier. Carrying its long-barreled German 75, it is a good example of the Nazis' skillful improvisation with salvaged equipment.

CAPTURED PHOTOGRAPH shows Nazi gun crew on chassis. Head-on, weapon is high, has an angular silhouette. Man at left holds hand signal.

FRENCH LORRAINE chassis with long-barreled 75 has clumsy, off-center look. Weight of lightly armored Lorraine is only 7½ tons, length 14 ft.

SHORT RECUPERATOR AT BASE OF BARREL DISTINGUISHES 75-MM. ANTI-TANK GUN FROM THE CAPTURED 76.2-MM. GUN ON SAME CHASSIS (P. 14)

CZECH CHASSIS

Mounts good 75-mm. gun

Czech factories now in German hands are turning out a prewar-designed chassis PzKw 38 which the Nazis use to carry their 75-mm. gun. It is a light, 30-m.p.h. mount, with high center of gravity, large overall dimensions and slight armor. Same mount also supports captured Russian 76.2-mm. at top of next page.

Recognition-wise the chief difference between 75 and 76.2 is in the recuperator which absorbs the gun recoil and which is situated at the base of the barrel. As shown on this page, the 75 has a short boxy recuperator. The Russian 76.2 has a long tubular recuperator. Another major difference is the size of the gun shield which on the 75 is large, five-sided and extends almost to the tracks, while on the 76.2 it is small and seems to be perched high above the chassis.

Development in crew protection based on battle experience with the Czech-mounted 75 may be seen by comparing the guns at top and bottom. Top picture not only shows higher crew compartment extending further to rear but illustrates recent mounting of gun within a curved metallic sheath which rides around with the barrel and affords greater gun traverse.

HEAD-ON VIEW of this self-propelled Czech-mounted 75-mm. gun captured in Africa shows tall narrow, almost pyramidal, silhouette which the Germans have never beer able to eliminate.

KNOCKED OUT in the First Army's attack at Kairouan, this piece of wreckage shows great protrusion of 75-mm. barrel, also radio antenna and four large bogies with two return rollers.

13

HEAVIER

76.2-mm., 88-mm., 150-mm.

The German arsenal of self-propelled equipment grew by leaps and bounds as Polish, Czech, French and Russian stores fell into their hands in huge quantities. Adept at makeshift and alert to fresh uses for old weapons, the mechanically clever German gun crews wasted nothing. Their ingenuity in a war of lightning speed and long supply lines has enabled them to travel far on captured ammunition as well as ordnance.

The six self-propelled gun mounts on these two pages include a Russian weapon, a French chassis, a Czech chassis and two old German 150-mm. howitzers. Only one chassis, Ferdinand (*below*), was designed for the gun it mounts. The captured Russian 76.2-mm. gun (*upper left*) is mounted on the light Czech PzKw 38 chassis. The 150-mm. howitzer (*lower left*), which has been highly efficient against tanks and fortifications, uses the obsolescent French Lorraine chassis. This howitzer's great weight, mounted on such a light 22-m.p.h. chassis is an excellent example of German operational skill.

Three 150-mm. howitzers are pictured at right. The top one was photographed i Italy at the time of Badoglio's capitulation to the Allies. It is an old howitzer, one which the Germans would use only if they were in

CAPTURED RUSSIAN 76.2-MM. GUN at Tripoli has tubular recuperator ⅓ the barrel length, small conical gunshield set high above PzKw 38 chassis. Ammunition carrier trails behind.

FRENCH CHASSIS captured in Western Desert carries 150-mm. howitzer (*above and below*). Coffin-shaped crew compartment, set well aft, is lightly armored, appears bulky and topheavy.

FERDINAND, enormous squat 88-mm. gun, is heavily armored, with 8-in. forward turret wall,

WEAPONS

are tough and dangerous

reat need of self-propelled artillery. The Mark IV chassis (*right, center*) is the most important of the four 150-mm. mounts. So far this self-propelled gun has been used only in small numbers on the Eastern front where it has not been too successful. Germans like it because its domestic chassis is more familiar to maintenance personnel and because its 22 tons can support a 150-mm. recoil without the use of a spade (shock absorption mechanism dug in at rear of mount). The Mark II chassis (*bottom right*) which supports another 150-mm. howitzer is a lower, more easily camouflaged version of the chassis carrying a 75 on page 12.

Most propagandized Nazi weapon is the 88-mm. gun. Originally a semimobile AA gun, the 88 was later given a more mobile mount, making it dual purpose (AA-AT). These towed 88's, Rommel's pets, ambushed and knocked out 230 of 300 British tanks at Knightsbridge in North Africa on June 13, 1942. Later the Germans mounted the 88 on the Mark VI tank and now on the 70-ton Ferdinand. Ferdinand hides and lies in wait for enemy tanks. After a recent Nazi onslaught north of Belgorod, the countryside for miles around was littered with Nazi tanks, Ferdinands. Russians moving faster than the 12-m.p.h. tank-busters blasted their vulnerable tops with high-angle fire.

GERMAN TROOPS ride through Pavia, Italy, in September on 150-mm. howitzer with PzKw 38 mount. Steep, box-shaped crew compartment is well forward. Top appears uncovered.

MARK IV CHASSIS with 150-mm. howitzer has eight bogies. The slanting gunshield has un- usually heavy armor. Below: 150-mm. howitzer on a Mark II mount with sloping armor.

has crew of six. Unique suspension system has no return rollers to take up slack in the track.

LIBERATORS OVER NORTH PACIFIC WATERS ON PARAMUSHIRO RAID SYMBOLIZES THE GLOBE-GIRDLING ACHIEVEMENTS OF U. S. AIR POWER

U.S. BOMBERS

Bombing planes of the USAAF excel in range, accuracy and firepower

U. S. bombardment aviation has been doing two big jobs in this war. It has been running interference for ground and sea forces by knocking out airfields, gun positions, communications, shipping and supplies on all U. S. fronts. It has also been carrying out U. S. ideas of airpower by going after factories which supply the Axis war machine in Europe.

The first job, while important, does not represent a revolutionary use of bombing planes. The second, as carried out by the USAAF, does. For American airmen have taken a clumsy and vulnerable weapon, the heavy bomber, one which other air forces risk only at night, and used it to achieve precision standards by day.

Precision has always been the main goal of U. S. airmen. They hoped to attain it with their accurate bombsights and with planes which could fly high enough and fast enough to avoid anti-aircraft and fighter opposition. Flying Fortresses of 1935 could do it; heavy bombers of 1943 cannot. But their withering

firepower has enabled them to smash their way to their objectives—and back.

In the drive for greater precision, two departures from conventional bombing tactics have been introduced. One of these is skip-bombing, a strictly American invention. Originally devised for obtaining greater accuracy at sea, it enabled skip-bombing mediums and heavies to sink 22 Jap ships in the Bismarck Sea. Notable success has also been achieved against land objectives, especially on Pantelleria. Second new method now in use is pattern bombing, a foreign invention which the AAF has refined for use on occasion. Instead of having each plane make its own run, lead bombardiers do the sighting for groups of 18.

A sharp rise in Nazi fighter opposition has so far failed to stop the AAF. They have countered with new formations, added gun turrets and a greater use of fighter cover at long range. Still newer developments—interchangeable noses and bigger and faster bombers—are on their way to meet whatever the Axis can offer.

A-20

Fast and heavily armed, it is an ideal attack plane and light bomber

Most versatile of the USAAF's heavier planes is the A-20. The A-20, also known as Boston and Havoc, has performed as a day and night fighter, attack-bomber, shallow dive bomber and medium-altitude bomber at short range. Fast enough to hold its own against most enemy fighters, it can also almost suspend its movement in the air over a small operational area because of its large flap surface.

As a night-fighter it carries tremendous firepower and played a prominent part in breaking up mass raids over England in the winter of 1940–41. As a bomber it has seen action in virtually every war theater and is one of the few American planes in operation under tough fighting conditions faced by the Red Air Force. A-20's carried out the first U. S. raid over Europe. On July 4, 1942 they smashed German airfields in The Netherlands.

RECOGNITION: The A-20 is a three-place, shoulder-wing monoplane equipped with two radial engines housed in underslung nacelles extending considerably beyond the wing's trailing edge. Distinctive are its tall fin and rudder, the marked dihedral of the tailplane and the swept-up aft section of the fuselage. The wing's leading edge is straight while the trailing edge tapers sharply. A solid nose has been built into the night-fighter version, the P-70.

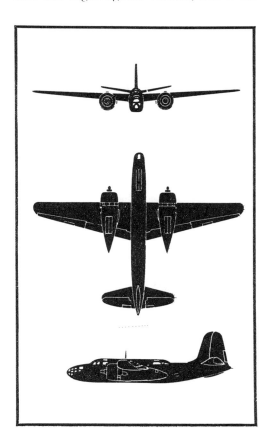

A-20's **IN FORMATION** show shoulder wing, tall fin and rudder and a gracefully turned-up after section. Center section of underside of A-20's fuselage has a definite break in contour.

FUSELAGE OF A-20 is tall and slender head-on (*above*). Picture below gives exceptional view of clear silhouette made by shadow. Note wing's trailing edge has strong forward sweep.

BOMBING RABAUL, B-25 Mitchell sweeps over burning Jap freighter. In background, Jap warehouses and oil tanks go up in black smoke.. Modified gull wing, caused by dihedral inboard of engine nacelles, is very apparent. Top turret forms projection between fins and rudders.

B-25

Steady rugged Mitchell

is consistent performer

Along with doing a great deal of the routine bombing in Tunisia, Italy, China, Burma and New Guinea, the B-25 has two important "firsts" to its credit. It was the first U. S. Army plane to sink an enemy submarine, and B-25's were flown by Major General Doolittle and his men to bomb Tokyo.

The B-25 is a consistent plane, easy to handle and predictable in behavior. It depends on ruggedness and heavy armament to bring it home. There are two .50-cal. machine guns in the plane's nose; two each in top and belly turrets. Some models carry guns in the tail as well.

RECOGNITION: The B-25 is a twin-engine mid-wing monoplane. Outstanding features are squarish twin fins and rudders; the gull-wing effect created because dihedral does not extend outboard of nacelles.

TWIN-TAIL ASSEMBLY and protruding nacelles give B-25 a distinctive appearance from below. Its ability to take off from a carrier's deck led to choice by Doolittle for Tokyo raid.

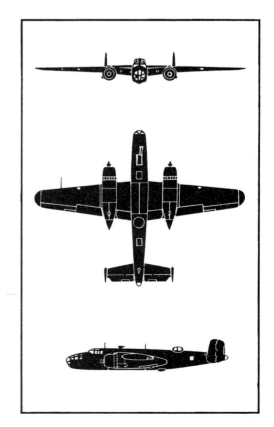

B-26

Terrific punch features this fast medium bomber

In speed, range, bomb load and armament the B-26 is unique among medium bombers. Its two 2,000-h. p. Double Wasp engines give it tremendous power for its size, which has paid off in performance. Most heavily armed medium bomber in operation, it carries two waist guns in addition to two .50-cal. weapons each in nose, top turret and tail. This firepower makes the B-26 a murderous ground-strafer.

The B-26 has been called one of the hot planes of the war (i. e., hard to handle). But in the hands of a man who can adapt himself to its tricks, it is a formidable weapon. Contrary to recent reports it is not being taken out of production and will continue to see plenty of action. Its present performance from British bases is noteworthy.

Strangely enough, impromptu torpedo-carrying at the Battle of Midway marked one of the B-26's first operational appearances. Its torpedo-carrying career continued in the Aleutians, but for the present it is functioning as a medium bomber, making French and Dutch airfields untenable for the Luftwaffe.

RECOGNITION: Perfect streamlining of its cigar-shaped fuselage is perhaps the B-26's best recognition point. It is a shoulder-wing, twin-engine monoplane. Both the trailing and leading edges of the wing taper sharply but head-on the wing is absolutely straight. Fuselage extends to a sharp point beyond tall fin and rudder.

ON ROME RAID, sleek Marauder bombers head for Ciampino Airdrome to the south. Tall fin and rudder set well forward, symmetrical nose and the shoulder wing help identify B-26.

MARAUDER VIEWED HEAD-ON has been compared to flying torpedo and man-eating shark. Absence of dihedral in wing contrasts with pronounced dihedral of B-26's tailplane.

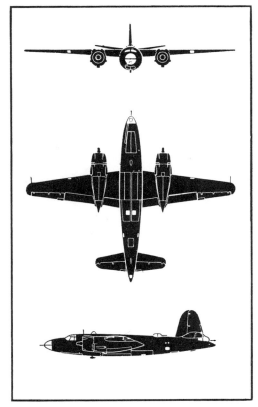

B-17'S IN FORMATION CAN BE SPOTTED BY TALL FINS, CHARACTERISTIC PATTERN FORMED BY TAILPLANE, RUDDER, FUSELAGE. BELLY TURRETS A

B-17

Flying Fortresses have

captured public's fancy

Darling of the American people is the Flying Fortress, the B-17. Developed in 1935, the Flying Fortress represents the essence of U. S. air philosophy. It was built for speed, range and altitude to do precision work.

Before the U. S. entered the war, 50 B-17C's were lend-leased to Great Britain. After two raids on Brest they were relegated to Coastal Command because of

their limited loads. First B-17 to reach combat with the U. S. was the D model, a vulnerable ship, especially from the rear. Tail guns were improvised for early fighting in the Java Sea and the South Pacific before the improved B-17E got into action.

The E was a real change from earlier models, incorporating top, tail and belly turrets. In redesigning the whole tail structure, Boeing engineers built into the B-17

CHIN TURRET FEATURES B-17G, NEWEST OF FORTRESSES, MATERIALLY CHANGING SHAPE OF NOSE

BALL TURRET, HIGH FIN, DIHEDRAL FROM THE WING ROOT ARE NOTEWORTHY IN HEAD-ON VIEW

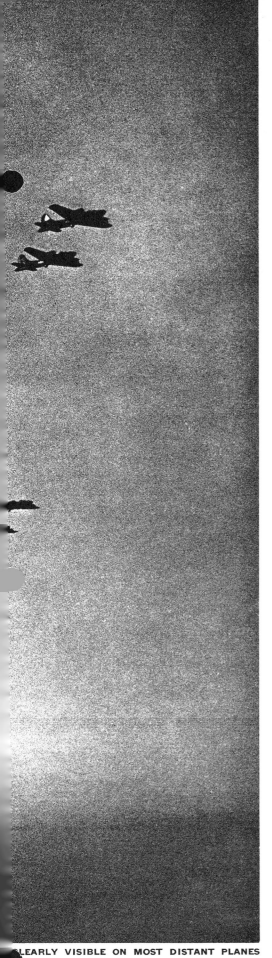

CLEARLY VISIBLE ON MOST DISTANT PLANES

its most prominent recognition feature, a tremendous fin. Now in use are B-17F & G. The former differs from the E only in internal details. The latter has added a chin turret to meet attackers coming in head-on.

RECOGNITION: Its long and narrow fuselage and the huge fin best distinguish the B-17. Dihedral stems from the root, and the edges of the wing taper equally. Wide tailplane has the same shape as the wing.

OPEN BOMB BAYS SHOW B-17'S READY FOR RUN

B-24

Long-range Liberators have performed superbly on important missions

The other half of the USAAF's heavy bombing team is the B-24—the Liberator. It has flown on some of the toughest runs of the war—Ploesti, the Kuriles, Wiener Neustadt and The Netherlands East Indies. To an ever-greater extent it is teaming up with the B-17 in pounding Germany.

When viewed head-on, the B-24 looks like a box car, and the ability of the thin Davis wing to get the bulky fuselage into the air seems aerodynamically impossible.

The Davis wing, however, is practical and is important both from the technical and recognitional standpoints. It is extremely thick at the roots, thin at the tips. The plan form of the wing is narrow and tapers almost to a point. The wing, which was worked out by formula rather than the trial and error wind-tunnel method, has a small surface that produces very little drag.

Deficient armament in early models has been remedied by adding a nose turret and a retractable belly turret. The Liberator now has ample firepower to slug its way to and from its targets. Despite its apparent clumsiness, it matches the speed of its longer, leaner stablemate, flying over 300 m.p.h. at a height of more than 30,000 ft.

RECOGNITION: The B-24 is a high mid-wing monoplane powered by radial engines. Dihedral of the long, thin wing is slight; wingtips are rounded, as are twin fins and rudders set outboard of the stabilizer.

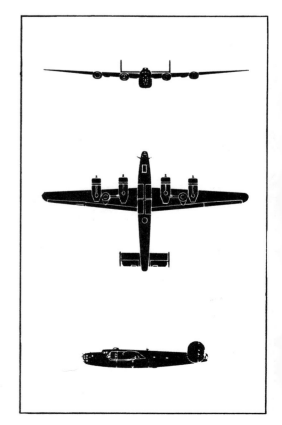

LONG, NARROW WING of B-24 tapers down like a knife blade. Seen from this angle, the fuselage, instead of looking bulky, shows remarkably clean design for such a big airplane.

NOSE TURRET represents latest addition to B-24's firepower which now equals that of B-17. Tailplane sits on top of fuselage, while rear gun turret is set right into elevator in tail structure.

LONGEST ROUND TRIPS undertaken by USAAF have been made by B-24's. RAF Coastal Command uses them extensively for anti-submarine work over the North Atlantic. Transport version of the Liberator, C-87, has a solid nose. Among famous passengers have been Churchill, Willkie.

For answers, see p. 50

H. M. S. ANSON, ONE OF THE NEWEST OF BRITAIN'S HARD-FIGHTING BATTLESHIPS, PLUNGES THROUGH A HEAVY SEA UNDER FULL HEAD OF STEAM

ROYAL FLEET

ITS SHIPS ARE WINNING THEIR FIGHT

For four years the Navies of the British Commonwealth have been at sea under battle orders. Months on end, ships have taken the buffets of hard steaming and the pounding of the sea. They have made port only for supplies and repairs, returning immediately to the almost daily sea fighting on the oceans of the world.

That the British could undergo the rigors of a four-year war and still remain among the rulers of the seas is as much a tribute to British shipbuilders and designers as to British courage and seamanship. The ships of the Royal Navies are fighting ships. They frequently lack the fine developments of German and American warships, but they are eminently suited to their job of patroling the farflung sea frontiers of the British Empire.

Even the most modern British ships are conspicuous for their lack of such refinements as streamlining, a fad carried to extremes in the beautiful but ineffective Italian ships. The superstructure of a British warship is a square bulky mass. Its flat surfaces and straight lines make it quick and inexpensive to build, easy to repair. Even the matter of painting the ship is facilitated by this structure.

The design of British ships is colored by the British philosophy of battle. Because of the long lines of communication between the Dominions and the island kingdom, it is necessary for the big ships to be at sea for long stretches. Overly complicated structural arrangements must be avoided so that repairs can be made at sea or at outlying bases. Moreover, it is

accepted as a first premise that warships are made to fight, and that in fighting some ships will be lost. For this reason, original construction costs must be kept as low as is practical. In round figures two King George V's could be built for the price of one North Carolina.

All of this has had an effect on their appearance and hence on their recognition. The ships of the King George V Class, for example, have a certain beauty (*see above*), but it is functional beauty like that of a steel mill or grain elevator, not that of a pleasure yacht. Tower bridges are fortresses in looks as well as fact. The broad stacks are set bolt upright. The decks are straight from bow to stern with no rakish lines. British ships are easy to recognize, easy to sail and hard to beat.

In the 43 silhouettes printed on these pages, the sizes and shapes of the major warships of the Navies of the British Commonwealth are presented in one spread. Among these are four which do not appear in the Recognition Training List published in the November issue of the *Journal*: the "S" Class destroyers, the light cruisers Belfast and Adelaide, and the minelayer Abdiel. Missing from the grid are silhouettes of the new Lion Class battleships, information about which must be withheld temporarily for security reasons.

Though most of the British capital ships are fairly old—some of them having been laid down during World War I—they have been frequently modernized with consequent changes in appearance. On the other hand, the present strenuous, drawn-out war at sea has meant heavy losses in the lighter ships and the necessary production of many new classes. The best intelligence currently available has been made use of to incorporate these changes in the grid.

Though the silhouetted ships are the most important British ships from the viewpoint of firepower, in numbers they are greatly outranked by the many small patrol and escort craft. A grid of these ships and small U. S. naval vessels, which create one of the greatest problems of recognition, will be presented in an early issue of the *Journal*.

SCALE: EACH SQUARE EQUALS 100 FT.

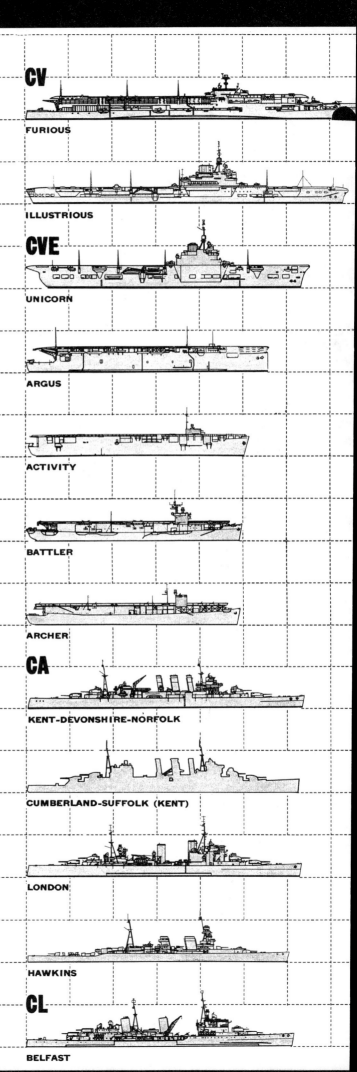

CV

FURIOUS

ILLUSTRIOUS

CVE

UNICORN

ARGUS

ACTIVITY

BATTLER

ARCHER

CA

KENT-DEVONSHIRE-NORFOLK

CUMBERLAND-SUFFOLK (KENT)

LONDON

HAWKINS

CL

BELFAST

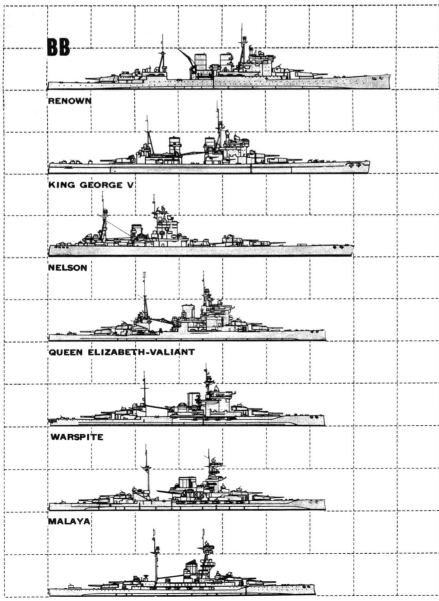

BB

RENOWN

KING GEORGE V

NELSON

QUEEN ELIZABETH-VALIANT

WARSPITE

MALAYA

ROYAL SOVEREIGN

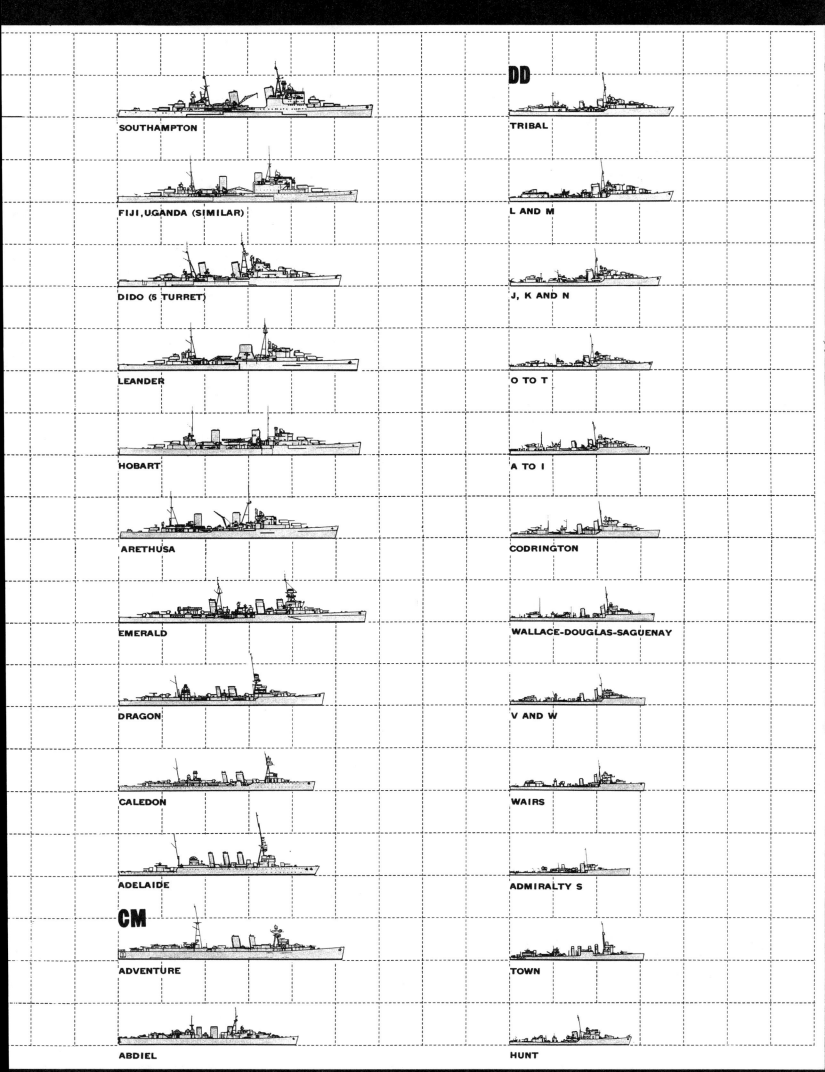

DD

SOUTHAMPTON

TRIBAL

FIJI, UGANDA (SIMILAR)

L AND M

DIDO (5 TURRET)

J, K AND N

LEANDER

O TO T

HOBART

A TO I

ARETHUSA

CODRINGTON

EMERALD

WALLACE-DOUGLAS-SAGUENAY

DRAGON

V AND W

CALEDON

WAIRS

ADELAIDE

ADMIRALTY S

CM

ADVENTURE

TOWN

ABDIEL

HUNT

BATTLESHIPS
OLDER CLASSES HAVE
FOUGHT IN TWO WARS

The eight British battleships which make up the Royal Sovereign and Queen Elizabeth Classes date from World War I. Units of both classes were at Jutland, while the Queen Elizabeth, which played a prominent role in the Dardanelles, was Beatty's flagship when the German High Seas Fleet surrendered off the Firth of Forth. In this war, the Royal Sovereigns have largely been used in patrol service. Prior to the outbreak of war, this class was slated for the scrap heap and so was never modernized.

Though older in years, the Queen Elizabeths are more modern tactically. They were the first oil-burning BB's of the world. Their design anticipated the "fast battleship" of today in combining the attributes of the dreadnought and battle cruiser. Originally built as two-stackers, they underwent modernization in the 1920's which trunked the two stacks into one. In the mid-1930's further modification brought the Warspite, Valiant and Queen Elizabeth up to date; the Malaya was altered somewhat less.

RECOGNITION: The four Royal Sovereigns are almost identical. All have wide quarterdecks, broad stacks set close to the tripod foremast, casemate batteries recessed amidships. Modernized Queen Elizabeths are similar in having massive tower bridges just forward of low broad stacks; hangars, cranes and catapults abaft the stack.

HULL FORM OF QUEEN ELIZABETH IS LONG OVAL WITH HEAVIEST SECTION

ROYAL SOVEREIGN CLASS distinguished at a distance by the long low hull from which projects a single broad stack and a comparatively light tripod foremast and bridge structure. Royal Sovereign and Revenge have a light pole mainmast; Resolution and Ramillies have a tripod mainmast.

H. M. S. RESOLUTION, the fourth unit of the Royal Sovereign Class, is unique in having catapult mounted on No. 3 turret. Like her sisters, she has old single-purpose casemated secondaries, and like most refitted ships, she has additional small anti-aircraft guns which cluster about the island.

TOWARDS STERN. ANTI-TORPEDO BLISTERS ADDED IN REFITTING MAKE HULL SEEM EXCEPTIONALLY BROAD IN CONTRAST TO RATHER SMALL TURRETS

THE MALAYA is least modernized of the Queen Elizabeths. Unlike Warspite and Queen Elizabeth, Malaya has chief weight of superstructure in the stack rather than in the tower. Small triangular deckhouse just aft of pole mainmast is an identifying characteristic of the class from the air.

H. M. S. WARSPITE'S blockhouse-like tower bridge is typical of later British battleship designs. Though ugly compared to streamlined Italians and Germans, square outlines make them economical to build and easy to maintain, vital considerations for a wartime building and repair program.

H.M.S. RODNEY has slightly less displacement than the Nelson but is almost identical in appearance. Chief distinction is the shape of the foremast. From the air, triangular tower and superstructure massed back of center, three large turrets on foredeck make class unmistakable.

H.M.S. DUKE OF YORK takes a heavy sea in the patrol of North Atlantic. Even in bow view, massive tower bridge, separated stacks

BATTLE

BRITAIN'S BEST

The ships on these two pages represent the greatest strength of England's battleline. The oldest of these, the battle cruiser Renown, has a fine fighting record. Off Narvik, she outgunned the Scharnhorst and Gneisenau and chased them back to port. In the Mediterranean, as the backbone of Force H, she kept a powerful Italian fleet penned behind the coastal minefields. The Renown's long cruiser lines give her a distinctive appearance and she is the only capital ship in existence with three twin turrets.

Rodney and Nelson were to be super-

NELSON CLASS (*above and below*) seems foreshortened when seen from abeam because superstructure is placed aft. Relatively heavy tripod mainmast contrasts with lighter masts of other British BB's. They are called the "Cherry Tree Class", i.e. they were "cut down by Washington."

H.M.S. RENOWN is the longest of His Majesty's ships. The island structure is separated, with two broad stacks and tower bridge forward

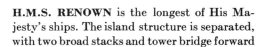

and light tripod mainmast mark her as King George V Class ship. Units of class have acted as transatlantic ferry for British personages.

KING GEORGE V, the name ship of her class, helped prove the superiority of British gunnery when she and the Rodney silenced the cornered

Bismarck in that bitter Atlantic duel. Like the modernized Queen Elizabeths, King George V ships have square-cut blockhouse style towers.

POWER

ARE NEW SHIPS

Hoods of 48,000 tons displacement but were caught by the limitations of the Washington treaty. To conserve space and weight, the nine 16-in. guns were concentrated forward so that these ships look like no others. Despite their reduced design they are the most powerful British ships.

Five units of the King George V Class have been commissioned. They were the first British battleships laid down after the abrogation of the limitations treaties but were probably designed during the treaty era. They are medium-sized but have more speed than older battlewagons.

of the catapult well deck and a long low deckhouse aft. Tall tripod foremast stands clear of tower and forestack, mainmast is light tripod.

H.M.S. ANSON looks massive, powerful when seen astern. Huge tower bridge gives bulk to superstructure; turret-mounted secondaries fill

out pyramidal mass. Profile of KGV Class (*below*) shows separated island, with wide-set stacks, tripod foremast distinct from the tower bridge.

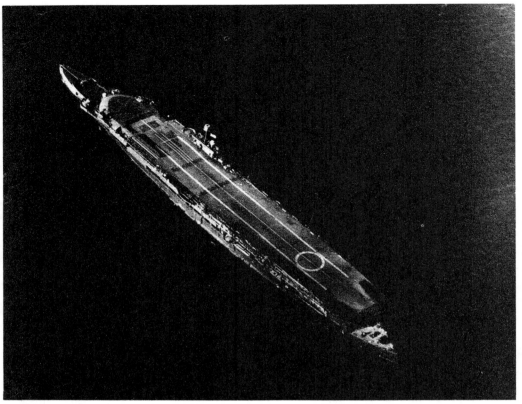
THE FLIGHT DECK OF H. M. S. FURIOUS STOPS SHORT OF POINTED STERN, WELL SHORT OF BOW

CURVED FORE EDGE AND OPEN BRIDGE OF

FLEET CARRIERS

HIT BISMARCK, ITALIANS

During the late days of World War I, a flight of planes took off from the deck of a converted cruiser, the H.M.S. *Furious*, flew to Tondern and attacked the German zeppelin sheds there. This was the first successful carrier-launched air attack. The ship from which the planes flew, having gone through two complete refittings, is still on active service.

Designed as a "large cruiser," to support an invasion of the Baltic, the *Furious* was intended to carry two 18-in. or four 15-in. guns. Before commissioning, however, she was transformed into a semi-aircraft carrier by building a flying-off deck from the bridge to the bow. Later a flying-on deck was added aft and still later the centerline stack and island were removed. In 1939

the present mast and island were added.

The chief strength of Britain's fleet carrier force is the four ships of the Illustrious Class. Among them they have built up an enviable battle record. It was planes from the *Victorious* which located the *Bismarck* and planes from the *Illustrious* which stopped her. The *Illustrious* also launched the planes which wrecked Taranto while the *Formidable* was a major element in the rout at Cape Matapan.

RECOGNITION: The Illustrious Class has a block shaped island on the starboard side amidships, a light tripod mast and pole mainmast. Flight deck is joined to sides of hull at bow and stern. Pairs of pillbox, dual-purpose twin mounts are set in each bow and quarter of symmetrical flight deck.

THE FLIGHT DECK INTEGRAL WITH HULL IS

LONG, LOW FOREDECK, ROUNDED LEADING EDGE OF FLIGHT DECK ARE FEATURES OF FURIOUS

VICTORIOUS' TOWER GIVE IT APPEARANCE OF SEASIDE HOTEL. NOTE HOW CARRIER'S FLIGHT DECK CURVES DOWN BOTH FORWARD AND AFT

APPARENT IN FORMIDABLE (*ABOVE*) AND INDOMITABLE (*BELOW*). ILLUSTRIOUS CLASS RESEMBLES U. S. ESSEX AND ENTERPRISE BUT IS SHORTER

AUXILIARIES
SMALLER CARRIERS
HELP SWELL FLEET

Prime development of the sea-air war since 1939 is the baby carrier used for escort and ferrying. Though this has been chiefly a U. S. development, the British and Japanese have both made use of it. The Royal Navies have chiefly used our small carriers but three ships of British construction are in auxiliary aircraft service.

One of these, the Argus, is one of the first aircraft carriers ever designed. Originally laid down in a British shipyard for an Italian steamship line as the S. S. Conte Rosso in 1914, her construction was halted by the outbreak of World War I. When the Admiralty decided to build carriers, the hull was converted to aircra

H. M. S. ACTIVITY HAS LONGER, NARROWER FLIGHT DECK THAN MOST CVE'S. SMALL ISLAND FAR FORWARD MIGHT CAUSE CONFUSION WITH JAPS

OPEN SPACE ABOVE LOW MERCHANT STERN AND PLUMB BOW DISTINGUISH THE ARGUS WHEN SEEN FROM ABEAM. BOW EXTENDS UP TO FLIGHT DECI

MERCHANT STERN AND CLIPPER BOW SET UNICORN APART FROM BIG BRITISH AIRCRAFT CARRIERS. THE ISLAND STRUCTURE IS ALSO LESS MASSIV

service, being completed in Sept. 1918. Since then it has been three times refitted, the last time in 1939.

Two newer British conversions are the Activity and the Unicorn. The first is a converted British merchantman, not unlike our Bogue Class carriers. The second is converted from a naval auxiliary, originally designed as a Fleet Air Arm supply and repair ship. Because of its heavy island and general lines it resembles a combat carrier, particularly the larger Illustrious Class.

The main portion of the British escort carrier fleet is made up of ships almost identical in appearance with equivalent American carriers. These the Royal Navy refers to as "Woolworth carriers" (i. e. 5- and 10-cent class). They are divided into three classes: the Archer Class which is the British equivalent of the U. S. Long Island Class; the Battler Class, equivalent to U. S. Bogue's; and Trumpeter Class, equivalent to our Prince William Class. The Battlers and Trumpeters are identical.

RECOGNITION: Argus has plumb bow, low merchant stern and high freeboard. Activity resembles our Sangamons but its flight deck extends almost to the cruiser stern. Unicorn is unique and readily identifiable by its large island which resembles a Fleet carrier's.

IN MOST BRITISH-BUILT AIRCRAFT CARRIERS, FLIGHT DECK DOES NOT OVERHANG THE HULL. ACTIVITY'S DECK EXTENDS ALMOST TO RAKED BOW

THE SYMMETRICAL STRAIGHT-SIDED FLIGHT DECK OF H. M. S. ARGUS HAS SQUARE STERN EDGE, CURVES TO RECTANGULAR PROJECTION AT BOW

BATTLER CLASS CVE'S ARE ALMOST IDENTICAL TO U. S. BOGUE WITH ISLAND WELL FORWARD, STACK PROJECTING FROM EACH SIDE OF FLIGHT DECK

LAST OF THREE TBF'S DROPS ITS TORPEDO AS THE OTHER MEMBERS OF THE FLIGHT JINK AWAY AFTER LOOSING PROJECTILES. IN BACKGROUND ANOTHER FLIGHT MAKES

TORPEDO BOMBING

The best way to sink a ship is to stop it with a submarine mine. Masses of explosive, moored or afloat in the sea, will rip the bottom from any ship, weaken and buckle her plates beyond repair. But the mine kills only by accident. The ship must contact the mine's antennae or cross its audio or magnetic field in order to set it off. And it can kill a friend just as easily as a foe.

The torpedo is a modification of the super-destructiveness of the mine. Powered by compressed air, hot gases or electric motors, it can be directed at its target and sent on its lethal way at speeds up to 40 knots. It carries a lighter charge than a mine, but the possibility of scoring an effective hit is many times higher.

No weapon has played a more dramatic role in World War II than the torpedo plane. Used most effectively in the South Pacific and the Mediterranean, it has accounted for many naval losses. Some nations, notably the U.S., Britain and Japan, have used it with skill and daring; time and again their pilots have scored successes.

Experiments in torpedo carrying are almost as old as the airplane itself. In the U. S., Rear-Admiral Bradley A. Fiske began experiments for the Navy back in 1910. In Europe, Italian Captain Guidoni successfully dropped a 352-lb. torpedo from an 80-h.p. Farman plane in 1911. This work was sufficiently successful so that in August 1915, when World War I was well under way,

Flight Commander C. H. K. Edmonds of the Royal Navy could fly his Short 184 into the Dardanelles and sink a 5,000-ton Turkish freighter, the first victim of an aerial torpedo.

From then till now, aerial torpedoing has been a required subject for all naval air forces. Perhaps the most intent torpedoists have been the Japanese, who made their pilots practice under simulated battle conditions. This paid off in the early days of 1942 when the Japs ran up a heavy score against us, but in the long run their losses have slackened their daring.

Since early German war plans did not include naval action, the torpedo plane as such was shelved for land-based planes. Thus when the Nazis discovered that they needed torpedo bombers, they had to fall back on their old stunt of adapting what they had. The Italians, on the other hand, having to fight their war in their closed sea, the Mediterranean, made torpedo bombing their chief interest. Their peacetime maneuvers were spectacular and the morale of the torpedo pilots was the highest in the Regia Aeronautica. But the Italians never had much of an appetite for this war, and in the face of resistance the pilots have not pressed home their attacks.

Though we cannot overlook the early Jap successes torpedo bombing has reached its greatest heights with the British and U. S. Naval and Marine fliers. The British using the Fairey Swordfish

ITS RUN. IN BATTLE, THE PLANES MIGHT FLY STRAIGHT THROUGH, HOPPING MASTS

EARLY U.S. TORPEDO PLANE, flown from experimental carrier Langley, makes perfect drop from low altitude as Naval fliers learn their hazardous trade.

TORPEDO WILL ENTER WATER smoothly, proceed to the target. Often, in early attempts, torpedoes porpoised off at odd angles or failed to discharge at all.

HAZARDOUS COMBAT JOB
DONE BY NAVAL FLIERS

scored notable torpedo victories at Taranto, Cape Matapan and throughout the Mediterranean. In northern waters, they caught the Bismarck and stopped its career for good. Now that the Fleet Air Arm is using the TBF (which they call the Tarpon), they have a faster, huskier plane to take into combat, but the Royal Navy still has a soft place in its heart for the plane it calls "Old Stringbags."

The United States' torpedo career began tragically at Midway when Torpedo 8 gallantly flew their outmoded TBD's to almost complete obliteration. Yet, in this same battle, the world's best torpedo bomber, the TBF, was introduced. Since that time, in naval battles in the South Pacific and on anti-shipping missions the world over, the Avenger has come in to score.

Though torpedo bombing is one of the more dangerous jobs in naval war—the very nature of the attack requires that the pilot bring his plane into point-blank range, hold it steady before dropping his fish—the TBF has been a great success. In the great naval engagements in the Solomons last fall torpedo bombers held the turn of the battle in balance. Major George Dooley, leading Marine Corps VMTB 131, and Lieut. Comdr. Coffin, leading Navy's VT10, made enough runs to put 11 torpedoes into a Kongo Class battleship. Such magnificent fighting highlights a good weapon and good pilots.

TBF

U.S. NAVY'S PLANE IS BIG, VERSATILE

At the time of the Battle for Midway, the U. S. Navy's standard torpedo plane was the Douglas-built TBD. This was a good plane in its day but the development of war planes had caught up to it and passed it. As a result its first combat experience was disastrous. Fortunately, a new American torpedo bomber was coming into operation. In fact, six TBF's had already arrived at Midway and more were rushed to fill the gap. Since then the newspapers have supplied a steady chronicle of its feats.

The TBF, or Avenger, is a big, sturdy and versatile plane. It has performed its prime task beautifully as the shattered hulks of the Kongo, Shokaku, Ryujo and a large part of the Jap merchant fleet will testify. Moreover, it has been the Navy's best scout carrier plane; its great belly being able to carry an exceptionally large radio installation. In missions against land targets, the TBF is a fine glide bomber capable of toting a one-ton bomb load. And at least one TBF is reported in use as an eight-man inter-island transport. The Avenger will carry a bigger load farther and faster than any other torpedo plane in action and will get its cargo and crew home even after severe battle damage.

RECOGNITION: Features are Grumman wing, deep-bellied fuselage, square-cut fin and rudder. Belly gunner's position forms marked step in underside of the fuselage.

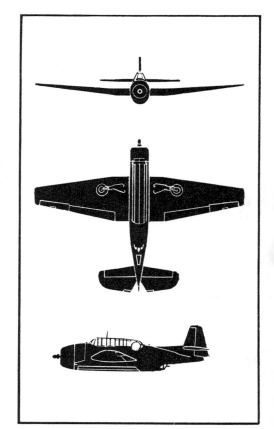

TWO VEE'S OF GRUMMAN AVENGERS MAKE GRACEFUL PATTERN OVER FLORIDA COAST IN TRAINING FLIGHT

TBF'S IN DRY RUN on the U. S. carrier Saratoga display characteristic attitudes of real torpedo attack. The nearest plane shows its chunky fuselage in straight flight while other planes in the group peel away after dropping their fish. In the background is an American destroyer of the Fletcher Class.

FALLING TORPEDO leaves trail of vapor as the compressed air motor begins to turn. Planes will now jink off line of approach and head for home.

AVENGER'S WING seems stubby in contrast to big heavy fuselage when seen in a quartering view; cockpit canopy projects well above fuselage barrel.

TORPEDO-CARRYING BEAUFORTS OF RAF COASTAL COMMAND, SHOWN ON PATROL, HAVE TAKEN HEAVY TOLL OF SHIPPING IN ENGLISH CHANNEL AND NORTH SEA

BEAUFORT
LAND-BASED TB OF RAF
ATTACKS GERMAN CONVOYS

Smashing Nazi convoys off Norway, France and the Low Countries is one of the main functions of the RAF's torpedo-carrying Beaufort. Faster and more heavily armed than the torpedo planes of the Fleet Air Arm, the Beauforts have penetrated harbors and fjords to deliver their attacks.

RECOGNITION: A mid-wing monoplane with two radial engines, the Beaufort can be recognized by the high cabin atop the fuselage, terminating in a gun turret. Horizontal tailplane has V-shaped cut-out. Dihedral is confined to outer panels of the wing.

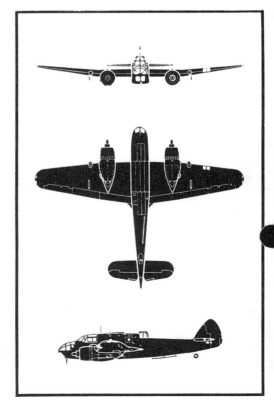

LONG, HIGH CABIN features side view of Beauforts. Familiarity with their fins and rudders is important, for it is identical on Blenheims and Beaufighters, other Bristol planes of the RAF.

BEAUFIGHTER SWOOPS LOW IN SIMULATED ATTACK ON CONVOY IN ATLANTIC. RECOGNITION AT THIS DISTANCE IS EASY BUT WOULD COME TOO LATE IN COMBAT

BEAUFIGHTER

BUILT AS FIGHTER, IT NOW SERVES AS TORPEDO BOMBER

Developed from the Beaufort, the Beaufighter is a faster, smaller, all-purpose plane which achieved success as a torpedo carrier in the Mediterranean. A workhorse of the RAF, it may be seen on all fronts. It can attack shipping either as a torpedo plane or as fighter escort for Beauforts.

RECOGNITION: The Beaufighter's wing, fin and rudder are identical with the Beaufort's. However, strong dihedral of the tailplane, engines set forward of fuselage, and a blister in place of the cabin-turret combination mark chief differences from prototype.

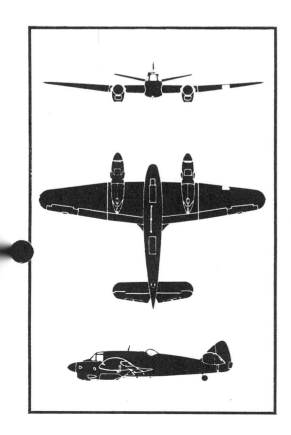

SOLID NOSE of the Beaufighter lies well aft of propellers. A newer model (*silhouette, left*) has inline engines. As a fighter the British call it the most heavily armed one now in operation.

ODD WING TIPS CURVING BACK FROM LEADING EDGE, TAILPLANE WITH LARGER ELEVATORS THAN STABILIZERS DISTINGUISH SWORDFISH FROM OTHER BIPLANES

PROMINENT COWL, HAYSTACK FIN AND RUDDER MARK SWORDFISH IN SIDEVIEW

STRUTS AND WIRES BETWEEN WINGS GIVE IT NAME OF "OLD STRING BAGS"

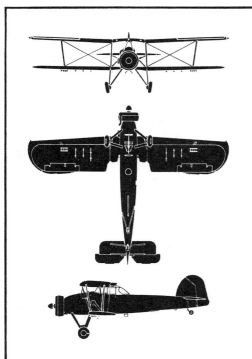

SWORDFISH

SANK ITALIAN FLEET AT TARANTO

Though the chief torpedo plane of the British Fleet Air Arm, the Fairey Swordfish, looks as if it did not belong in the same air with today's fighting planes, it has one of the most remarkable battle records of the war. To its credit lie the sinking of the major elements of the Italian Fleet at Taranto, the stopping of the Bismarck, the cutting of Rommel's sea supply lines and the battering of the Vittorio Veneto at Matapan. On one occasion, at Bomba Bay, three Swordfish, with one torpedo each, sank four enemy ships; the last torpedo blew up one ship which set another on fire.

The Swordfish is slow but makes up for it by being highly maneuverable and a good diver. After a high approach behind cloud cover, it dives, drops its fish and jinks for home. By flying low, the Swordfish makes it difficult for fighters to dive on it, turns inside them when they do.

RECOGNITION: The Swordfish is an old-fashioned biplane with a maze of wing struts and heavy truss undercarriage. Upper wing is swept back, lower one straight. Prominent nose cowling and extended elevators are other distinctive features. Latest version has a glazed-in cockpit cover as shown in the silhouette at left.

HIGH TAILPLANE MAKES BARRACUDA UNIQUE AMONG SINGLE-ENGINE PLANES. LONG NOSE HAS BULBOUS RADIATOR. COCKPIT IS FORWARD OF LEADING EDGE

BARRACUDA

GIVES NEW SPEED TO FLEET

AIR ARM'S TORPEDO ATTACK

To overcome the Swordfish's chief weakness, its slowness, the Fleet Air Arm has adopted the Barracuda, a fast, high mid-wing monoplane, as its newest torpedo-reconnaissance plane. Like the Swordfish, it is eminently fitted for the diving type of attack. In addition, its greater speed makes the Barracuda also useful for attacks at zero altitude at night or in heavy weather.

RECOGNITION: Most distinctive features are the high-set, strut-braced tailplane and large dive brakes projecting behind trailing edge of wing. The high mid-wing tapers from a thick wing root to a thin tip. The fuselage is long and sleek, with the nose projecting well ahead of the leading edge. Greenhouse extends from the pilot's cockpit to beyond the trailing edge of wing.

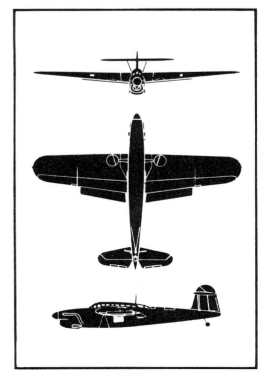

IN THE ATTACK, Barracuda's dive brakes are conspicuous below thickset wing; tailplane rides high above slender fuselage. In head-on view, cockpit canopy is also apparent above wing.

43

KATES MAKE A SUCCESSFUL TORPEDO ATTACK ON THE U. S. AIRCRAFT CARRIER HORNET DURING THE BATTLE OF SANTA CRUZ. CARRIER-BASED THEY RESEMBLE TBD'S

JAPANESE TB'S

ENEMY USES THEM SUCCESSFULLY

Spearheads of Japanese seapower in the Pacific and Indian Oceans have been the torpedo bombers of the Jap Navy. They accounted for much of the destruction at Pearl Harbor, sank the Prince of Wales and Repulse and contributed heavily to U. S. losses in the Solomons area.

Three planes, Kate, Betty and Nell, have made most of the Japanese torpedo attacks. Kate is a single-engine carrier-based plane designed primarily for torpedo action. The other two are big twin-engine medium bombers, able to deliver high-level as well as torpedo attacks.

Japanese maneuvers in peacetime emphasized torpedo practice under realistic combat conditions. While many planes were lost, a high degree of accuracy was achieved.

RECOGNITION: Kate is a low-wing monoplane powered by a single radial engine. Long, horizontal greenhouse accommodates crew. Pronounced dihedral of wing stems from points considerably outboard of fuselage. Fin is a high triangle with rounded top.

ONE KATE (CENTER) HAS JUST CRASHED WHILE ANOTHER EVADES ANTI-AIRCRAFT FIRE FROM AN ATLANTA CLASS LIGHT CRUISER IN THE SANTA CRUZ ENGAGEMENT

FLYING LOW, this Kate is headed towards U. S. S. South Dakota in the Santa Cruz air-sea fight. Heavy anti-aircraft fire broke up the attack.

KATE'S TORPEDO is clearly visible just before launching. Jap torpedoes can be dropped from a considerable height, carry heavy explosive charge.

NELL is a big plane, its 82-ft. wing span exceeding that of U. S. medium bombers. Angular wing has square tips; slender fuselage extends beyond the engines. Inboard twin fins and rudders also identify it.

BETTY is one of the newest Jap bombers. A twin-engine mid-wing monoplane, it can be identified by torpedo-shaped fuselage, triangular fin and rudder. Side blister, aft of wing, can be seen forward of marking.

PROMINENT ROUND NACELLES house inline engines of Nazis' fastest torpedo-carrying plane. Wing form is distinctive with straight center section, tapering outboard of the engines to thin wing tips.

JU-88
IS LATECOMER AS
TORPEDO BOMBER●

Most prominent omission from the Luftwaffe's ranks when war began was the torpedo bomber. Germany had but one carrier and did not plan an immediate naval offensive. Since limited resources demanded that only essential weapons be built, specialized torpedo-carrying aircraft were shelved in favor of the more versatile level bombers. A few old He-115's on coastal patrol did carry torpedoes but their performance was so mediocre that they had nothing more than nuisance value.

Late in 1941, however, a means had to be found for stopping the Murmansk convoys and the reliable He-111 was pressed into service for torpedo dropping. This was soon supplemented by the faster Ju-88. To train crews for these planes a torpedo-bombing school was set up at Grosseto in Italy, where the Nazis could take advantage of the Mediterranean experience of their Fascist ally.

Both Italian and German torpedo-bombing squadrons favor the low-level attack, particularly against convoys. They come in low, hopping the masts of the ships. By making their getaway at zero altitude, they make it difficult for the escorting vessels to fire without imperiling the ships of the convoy.

RECOGNITION: Wings tapering only on the outboard section, bulbous nose help identify Ju-88. Underslung radial-type nacelles project well ahead of the wing. Rounded rudder extends beyond tailplane.

CREW OF JU-88 is housed in extreme forward section of fuselage. Below: bombardier's position is in the small gondola below nose on starboard side. Torpedo bombing is but one of Ju-88's jobs.

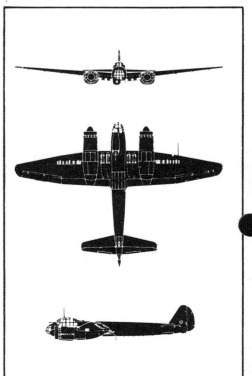

CHARACTERISTIC INDENTATION ON TRAILING EDGE OF THE WING AND OFFSET NOSE ARE DISTINCTIVE FEATURES OF HEINKEL 111. THE TAILPLANE IS A SMOOTH ELLIPSE

HE-III

IS A CONSTANT MENACE TO CONVOYS

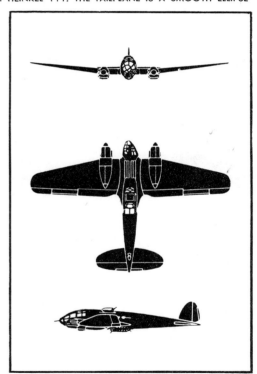

Torpedo bombing is a very important tactical operation but it is one which seldom involves a great many planes. It is reported that the Germans have never had more than 50 torpedo planes in a state of "crewed serviceability," i. e., in good shape with trained men to fly them. Of these, the majority up to this year have been Heinkel 111's, at least two squadrons of which were ready for action in April 1942.

The Heinkel 111 is by no means an ideal torpedo bomber. It is at best a fair makeshift. Being large, it has the advantage of carrying two torpedoes. Being rugged, it can frequently get home after it is hit.

However, its size works against it in that it makes the plane a particularly good target in an always risky business.

The two torpedoes carried by the He-111 may be of either German or Italian make. The German one, the F5B, carries a somewhat heavier charge, but the Italian F5W has a speed of 36 knots, 3 knots more than the F5B, and a somewhat greater range. F5W has further advantages of a more sensitive warhead and a higher altitude of drop.

RECOGNITION: Noteworthy on He-111 are indentations at wing root, swept-back wing and elliptical tail-plane. In total form, the plane seems heavy-bodied, bat-winged.

ROUNDED CONTOURS of He-111 give it more grace than most German planes. The fin and rudder repeat the elliptical shape of horizontal tail surfaces.

NACELLES of the two inline engines project almost equally with the nose of the fuselage. Belly gunner's gondola is prominent in quartering views.

QUIZ NO. 3: TANKS & ARMORED CARS

For answers, see p. 50

BRITISH VS. JAP

Ranging the skies over Eastern Asia and the South Pacific are two fighter planes that are likely to be confused. One, the Hawker Hurricane, is well-known to pilots and gunners in the European Theater of Operations where few, if any, members of the armed forces have seen its twin—Tony—first Jap fighter to appear with an inline engine.

On this page are four views of each plane to be studied. Outstanding difference between them lies in the tail structure. Whereas Hurricane's tailplane forms a perfect ellipse, Tony's is almost triangular with straight trailing edge, sharp taper on leading edge. Both planes have cutaway in elevator. The Hurricane's rudder extends beyond tailplane trailing edge; Tony's ends flush. Hurricane's fin and rudder are smoothly rounded, Tony's are high. Hurricane's radiator is set closer forward under cockpit than Tony's, and for service in both Asia and Africa it is equipped with an extra large scoop directly under the nose,

(For key to numbers, see p. 50)

NEWS & MISCELLANY

NEW SILHOUETTE

A provisional silhouette of the new Japanese twin-engine aircraft, first photographed in the Army Air Forces' raid on Wewak (*see Journal, Nov. issue*), is given below. Further data is not available.

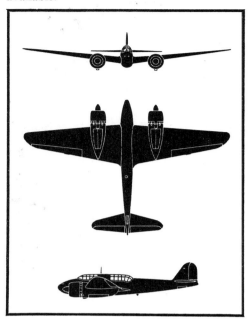

NEWS

According to the latest information available the enemy aircraft most likely to be encountered in the Mediterranean area are as follows:

Fighters:
- Me-109 (Fighter-Bomber)
- Me-210 (Fighter-Bomber)

Light Bombers:
- Ju-88 (High altitude recco)
- Ju-86

Medium Bombers:
- He-111
- Do-217

Reconnaissance:
- FW-200

Transports:
- Ju-52

•

The Japanese fighter formerly referred to as "Hap" (*see Journal, September issue, p. 31*) has officially been renamed "Hamp."

•

Information from the I Troop Carrier Command indicates that in aircraft recognition training, emphasis should be placed on the C-47 and the C-53 type of aircraft carrying the external para-racks (sometimes called equipment bundle racks) as these racks might be mistaken by ground forces and naval forces as external bombs.

TRAINING FILMS

A series of new Recognition Training Films are being produced by the Army, Navy and the British working in cooperation. The WEFT series are not recommended as they are obsolete and suitable only as a stopgap until new films are released.

Every training motion picture and film strip is assigned a serial number. Letters used in this series have the following meanings:

First letter (type of visual aid):
  M—motion picture
Second letter (source)
  N—United States Navy
  A—United States Army
  B—British

MN-491   Identification of TBF
MA-2286a Recognition of the Hudson III
MA-2286c Recognition of the Grumman F4F
MA-2286e Recognition of the Catalina PBY-5
MA-2465   Identification of Jap Zero
MA-409a   Identification of Aircraft, Gen'l Characteristics & Types of U. S. Military Planes
MA-409b   Identification of Aircraft, Distinguishing Features of U. S. Military Planes
HA-409ad Identification of Aircraft, The North American B-25, Medium Bomber

•

Quizcraft Series:

MB-1432a (Navy) Quizcraft I (9½ minutes) T. F. 1-3600 (Army)
How to identify the Super-Marine Spitfire, the Hurricane, Ju-88, Halifax and Blenheim 4.

MB-1432b
T.F. 1-3601   Quizcraft II (9 minutes)
Shows the Curtiss Tomahawk, Bell Airacobra, Junkers 87-B, Lockheed Hudson and Wellington Bomber in different attitudes of flight and the audience is asked to identify them. They are named by commentator and some of their prominent features pointed out.

MB-1432c   Quizcraft III (9½ minutes)
T.F. 1-3602
A Defiant, Stirling, Bristol Beaufighter, Manchester and Catalina are shown in flight as the commentator asks if you can identify these planes. The names of the planes are given and their principal identifying features are discussed briefly.

MB-1432d   Quizcraft IV (9 minutes)
T.F. 1-3603
Shows the Maryland Bomber, Messerschmitt 109-E, Sunderland Flying Boat, Whitley Bomber and Douglas Boston Mark III in various attitudes of flight and audience is asked to identify them. Their names are given by the commentator and some of their prominent features are pointed out.

MB-1432e   Quizcraft V (10 minutes)
T.F. 1-3604
A Fulmar, Messerschmitt 110, Heinkel III, Bristol, Beaufort and Mustang are shown in various flight attitudes as the commentator asks if these planes can be identified. Names of planes are given and their principal identifying features are discussed briefly.

MB-1432f   Quizcraft VI (9½ minutes)
T.F. 1-3605
Typhoon, Ju-52, Focke-Wulf 190, Lancaster, Mosquito

MB-1432g   Quizcraft VII (11 minutes)
T.F. 1-3606
Series of shots from different distances and angles of Mitchell, Liberator, Lightning, Marauder, Flying Fortress. The identification features of various planes are pointed out.

CORRECTIONS

Correction (*Journal, Oct. issue, p. 21*): German six-wheeled armored car has power on only the four rear wheels.

•

Corrections to be made to U. S. Navy Basic Slide List dated 19 July 1943:

Slide Numbers	Corrections
1762, 1840	Sally not Kate
1686A, 1687A, 1688A, 1689, 1817, 1959, 1967	
1968, 1969, 1970	All Baltimore, A-30 not A-31.
234	7 digits

•

The Division of Naval Intelligence has pointed out an error in identification of the ships in the photograph on page three of the November issue of the *Journal*.

By comparison with the center spread of the U. S. Naval vessels (*Journal, Sept. p. 26-27*) the ships may be correctly identified as belonging to the Benson or Livermore Classes. This error in recognition should not be attributed to the "Bumps."

QUIZ ANSWERS

QUIZ No. 1

Plane	In or Out of Range	Range
1. Rufe	In	2,000 ft.
2. F4F	In	750 ft.
3. Spitfire V	In	2,000 ft.
4. Me-110	In	1,800 ft.
5. Beaufighter	Out	3,000 ft.
6. Hurricane I	In	1,200 ft.
7. F6F	In	500 ft.
8. Oscar	In	1,800 ft.
9. F4U	In	750 ft.
10. Me-110	In	1,500 ft.
11. Tony	In	1,000 ft.
12. Rufe	In	1,500 ft.
13. Oscar	In	750 ft.

QUIZ No. 2:
1. C-60
2. FW-200
3. Whitley
4. Sunderland
5. He-177
6. Beaufighter
7. PV Ventura
8. PB2Y Coronado
9. Ju-88
10. Arado 196
11. Beaufort
12. Barracuda
13. Hampden
14. Blohm & Voss Ha-138
15. PBY Catalina
16. Beaufort
17. Blenheim
18. He-115

QUIZ No. 3
1. German halftracks
2. German PzKw III
3. British Churchills
4. British Covenanter
5. U.S. M 5A1
6. British Crusader
7. U.S. M-3
8. British Cromwell
9. British Valentine
10. German 8-wheeled armored car
11. German PzKw IV
12. Italian 4-wheeled armored car

KEY TO PLANES on p. 49:
Hurricane: 1, 3, 5, 7
Tony: 2, 4, 6, 8

ME-323

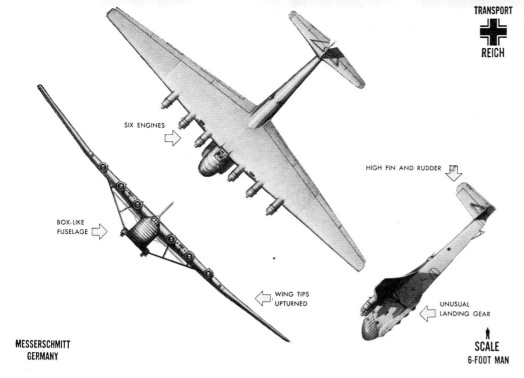

SIX ENGINES

HIGH FIN AND RUDDER

BOX-LIKE
FUSELAGE

WING TIPS
UPTURNED

UNUSUAL
LANDING GEAR

SCALE
6-FOOT MAN

MESSERSCHMITT
GERMANY

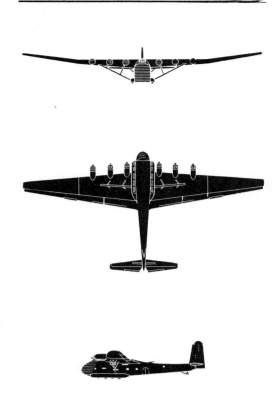

SPAN: 181 ft. **SERVICE CEILING:** over 21,000 ft.
LENGTH: 93 ft. 6 in.
APPROX. SPEED: 195 m.p.h. at 13,000 ft.

DISTINGUISHING FEATURES: Six-engine, high-wing monoplane. Very long wings are tapered to small, squarish tips. Flat center section is very thick. Long outer panels have marked dihedral. Nose-heavy, humpback fuselage tapers sharply aft of the wing. Landing gear consists of five wheels in tandem under each side of forward fuselage. Horizontal tail plane is long and slender, resembles wing in plan with cut-out in elevators. Extremely tall, narrow, single fin and rudder has slightly tapered edges and round tip.

INTEREST: The Me-323 is a modified, powered version of the Me-321 Gigant glider. During the final stages of the Tunisian campaign, P-40 Warhawks completely destroyed a large formation of these giants attempting to land supplies for the besieged German troops. With a full military load of about 40,000 pounds, some sort of assisted take-off, either a tug or rockets, is believed to be used. The nose of the fuselage is made up of two very large doors through which heavy equipment of all sorts can be loaded with ease.

NOTE: This page is to be cut along dotted lines (*above* and *below*), added to the proper nation's section in the Recognition Pictorial Manual. The dots indicate perforations.

D.F.S. 230

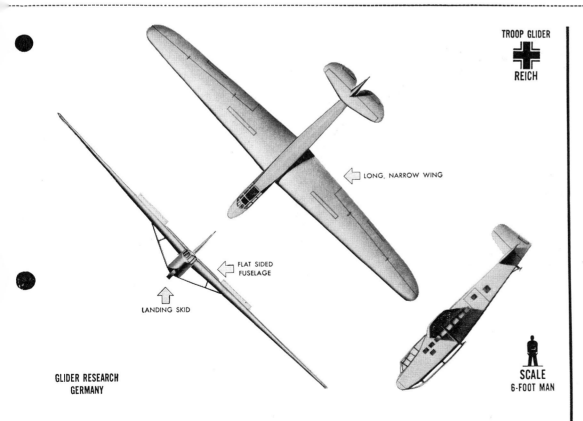

LONG, NARROW WING

FLAT SIDED
FUSELAGE

LANDING SKID

SCALE
6-FOOT MAN

GLIDER RESEARCH
GERMANY

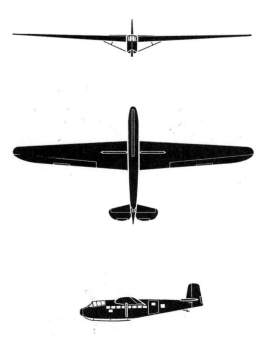

SPAN: 72 ft 4 in.
LENGTH: 37 ft. 6 in.
NORMAL TOWING SPEED: 110 m.p.h.

DISTINGUISHING FEATURES: High wing braced with single struts. Wing is long and narrow with slight taper on leading edge, tapered trailing edge, and small rounded tips. Fuselage long and narrow in plan and has straight top. Cross-section is rectangular. Horizontal tailplane has tapered leading edge with round tips and curved trailing edge with V cut-out. Tall, single fin and rudder is slightly tapered with blunt top.

INTEREST: The D.F.S. 230 is one of Germany's standard gliders and was used in occupation of Crete. Optimum gliding speed of this glider after release is approximately 70 m.p.h. Its landing speed in still air is from 35 to 40 m.p.h. It is a ten-seater of simple design.

A

B

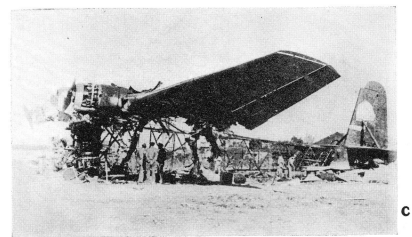

C

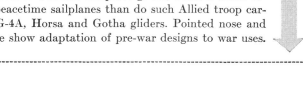

ME-323's motors turn a bulky, unmanageable glider into a valuable addition to Germany's aerial transport system. Though relatively slow, the Me-323 can carry tremendous loads, up to 120 fully equipped troops, or 40,000 lb., for approximately 500 miles.

DFS-230, a standard German ten-place glider, bears a closer resemblance to peacetime sailplanes than do such Allied troop carriers as the CG-4A, Horsa and Gotha gliders. Pointed nose and slender fuselage show adaptation of pre-war designs to war uses.

A

C

B

D

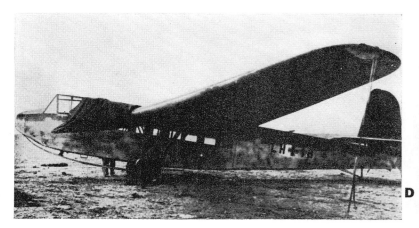

U. S. ARMY-NAVY JOURNAL OF
RECOGNITION

TANK-BUSTER

JANUARY, 1944

NUMBER 5

RESTRICTED

SHARE THIS COPY

QUIZ NO. 1
PACIFIC
THEATER

(For answers see p. 50)

U. S. ARMY - NAVY JOURNAL OF
RECOGNITION

JANUARY, 1944

NUMBER 5

PUBLISHED BY THE U. S. WAR AND NAVY DEPARTMENTS
COPYRIGHT 1944 BY STEPHEN R. CONNOLLY, 1ST LT., AIR CORPS

TBF SCURRIES LOW OVER WATER IN ATTEMPT TO AVOID MURDEROUS FIRE FROM U. S. CRUISER. SUCH MISRECOGNITION IS ASTONISHING

WHOSE ENEMY?

The picture above was taken from the deck of a U. S. cruiser during a recent action in the Pacific. Attached to the back was a caption which read in part: ". . . unidentified plane that appeared to be making a torpedo attack on the U. S. S. ———— is driven off by anti-aircraft fire." No mention was made of the fate of the plane; it was not reported whether it was damaged. We sincerely hope it was not, since the airplane is an American torpedo bomber, a TBF Avenger.

Into such weapons as the Avenger go innumerable hours of painstaking training of crews, of careful research, of exquisitely precise manufacturing. In combat such weapons have to be used with skill and courage to accomplish their purpose. But if they are not able to function because a trigger-happy or under-trained gunner knocks them out of the sky, it is plainly a case of fatal waste.

Faulty recognition, in the first instance, was bad enough, and that an American pilot was fired upon even worse. Most amazing, perhaps, is the fact that even after the picture was developed and printed, no one recognized the plane.

One of our prime weapons in this all-out war is recognition; it is a weapon we cannot afford to misuse. In fighting the enemy we must use every possible angle we can to win. The men fighting alongside us, manning our ships, planes and tanks, should at least be afforded the status of allies. Whenever they are mistakenly attacked, as in the picture above, a small bell rings on the enemy's cash register. And for us it registers No Sale.

CORRECTION The information relative to naval operations in the Aleutians which appeared on page 3, column 2, of the December, 1943 issue of the Journal has been found to be incorrect and should be disregarded.

RABAUL RAID

Navy carrier planes catch large Jap force at bay in New Britain harbor

These magnificent pictures of Simpson Harbor, Rabaul, are recognition news. Taken by a U. S. Navy photographer who rode as gunner in one of the carrier-based aircraft that made the attack, they are the most comprehensive pictures available of Japanese naval force.

Rabaul, the second biggest Japanese base in the Southwest Pacific, has been subjected to a constant pounding in the last few months by the combined forces of the Army and Navy. These raids reached a climax in mid-November when planes from U. S. carriers caught 23 Jap warships and several merchantmen at rest in the large land-locked harbor. Before the American planes returned to their ships, they left one cruiser and two destroyers at the harbor's bottom, one cruiser and eleven destroyers badly damaged. Thirty-one enemy planes were shot down during the bombing attack and 64 more were destroyed when they attempted a revenge blow at our carriers. Considering the strength of Japanese installations in these waters, it was a feat of great daring and enterprise.

These pictures reveal the large concentration of naval strength amassed by the Japs and tell better than any news story the consternation which hit our enemy with this surprise attack. The long white wakes of the ships scurrying for the harbor mouth show the frantic efforts of their commanders to evade bombs.

As a test of your knowledge of Japanese ships we have made a quiz of the picture at the top of this page. In it you should be able to identify heavy and light cruisers, destroyers, tankers, cargo ships and one hospital ship. The answers may be found on page 50.

PANORAMA OF SIMPSON HARBOR DURING HEAT OF RAID SHOWS LARGE

TAKEN EARLY IN ATTACK, this picture shows the Japanese ships getting underway. Short wakes indicate that the vessels have not yet reached full speed. Changes in the position of the landing strip at left and small volcano at the right show how far plane has moved between two exposures.

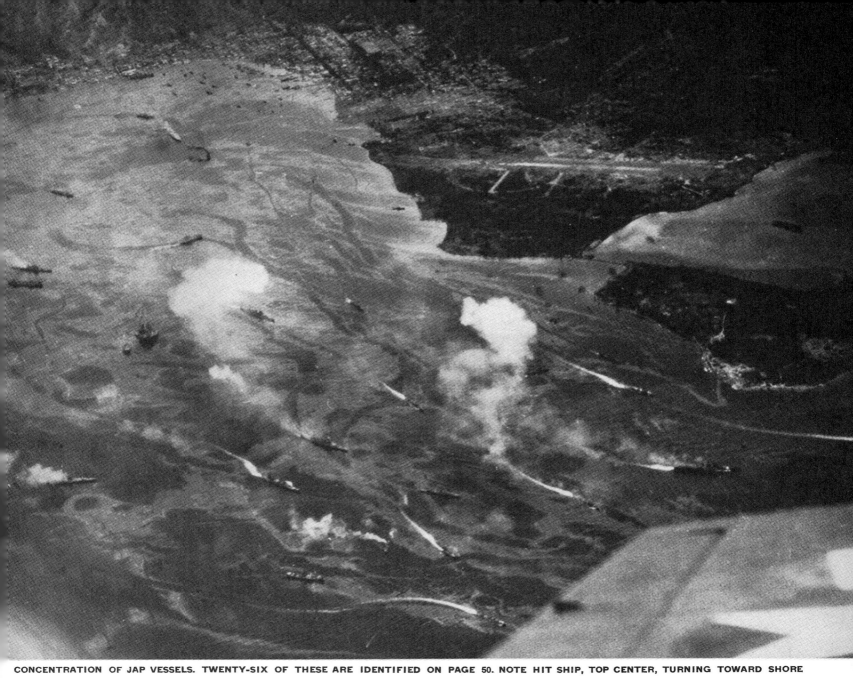

CONCENTRATION OF JAP VESSELS. TWENTY-SIX OF THESE ARE IDENTIFIED ON PAGE 50. NOTE HIT SHIP, TOP CENTER, TURNING TOWARD SHORE

CRISS-CROSS PATTERNS of wakes demonstrate turmoil of Japs' mad scramble to escape. At bottom left, cruiser has swung around sharply after being bombed, seems to be burning, as fleet jams harbor mouth. From the airfield at left rose swarms of Jap planes of which 95 never returned.

B-24 重爆	PB2Y 哨戒兼爆撃	B-19 重爆	B-17 重爆
全幅 33.53米 尾翼ハ矩形ヲナシ双垂直翼ナリ 細キ「ダイヤモンド」型翼、長キ矩形ノ胴体 等ヨリ知ル之	全幅 35.05米 尾翼矩形 B-24ト相異 太キ艇体、矩形ニ近キ翼及矩形翼端	全幅 64.62米 尾翼ハ普通型 三角形ノ長キ翼、長キ機首 巨大機	全幅 31.7米 太キ「ダイヤモンド」型主翼 三角形尾翼、太ク厚キ胴体 短キ機首、先端ハ円形ヲナス

A-20A 襲撃機	PBM 哨戒兼爆撃	PBY-5 哨戒兼爆撃	P-38 駆逐機
全幅 18.6米 後方ニ頂点ヲ有ス三角形ノ主翼 「ダイヤモンド」型尾翼、単垂直翼機 ハ一見猫背ノ恰好ヲナセリ	全幅 35.97米 飛行艇 上反ル尾翼、双方ノ方向舵ハ 内方ニ傾斜ス	全幅 31.7米 飛行艇、双胴ニテ四角形ノ主翼 ヲ有スルハ本機ノミナリ、 機首短ク胴体太シ	全幅 15.85米 化樹種、翡遠、テルヘツキ持機 入、細長キ両翼双胴、双垂直翼ハ ニテ尾翼ニテ連結ル

F2A 戦闘機	F4U 戦闘機	F3F 戦闘機	SBD 索敵兼爆撃
全幅 10.67米 ズングリセル胴体 F4Fト相異 翼端尾翼ノ滑カナル曲線	全幅 12.19米 逆カモメ型翼、又ハ殆ド凡ユル 方角ヨリ顕著ニ見ユ 狭キ尾翼	全幅 9.75米 海軍ニテ現戦使用中ノ複葉機 1 短ク太切ノ張、ベル胴体	全幅 12.8米 急降下爆撃機 「ダイヤモンド」型主翼並ニ尾翼、急 ニ後退セ翼、ニ開ク隔器

SB2A 索敵兼爆撃	SB2U 索敵兼爆撃	SBC 索敵兼爆撃	A-24 襲撃機
全幅 14.33米 圓味ノアル翼、長キ機首	全幅 12.8米 F4Uト同様ニ見ユ、F4Uト相異 四角形ノ翼、翼端 但シ尾翼ハF4U ト同ジク「ダイヤモンド」型	全幅 10.36米 複葉機 急激ニ後退セル上翼、胴体長	全幅 12.8米 SBDト同型ナリ 陸軍ニテ使用 主翼並ニ尾翼ハ「ダイヤモンド」型

B-18A 中爆	B-23 中爆	B-25 中爆	B-26 中·爆
全幅 27.43米 三角垂主翼 膨ミ… レ胴体 戰ニ似タル機首	全幅 27.43米 B-18Aト相異 尾翼長ク其先端ニ銳座アリ 胴体ハ稍細ク機首丸味ヲ帯ブ	全幅 20.42米 主翼ハA-20Aニ相似ス A-20Aト相異 尾翼ハ双垂直翼、矩形ラス	全幅 20.12米 主翼ハダイヤモン ド型 發動機ハ大キク翼ノ前方ニ 可成ク突出シアリ

P-39 驅逐機	P-40 驅逐機	P-43 驅逐機	F4F 戰鬪機
幅 10.36米 動機水冷 長…先…レ機首（側面ヨリ …場合 各キ操縦室 空氣取入口隆起	全幅 10.97米 發動機液冷 先細ノ機首ヲ有スルモP-39ノ如ク細長 クラス、機首及カ…ス、獨特ノ三角形擴	全幅 10.97米 ツシングリセル切株ノ如キ機首 翼ノ前緣ヨリ後方ヘ「カーブ」ヲ描キ タル肉切庖丁ノ如キ主翼	全幅 11.58米 四角形主翼 五角形ノ尾翼

-17A 襲擊機	SB2C 索敵兼爆擊	TBD 雷爆擊機	SBN 索敵兼爆擊
幅 14.02米 D及A-24ノ同 機… 及尾翼… …車輪…相接觸…小サキ機首	全幅 15.24米 「カーチス」ノ典型的三角形翼 …角形ノ機首	全幅 15.24米 非常ニ深ミアル三角形翼、尾翼ノ 方向ニ同ジ先細トナル、尾翼ハ之ト 反對ニ三角形ラナス	全幅 11.89米 SB2A及F2Aト同一ノ丸キ「ブリスター」 翼ヲ有ス、短キ機首、細キ胴体

JAPS STUDY U.S. PLANES

INVASION CONVOY STEALS INTO CASABLANCA IN DARK HOURS OF MORNING. THE PASSENGER LINER IN FOREGROUND HAS BEEN CONVERTED TO

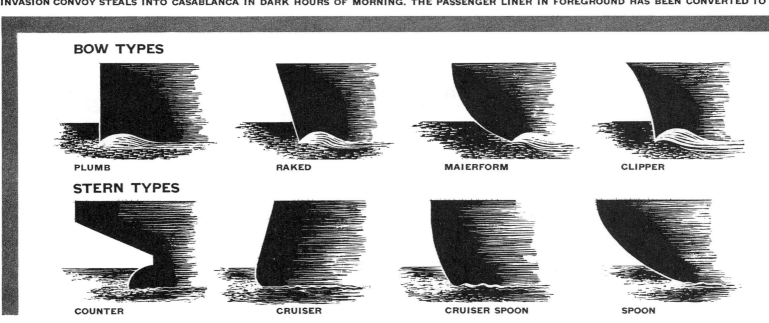

BOW TYPES

PLUMB   RAKED   MAIERFORM   CLIPPER

STERN TYPES

COUNTER   CRUISER   CRUISER SPOON   SPOON

TROOP TRANSPORT. SHIPS IN DISTANCE ARE WAR-FITTED CARGO VESSELS

MERCHANT SHIPS

The battle of transportation rages incessantly on a world-wide front

First to serve in time of war is the Merchant Marine. Without it battles cannot take place. Planes, guns and men cannot fight; food, oil and ammunition cannot reach the field. Even before the U.S. entry into the war, lend-lease shipments ran the U-boat gantlet to Britain and Russia, helped hold the civilized world together. Sailing the long sea lanes of the world, alone or with little protection, ships went down faster than they came off the ways. But the endless procession of ships kept fanning across the oceans to the battlefronts and, gradually, as more of them left the shipyards and convoy protection increased, there were merchant ships enough to launch a second front in Africa and an offensive in the Pacific.

The chart below shows how to spot merchant ships according to differences in hull and superstructure. A further description of their characteristics and duties appears on following pages. Learning to know ship types is easy and very important. The kind of ships in an enemy convoy indicates projected strategy. Tankers may mean only a refueling operation; freighters, a garrison reinforcement. Attack-cargoes and transports may be the prelude to grand-scale invasion. A complete presentation of merchant ships is given in Navy Department manual ONI 223-M, Merchant Ship Shapes.

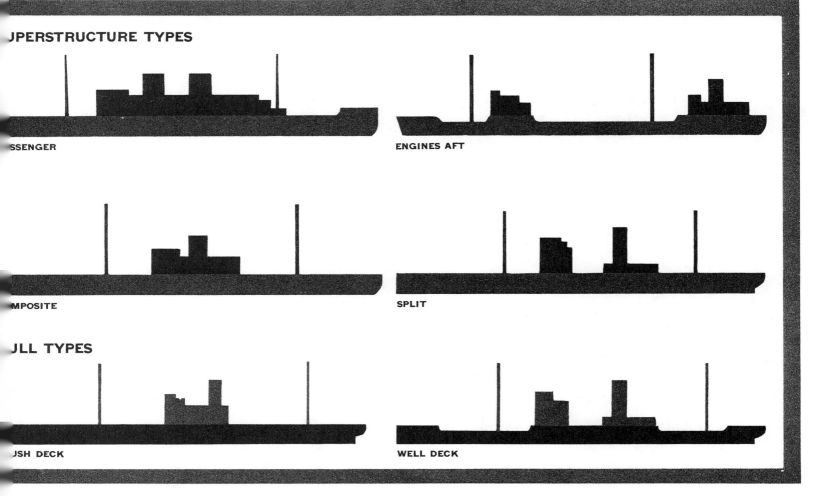

SUPERSTRUCTURE TYPES

PASSENGER

ENGINES AFT

COMPOSITE

SPLIT

HULL TYPES

FLUSH DECK

WELL DECK

PASSENGER SHIPS

Peacetime luxury liners, stripped for action, transport thousands of men to fighting fronts

The years before the war saw the principal countries of the world rivaling each other to build the biggest, fastest, most luxurious passenger liners. Liners like the Normandie, Queen Mary, America, Rex, Ile de France, Bremen and Europa, too expensive to be operated by private enterprise, were subsidized by their governments for the sake of national prestige. Liabilities in peacetime, they have become tremendous assets as high-speed transports and hospital ships. Lavish ballrooms and cocktail lounges, exquisitely appointed suites and dining salons have been shorn of finery and transformed into dispensaries, mess halls and living quarters. The Queen Mary (below), third largest of the luxury liners, can do 34 knots, 10 more than the fastest submarine. More than once in the early days of the war she relied on her speed to dash unescorted through U-boat hunting grounds. On decks, in cabins and holds, she can pack as many as 20,000 troops, once carried a fully-equipped division from Britain to Suez. The America, now called the West Point, largest U. S.-built passenger liner, has the latest safety equipment, cruises at 22 knots and carries 12,000 troops besides her regular crew.

Passenger ships are the easiest of all merchant vessels to recognize. Prominent in size, they have unusually high center superstructure made up of several decks extending for at least a third of the hull length. Long rows of lifeboats or small landing boats and rafts, large funnels, numerous ventilators make it impossible to confuse them with ships of any other type. Besides fore and mainmasts, some have "jury masts" on superstructure, prominent kingposts on hull or superstructure.

The Queen Mary (below) and the West Point (right center) exemplify the most modern passenger-ship designs. Their raked bows cut cleanly through the water. Their funnels are short and fat. All the lines of the hull and superstructure have a swept-back streamlined look. The Wakefield, ex-Manhattan, (lower right) has an older design counter stern which differs from the cruiser sterns of the first two vessels. Otherwise she looks very much like the West Point above her. The plumb bow and stern, tall, thin, coal-burning stack and severely squared contours of the World War I vintage President Line vessel at top right make her the ugly duckling of the passenger fleet.

HOG ISLANDER, "A SHALLOW FLOWER BOX WITH

WEST POINT, EX-AMERICA, LARGEST U.S. SHIP, HAS

QUEEN MARY is the world's fastest passenger ship. Her massive raking funnels go with enormously powerful engines. Solid, twelve-deck superstructure spreads over ¾ of hull.

A POT IN MIDDLE," WAS BUILT IN FIRST WAR WITH OLD-STYLE PLUMB BOW AND ODD STERN, HAS CARGO-HANDLING KINGPOSTS ON FOREDECK

STREAMLINED SUPERSTRUCTURE OF MODERN DESIGN. BELOW: THE WAKEFIELD, EX-MANHATTAN, HAS OLD-STYLE COUNTER STERN, PLUMB BOW

ANCHORED AT ADAK HARBOR IS AN OLD COASTAL CARGO SHIP (LEFT) WITH ENGINES AFT, AN OLD WELL-DECK PASSENGER-CARGO LINER AND AN LST

PASSENGER-CARGO SHIPS

Cruise ships and fruit liners carry assault forces to invasion shores

Armed and commissioned for fleet service are many passenger-cargo ships that once plied the warm waters off South America with loads of beef or bananas. Half freighter, half passenger vessel, these ships have several decks to accommodate passengers, kingposts and booms for loading cargo hatches. They are slower and smaller than passenger liners, have a deck superstructure extending more or less one-third the length of the hull, and one funnel. As transports (AP), attack transports (APA) and headquarters ships (AGC) they perform many dangerous missions. Attack transports carry men and equipment into battle areas, then also serve as bombardment ships to cover landings. Headquarters ship serves as the brains of the landing operation, maintaining communications between the various arms of the attack group.

SMALLER TRANSPORT HAS TALL RAKED STACK, HIGH BOW AND LOW COUNTER STERN, NAVIGATION BRIDGE RISES ABOVE DECKS OF SUPERSTRUCTURE

U.S.S. CHARLES CARROLL CARRIES A DOZEN SMALL LANDING CRAFT ON DECK. SHE WAS BUILT AS THE DELURUGUAY IN 1940, CARRIED 63 PASSENGERS

OLD PLUMB BOW, PLUMB STERN SHIP HAS SQUARE SUPERSTRUCTURE, TWIN GUN SPONSONS FORE AND AFT. NOTE KINGPOSTS ON SUPERSTRUCTURE

U.S.S. JAMES O'HARA IS AN ATTACK TRANSPORT OF RECENT DESIGN. TOPMASTS ARE STEPPED-ON TRUSS MEMBERS OF HEAVY GOAL-TYPE KINGPOSTS

THE JOHN C. CALHOUN, a Liberty ship, has a composite superstructure housing crew and navigation bridge. A catwalk and small temporary decks have been set up to allow crew to pass over deck cargo. Three heavy kingposts support several booms each, two have stepped-on topmasts.

U.S.S. AQUILA, an attack-cargo vessel, is a modern Danish freighter capable of a speed of 13 knots, used to carry equipment for landing operations.

CARGO SHIPS
Backbone of the merchant fleet

Most numerous and important ship of the Merchant Marine is the slow-and-steady pack-horse freighter which bears the brunt of war transportation on hazardous convoy journeys that take half again as long as in peacetime. All ship shapes and sizes make up the cargo fleet, from old tramps to sleek new steamers. A small superstructure housing the crew is located amidships and is sometimes of split construction with bridge and engines separate. Stalwart kingposts and cargo booms deposit the load in the hold

THIS TYPICAL MARITIME COMMISSION FREIGHTER HAS SUPERSTRUCTURE AFT OF AMIDSHIPS, IS SLIGHTLY FASTER THAN LIBERTY SHIP

SPLIT SUPERSTRUCTURE, with bridge and engine rooms separate, appears on Hog Island freighter, one of which was launched every four hours of World War I. In this war she is covered with anti-aircraft cannon. Angular counter stern, sharp lines of well decks and plumb bow are typical.

through large hatches on the deck. In normal times cargo is all stowed below but now, to increase capacity, some material is piled on the weather deck.

The United States is the biggest builder of cargo vessels, although ten years ago we did not have ships enough to carry more than a third of our foreign trade Mass-produced Liberty ships and other Maritime Commission designs have been our answer to Allied war losses. Designed in close collaboration with the Army and Navy, these new ships are readily adaptable for use as fleet auxiliaries. The hard-working Liberty ship now carries about one quarter of all United Nations tonnage. Fifteen of these ships are needed to transport the equipment of a single armored division. To keep that division supplied with its daily requirements of 650 tons of gasoline, 600 tons of ammunition and 35 tons of food necessitates the arrival of a Liberty ship every eight days of the war.

LIBERTY SHIP awaits unloading during bombardment of Gela in Sicily. This pre-fabricated vessel has flush deck, attains speed of about 10 knots.

MODERN ENGLISH FREIGHTER OF FORT, EMPIRE OR OCEAN TYPE LIES VERY LOW IN THE WATER, HAS DISTINCT SPLIT SUPERSTRUCTURE

ESSO NEW ORLEANS, NOW THE FLEET'S CHENANGO, ONCE SAILED AROUND THE WORLD FOR STANDARD OIL COMPANY. HER CATWALK RUNNING FORE

TANKERS AND COLLIERS

The fuel that keeps the United Nations fighting is carried thousands of miles

The bombardment of Germany would stop today were it not for the priceless loads of oil and high-octane aviation gasoline carried by merchant ships. The tough, nerve-racking job that tanker crews have sailing their 10-knot vessels through sub-infested waters is an heroic story of the war.

Tankers ride low in the water, their holds filled with crude oil, gasoline and kerosene. Bulkheads prevent shifting of cargo in a rough sea. Weather deck of a loaded tanker is almost constantly awash, and an elevated catwalk running fore and aft is neces-

sary. Engines are aft for safety's sake, and heavy cargo gear is generally absent. On larger tankers, bridge is located amidships.

Faster tankers, with greater than "fleet speed," are part of our Maritime Commission building program. Traveling with the fleet as naval auxiliaries, tankers can refuel warships on the move. The Japanese in the 1930's built a number of fast, 18-knot tankers, probably with the war in mind.

Engines-aft cargo types, like tankers, are built to carry bulk cargo in compartments in the hold, but collier cargo is dry rather

than liquid, consisting of coal, ore or grain, often timber, etc. Many large cargo hatches appear on the weather decks of colliers together with a number of short heavy kingposts to lift the cargoes. Engines are often aft. The bridge is amidships, aft or forward. Some cargo types are loaded by pier machinery; others, like the one at bottom right, have cranes of their own for self-loading. The chief difference in appearance between tankers and cargo carriers is the absence of catwalk and prominence of loading gear in the latter.

U.S. OIL TANKER with well deck, riding light at anchor, stands high out of the water. Her bridge is just forward of amidships, engines are aft.

Two tall masts for signaling equipment stand on either side of bridge. Raking bow and cruiser spoon stern show that vessel is of a fairly new design

BERWINDVALE, a pier-loading collier, has its engine aft, bridge structure forward of amidships. Between these two prominent recognition points is a long expanse of well deck interrupted only by kingposts. Hatch covers are large for easy handling of bulk cargoes like grain and coal, metal ores.

THE ACHILLES, a self-loading collier, has a long crane thrusting out over rows of hatches on the weather deck. The bridge is forward, engines are aft. Crew quarters above the engines are unusually large. The tall, thin funnel shows that the Achilles burns coal. She has a marked spoon stern.

17

1930

BOEING MONOMAIL served either as a mailplane or transport. The outline of its long, sleek fuselage was carried over into later Boeing airplanes.

1931

PIONEER HEAVY BOMBER, B-9 resembled Monomail in basic design of wing and tail but had machine-gun position projecting beyond engines.

AIRPLANE GENEALOGY

Development of airplane families
gives valuable recognition clues

Automobiles were very easy to recognize in the late twenties. Each manufacturer had his set of doodads, and before streamlining came along to take away the square corners and distinctive hoods, every kid on the block was a recognition expert. But streamlining by no means made it impossible to recognize cars; radical changes took place, but individuality survived.

Accompanying the modernization of design was a series of mergers which resulted in "families" of cars. The result was that one could sometimes tell who built a car before getting close enough to give the exact make.

To some extent the same sort of family grouping has become apparent in the development of aircraft. The cluttered designs have given way to cleaner, more uniform models, and hard and fast military necessities allow little leeway in placing engines, turrets and cockpits. Nevertheless, family features survive, and even to the relatively untrained eye, the distinctiveness of a part like the Bristol fin and rudder (December *Journal*, page 40) is obvious.

WITH 13 MACHINE GUNS, EIGHT OF THEM IN TURRETS, BOEING'S LATEST HEAVYWEIGHT, THE B-17G, IS POTENT THREAT TO GERMAN AND JAPANESE

1943

"PROJECT 299," built over eight years ago, has unmistakable Flying Fortress airframe. Note side and belly blisters, indentation under nose.

RAF's B-17C had flat panels in place of blisters and "bathtub" gun position under fuselage. It was first of the B-17's with smooth nose contour.

Any system of recognition depending on a search for family features is likely to be bad, for it would contradict the principle of seeing the plane as a whole. But when positive identification is impossible at first glance, the pilot or gunner is very likely to start grasping at clues such as the shape of the nose, the fin or a nacelle. At this stage a knowledge of family features can help enormously.

It must not be assumed that manufacturers keep family features in all of their planes. But familiarity with the developments shown on the following pages may add materially to one's interest in recognition.

Typical in the history of airplane design has been the evolution of the Boeing B-17G. First plane recognizable as its ancestor was the Monomail, a heavy monoplane designed in 1928-29. Built for speed, it had the long, sleek fuselage which has characterized the entire Fortress series. Logical military successor to the Monomail was the B-9 which appeared in 1931. It did 186 miles per hour at a

height of 6,000 ft., a sensational performance for heavy planes of that time.

In 1934 the Army Air Corps announced a competition for a new bomber. The number of engines was not specified, and Boeing engineers decided on a four-engine plane which could out-perform all competitors. Known as "Project 299," the plane first flew in July, 1935. Although it crashed in October as the result of a take-off with a locked elevator, its performance was such that additional four-motored Boeings were ordered.

With its assortment of blisters and its smaller fin, the 299 is, in the military sense, a far cry from the well-armed B-17G. Perhaps the most important transition was from D to E. since it meant redesigning the whole tail structure to house a gun turret and adding other turrets on the back and belly. But through all the developments which have added armor, horsepower and firepower to the B-17, the basic airframe has been retained. The forthcoming Boeing bomber, B-29, will be predicated on the same fundamental design.

FIGHTERS. INCORPORATING MANY CHANGES RESULTING FROM COMBAT EXPERIENCE, IT DIFFERS SURPRISINGLY LITTLE FROM THE EARLY FORTRESSES

1933

DELIVERED TO THE ARMY IN 1933, B-10'S WERE STANDARD EQUIPMENT AS LATE AS 1939 WHEN THEY SERVED AS PART OF PANAMA CANAL DEFENSE

MARTIN AND CONSOLIDATED

Land-based bomber and big flying boat can be traced to earlier models

Light and medium bombers have comprised Glenn L. Martin's greatest contribution in the building of landplanes. Beginning with the XB-907, a steady series was produced including the famous B-10, a later export version, the Martin 139, the 167 or Maryland, and 187 or Baltimore.

The B-10, whose prototype was delivered to the Army in 1933, was actually used in combat early in 1942 together with the Martin 139 by pilots of the Netherlands East Indies Air Force. A dozen of these outmoded planes were credited with sinking 26 Japanese ships.

Specific needs of the RAF's desert campaign governed the development of the Baltimore, a heavier version of the Maryland. The earlier plane, built to French specifications, stressed maneuverability which the British sacrificed for bomb load. Successful in the Mediterranean, it has been used almost exclusively in that theater.

BALTIMORE WAS TEST FLOWN IN JUNE 1941, TWO YEARS AFTER MARYLAND. DEEP BELLY, TAIL ASSEMBLY SHOW DEFINITE RESEMBLANCE TO B-10

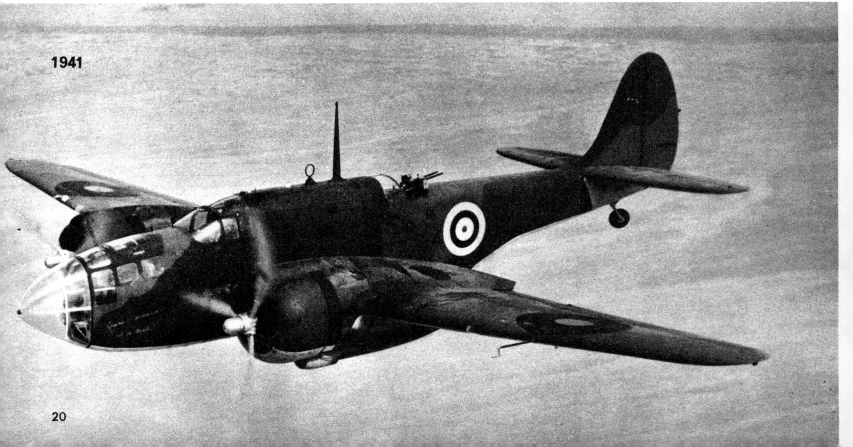

1941

FIRST OF SESQUIPLANE TYPES, CONSOLIDATED P2Y-1, IS 1932 MODEL. NACELLES WERE UNDER WING, NOT BUILT INTO IT. NOTE TWIN RUDDERS

Consolidated flying boats now serving the U. S. Navy and RAF Coastal Command date back to 1928 when the PY-1 was delivered to the Navy. Originally a monoplane, this ship went through the sesquiplane stage (*above*) with a small lower wing at the top of the hull. It finally emerged as a parasol-wing monoplane with a single fin and rudder.

In 1933 the Consolidated boats flew 2,039 miles non-stop to break the existing straight-line distance record for seaplanes. Among other PY and PBY records are the first formation flight from San Francisco to Honolulu (January 1934) and another distance record of 3,443 miles from Norfolk to San Diego via Coco Solo (1935), this last by the PBY-1 prototype.

Appearing in 1938, the PBY-4 was longer, heavier than its predecessors and was first to have blisters. The model now in use is the well-known Catalina, PBY-5. Amphibian version is the PBY-5A.

PBY-1 could very easily be taken for the latest Catalina. Nose resembles that of P2Y-1 and high stabilizer survived in switching to the single tail.

PBY-5'S SIDE BLISTERS PACK STRONG DEFENSIVE PUNCH. RETRACTABLE FLOATS BECOME WINGTIPS WHEN LONG-RANGE CATALINA IS IN FLIGHT

HAWKER, CURTISS

Typhoon, Warhawk climax two famed fighter lines

The Hurricane and Typhoon, built by Hawker Aircraft Ltd., have a definite link to their common ancestor, the Fury biplane. Despite inevitable changes involved in the production of the first monoplane, the basic fuselage design of the Fury was retained. The Hurricane design crystallized in 1934 when the Merlin engine became available. The prototype was test-flown in 1935. Mainstay of the Fighter Command until Spitfires appeared in quantity, Hurricanes bore the brunt of the fighting in the Battle of Britain.

The powerful Typhoon entered combat in August, 1942. As was the case with the Thunderbolt, the plane was designed to exploit a powerful engine, in this case the Napier Sabre. Its huge radiator and the rudder extending below the fuselage give the Typhoon quite distinctive features. Nevertheless, in the outline of the wing and shape of fin and rudder, the influence of the earlier models is clearly apparent.

In the development of the Curtiss series of fighters two noteworthy features are apparent. One of these is the change from a radial to an inline engine. The other is the complete abandoning of one model and a consequent falling back on an earlier design.

With the trend towards liquid-cooled engines, Curtiss tried a completely new design to house the new Allison and built the P-37 (*right*). When it proved impractical, the P-36 fuselage and wing were used for the installation of the inline engine, resulting in the first of the P-40 series. After this unorthodox start, the subsequent changes to the P-40F (*below, right*) were the logical ones dictated by the need for more firepower, greater speed and ability to perform at considerably higher altitudes.

LAST OF THE BIPLANES made by Hawker was the Fury. Despite its open cockpit, fixed landing gear, maze of struts and wires, it contained many features of the speedy Hurricane.

1935

HURRICANE PROTOTYPE has characteristic hump, still most prominent recognition feature. Tailplane struts were soon found unnecessary.

1942

TYPHOON in fighter version carries four 20-mm. cannon or 12 .303-cal. machine guns. Speed and ruggedness make it an ideal fighter-bomber.

1936

STANDARD FIGHTER of the U. S. Army Air Corps in 1938–39 was the P-36, with single-row radial engine. Its prototype had twin-row radial. P-36 was flown by the French over the Maginot and Siegfried Lines. Switch to liquid-cooled engine was the only major change in the first P-40.

1937

FREAK SHAPE of the P-37 with heavy tail and cockpit far to the rear, represented break from the earlier designs, was abandoned after a brief trial. It was the first modern Curtiss fighter plane to have the Allison engine, was also equipped with turbo-supercharger and inner coolers.

1941

WARHAWK, P-40F, introduced the Merlin engine to Curtiss series. Also Merlin-powered is P-40L. All other models including P-40P have Allison engine, shallow airscoop atop nose. Representing variations only in details, later P-40 models have not changed from recognition standpoint.

23

QUIZ NO. 2 GUNNERY

This is a fixed gunnery quiz. Like the free gunnery quiz in the December issue of the *Journal*, it is double-barreled. All servicemen should be able to recognize the airplanes. Fighter pilots, trained in the use of the 50–100 mil sight, should be able to tell whether they are in or out of range and just what the range is. For reproduction reasons all the planes are centered in the sight rings. Please note particularly: these pictures do not indicate the correct point of aim position or the correct angle of bank.

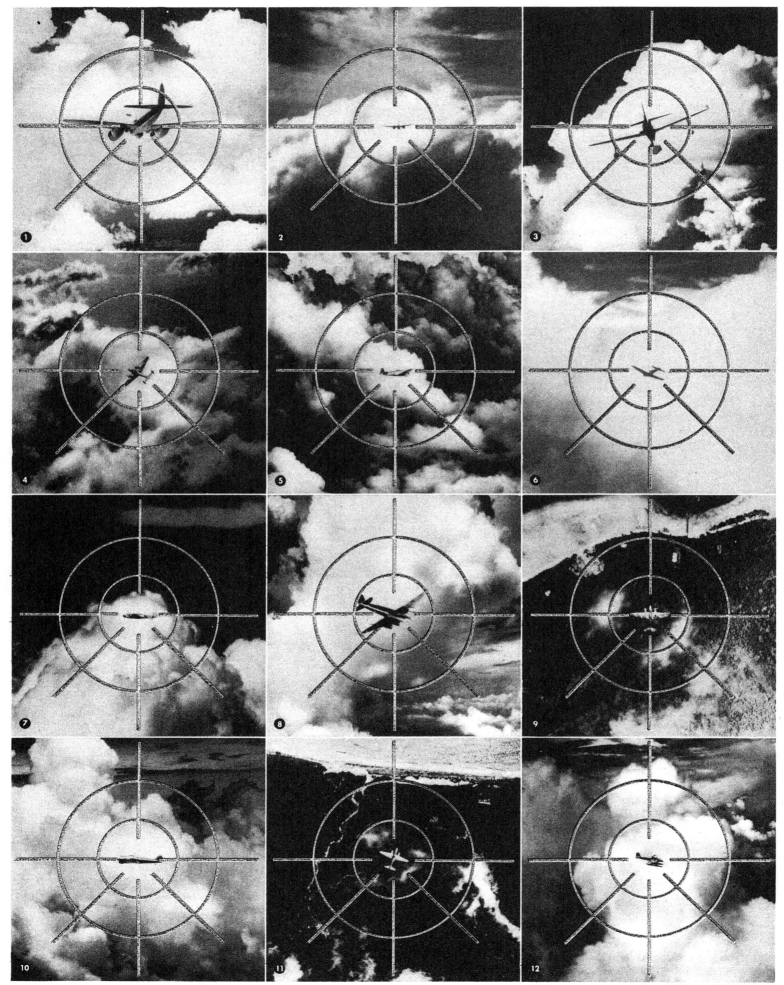

For answers, see p. 50

FAST NEW DESTROYER ESCORTS LIKE U. S. S. BARON (ABOVE) ARE HELPING MAKE SEAS SAFE FROM U-BOATS

THE SMALL STUFF

THEY FIGHT A TOUGH, UNPUBLICIZED WAR

Though the big ships get the press notices, a major naval job of this war is being done by a motley assemblage of small craft: minelayers, minesweepers, corvettes, frigates, gunboats, sub-chasers, motor torpedo boats and patrol and escort vessels of all shapes and sizes. On these ships falls the steady grind of convoying merchantmen, sweeping enemy waters and landing troops on hostile beaches, raiding enemy convoys and, perhaps toughest and most important of all, the deadly dull routine of coastal patrol. With amphibious warfare certain to increase in all theaters of war, these minor combatant types will see more action than ever before.

Since these small ships make up the great bulk of the Navy, since they are in all fields of sea action, and since the small ships of all navies look very much alike, they constitute the greatest naval recognition problem of all. The men who man our small craft are engaged in a most hazardous business. It is not for nothing that the personnel on sub-chasers, minelayers and sweepers and PT boats often refer to themselves as the suicide fleet. It is therefore particularly important that they should not be subjected to the fratricidal dangers of misrecognition. Soldiers and seamen in every activity can best protect themselves and their friends by knowing intimately the contours of the vessels on the following pages.

On the two pages immediately following, the minor warships of the U. S. are arranged in silhouette on a comparison grid, each square of which represents 50 ft. They range in size from the 453 ft. of the U.S.S. Terror, a minelayer, to the 80 ft. of the PT boat. This grid may be removed from the magazine and mounted on a bulkhead or wall. Further information about small naval craft will be found in manual Minor Combatant Craft, ONI 54-MC.

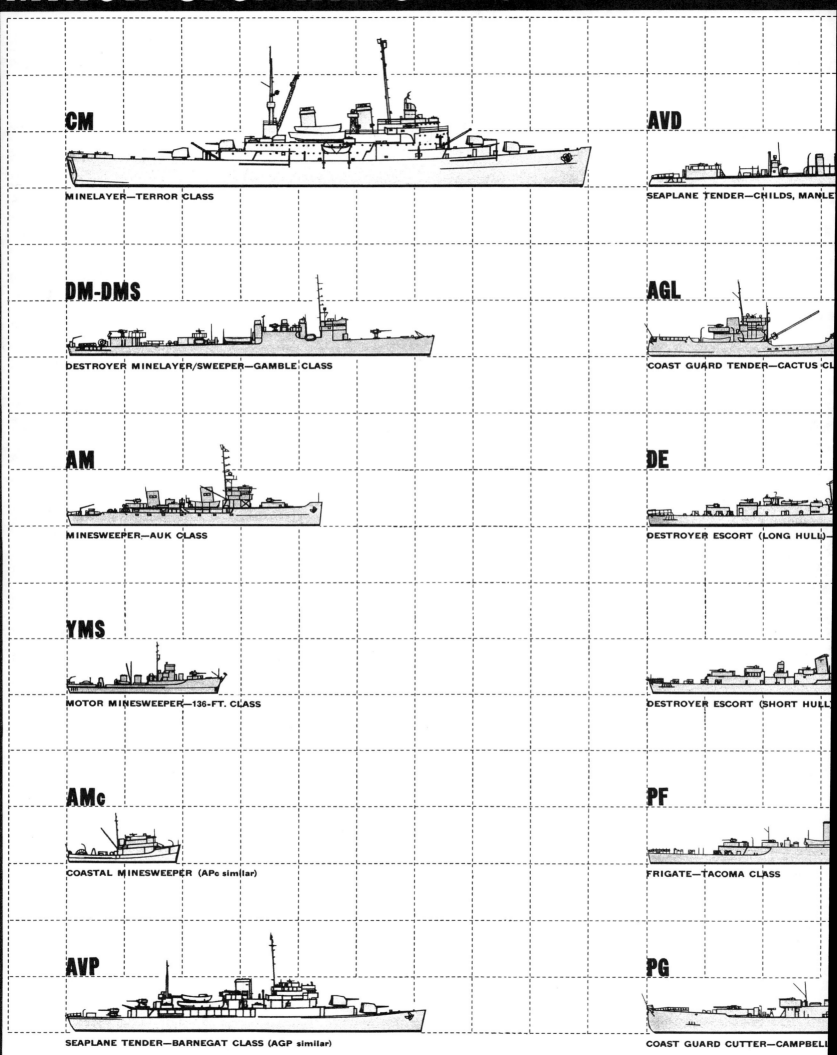

MINOR U.S. WARSHIPS

CM

MINELAYER—TERROR CLASS

DM-DMS

DESTROYER MINELAYER/SWEEPER—GAMBLE CLASS

AM

MINESWEEPER—AUK CLASS

YMS

MOTOR MINESWEEPER—136-FT. CLASS

AMc

COASTAL MINESWEEPER (APc similar)

AVP

SEAPLANE TENDER—BARNEGAT CLASS (AGP similar)

AVD

SEAPLANE TENDER—CHILDS, MANLE

AGL

COAST GUARD TENDER—CACTUS CL

DE

DESTROYER ESCORT (LONG HULL)—

DESTROYER ESCORT (SHORT HULL

PF

FRIGATE—TACOMA CLASS

PG

COAST GUARD CUTTER—CAMPBELL

SCALE: EACH SQUARE EQUALS 50 FT.

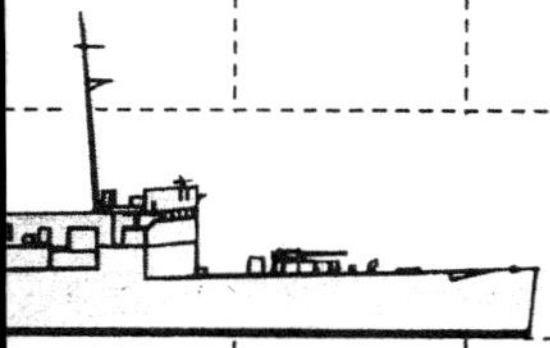

ES (APD similar)

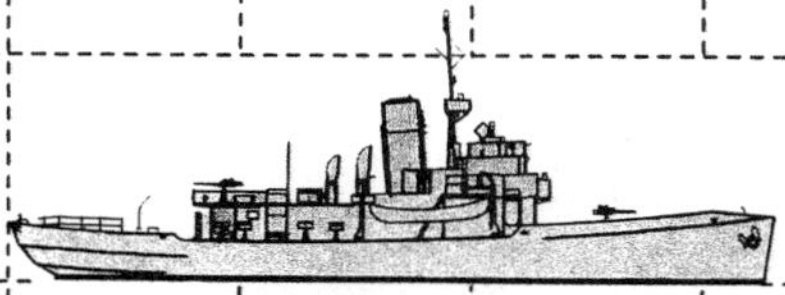

COAST GUARD CUTTER—"A" CLASS

SC

SUBMARINE CHASER—SC 497 CLASS

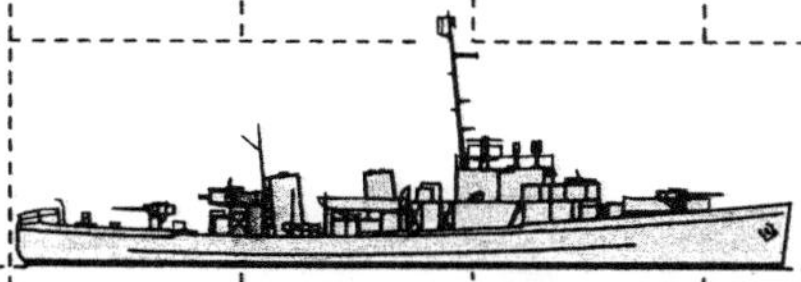

AT

COAST GUARD CUTTER—"B" CLASS

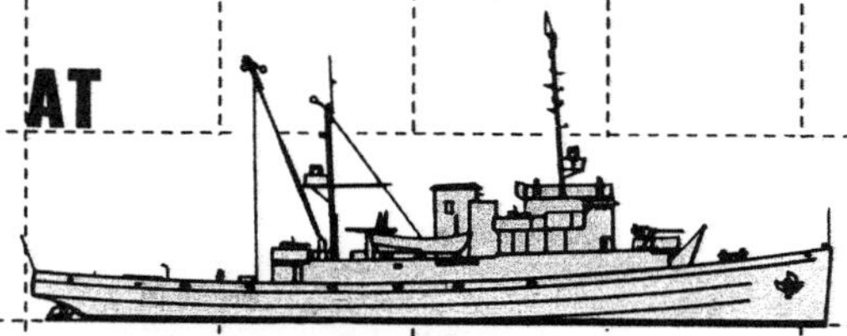

OCEANGOING TUG—NAVAJO CLASS

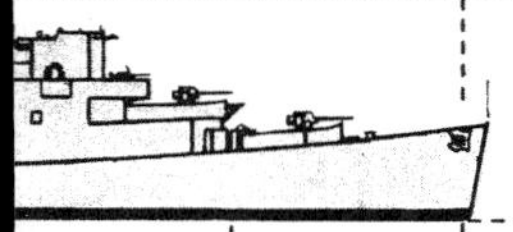

CLASS

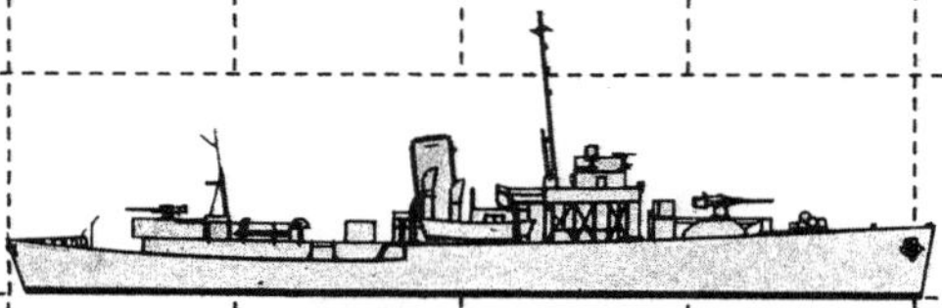

CORVETTE—TEMPTRESS CLASS

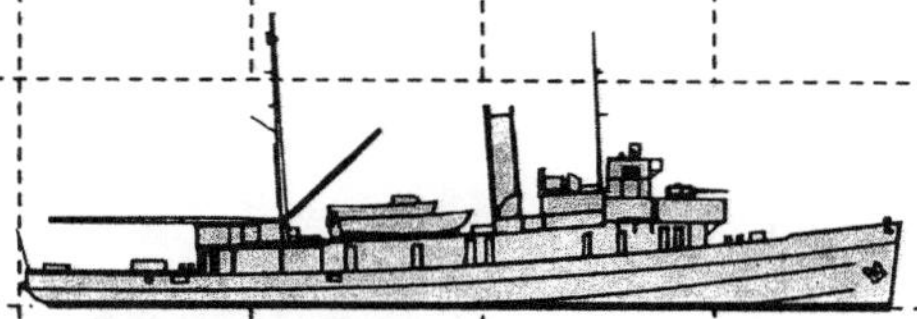

OLD "BIRD" CLASS

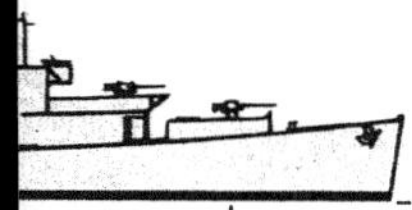

PC

YN

CLASS

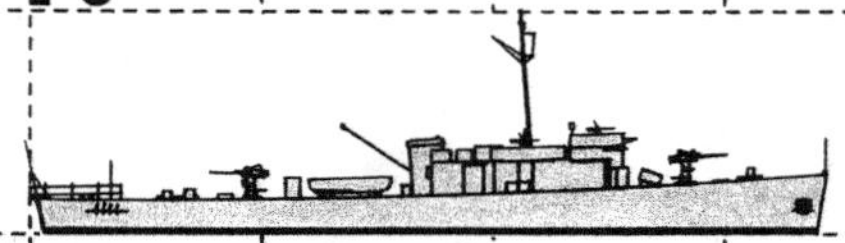

SUBMARINE CHASER—PC 461 CLASS

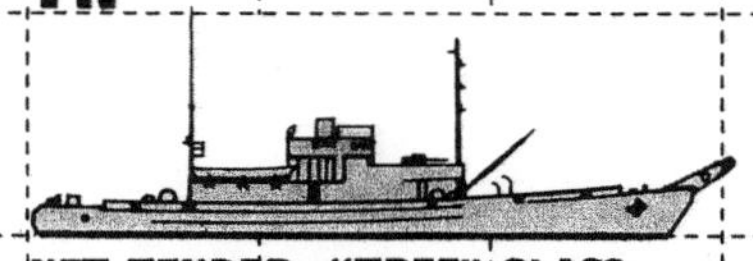

NET TENDER—"TREE" CLASS

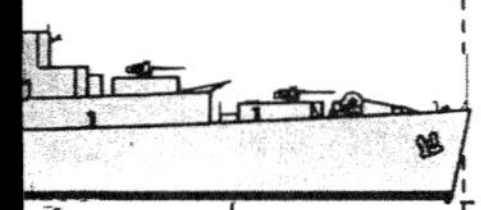

PCE

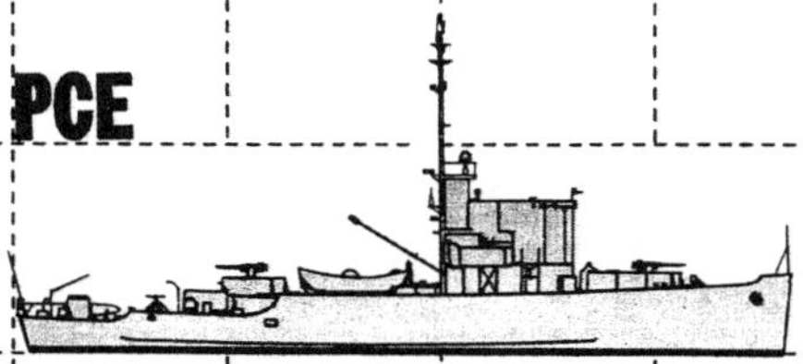

YP

PATROL ESCORT—PCE 827 CLASS

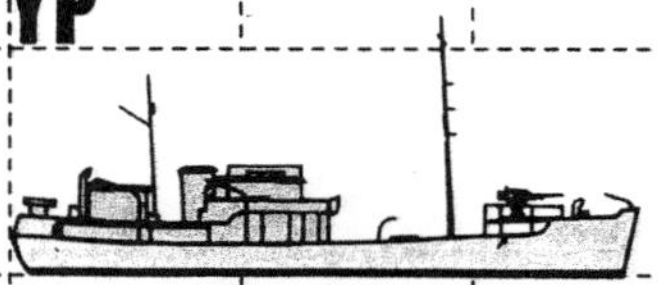

DISTRICT PATROL CRAFT—CONVERTED TRAWLERS

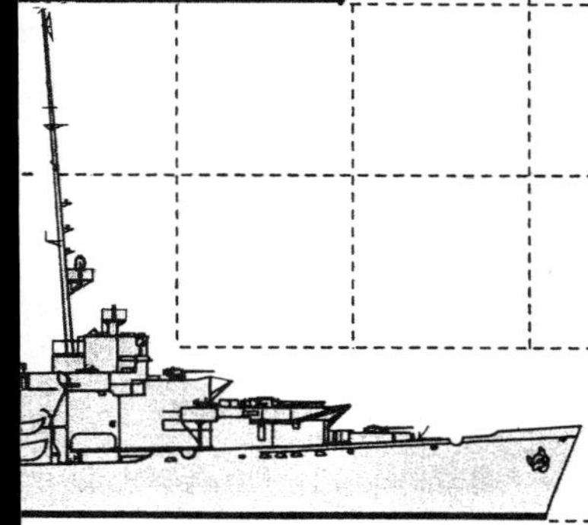

PCS

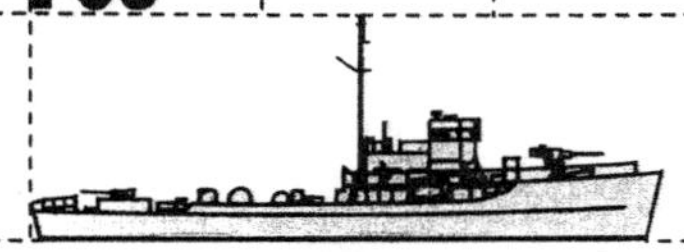

PT

SUBMARINE CHASER—PCS 1376 CLASS

MOTOR TORPEDO BOAT—PT 103 CLASS

SUBMARINE
CLEAR SEA LANES

In sub-chasing, the number of ships available is a lot more important than their armament and size. When only a few escort vessels were available to accompany a convoy, they had to stick to their slower, clumsy charges, screen them from marauders. But now that spare sub-chasers are at hand, they can detach themselves without weakening the convoy's defense, can chase individual U-boats, spotted either by the detecting devices they carry or by carrier and land-based airplanes, and pound away until their quarry is sunk.

Three types of the small, easy-to-build anti-submarine vessels of the U. S. Navy are shown on these pages. They are classified as PC's, PCE's and SC's, but these classifications are not so rigid as those of the major types, are used chiefly to describe the vessel. For one thing, PC's may operate either as patrol craft or submarine chasers. For another, some PC and PCE units have been converted to AM's. Remembering this is essential, for an observer may make the fatal error of deciding that a PC cannot be a PC simply because there is no tactical need for sub-chasing in his area.

Though frail-looking, PC's are capable of getting in and mixing it with subma-

PC IS 173-FT. steel sub-chaser. Side view emphasizes pole mainmast and single island from stack to bridge set forward. Flush deck, guns, raked bow may also be observed from this angle.

TALL MAST OF PC, shown above and below, stands out in aerial view. Unusually low funnel is nearly buried against deckhouse forward, giving the craft the appearance of a cabin cruiser.

SC IS SHORTER than boats of PC class, has no stack. Wooden 100-foot vessel has one deck

STALKERS

FOR OUR CONVOYS

rines. Their skippers are perfectly willing to ram subs in order to complete the kill. By attacking submarines, even when they fail to sink them, the small escort boats are doing an extremely valuable job. When a U-boat dives several hundred feet, it has a very good chance of escaping destruction, but it is certainly in no position to threaten any merchantmen. The small sub-hunting craft, the terriers of the fleet, help keep the sea lanes open for the successful passage of men and weapons to the fighting fronts.

RECOGNITION: The PC is a 173-ft. steel flushdecker. Its short capped stack is close up against the superstructure. The bridge looks enough like a sub's conning tower to cause confusion at long range. Deck guns are mounted both fore and aft, while depth bomb racks are ready for action at the ship's stern.

PCE's have high freeboard forward, broken two-thirds of the way aft. Longer than PC's, they have no stack. Superstructure is taller and more pronounced than on a PC.

Like the PC, the SC is frequently mistaken for a submarine. It is a 110-ft. flushdecker with a pole mast, deck gun forward.

LONGER AND TALLER than PC, PCE is designed for a great variety of uses. Note high freeboard forward breaking down to low stern. Bridge looks like fort forward of tall pole mast.

PC HAS TALL MAST, low flush-deck hull. Both PC and SC (*below*) have been mistaken for subs because of low silhouette, conning tower-like bridge, resemblance of wake to that of sub.

gun forward and depth charges at stern. From his angle it shows a resemblance to the PC's.

DESTROYER ESCORT REUBEN JAMES HAS NARROW LINES OF DESTROYER BUT SIMPLER SUPERSTRUCTURE

TALL MAST in contrast to foreshortened hull makes DE 162, U. S. S. Levy, look diminutive. Actually, short hull DE's are almost 300 ft. long.

NEW ESCORTS REPLACE DD'S

GUARD CARGO SHIPS

The new destroyer escorts and large Coast Guard cutters have made the protection of Allied convoys a much surer, simpler business. They have relieved faster and more heavily armed destroyers for fleet action. The steel-hulled DE's are made in two versions: long hull and short hull. They also differ slightly in armament; the short hull DE does not mount torpedo tubes. Cutters and gunboats, the PG's, range in size from the Spencer Class, slightly larger than a DE, to A and B Class cutters of half this size.

RECOGNITION: Both DE's somewhat resemble U. S. destroyers, are chiefly distinguished by their simplified superstructure and by the absence of full gun shields on the main batteries. The long hull DE has a bank of torpedo tubes abaft the stack. Large PG's have a much broader beam and higher and heavier superstructure than the DE's. A-Class cutters have one tall stack while B-Class ships have two squat stacks.

CAMPBELL CLASS CUTTER on convoy duty receives line for the transfer of messages from squadron leader. Notice raised gun platforms aft of superstructure and raised gunwales aft. Class carries heavy guns to battle any U-boat but main weapons are depth charges seen on stern.

U.S.C.G. SPENCER has at least one U-boat to her credit, having depth-bombed and outgunned a German submarine while engaged in convoy duty in Atlantic. In this view, several of her very effective guns are seen. Numerous AA and dual-purpose guns protect her from attack.

U.S.S. VIXEN is the former pleasure yacht Orion, converted to wartime duties. Many such conversions were made in the early rush of war preparation before naval building program was in full swing. They retain original appearance plus some deck guns and depth-charge gear.

SWEEP OF PT BOATS rides the leader's wake in spectacular maneuver. These small craft, often referred to as mosquito boats, have engaged in the most daring of naval actions against overpowering enemy odds.

In the English Channel, British and German types have kept up a constant guerrilla warfare since Sept., 1939. Too small to identify by detail, PT's are best spotted by their tremendous foaming wakes and broad decks.

MINELAYER, WEEHAWKEN, HAS HIGH DECK CUT AWAY AFT FOR DROPPING MINES AND CLOSELY-SPACED STACKS

BIG & LITTLE

MINOR COMBATANT TYPES RUN

FROM HUGE CM'S TO TINY PT'S

Biggest minelayer of the U. S. Fleet is the new U. S. S. Terror; smallest active warship type is the PT boat, the Navy's fastest craft. Between these extremes fall the other classes illustrated on these pages. The bulk of our minelaying falls on the big. CM's which carry large stores of mines to distant areas, plant extensive fields. Some are new, designed-for-the-job ships like the U. S. S. Terror (below); others are converted train ferries or ex-merchantmen. Newcomers in this war, the PT boats are high-powered, high-speed craft equipped with either two or four torpedo tubes. In action they cast a very large bow wave and wake which helps to identify them at a distance or from the air (see *Journal*, October issue).

NEWEST, BIGGEST MINELAYER is the U. S. S. Terror, a finely designed, modern-looking ship. Two short capped stacks rise from a massive island superstructure. Foremast is a heavy pole between fire director and forward stack; mainmast is a lighter pole supporting a large boom. The Terror carries its main battery in four turrets—two forward and two aft. Her superstructure has the same clean lines as our Iowa Class battleships.

FLEET MINELAYING is frequently handled by the converted destroyers classified as DM's. In a large naval battle, these craft might sweep across the path of the enemy fleet, sow deadly floating mines in line of advance. Except for mineracks and amidships structure, they resemble old DD's.

NEW LIFE FOR FLUSHDECKERS

In the new guise of minelayer, minesweeper, seaplane tender or high-speed transport, many World War I flushdeck destroyers are back at sea. Sisterships of lend-leased destroyers (many of which underwent similar conversions in Britain), these older "cans" have taken on many auxiliary jobs where the destroyer's speed and offensive and defensive power will pay off. Minesweeping versions often move in before all other attack forces to clear the waters so our landing barges can carry the invaders safely to the

MINESWEEPING GEAR, which consists of paravanes, cable reels and cranes, is distinctive feature of destroyer minelayer/sweeper. Pulled out to side by paravane, minesweeper's cable catches mooring cable of mine and leads it to paravane which severs it. Mine can then be discharged by gun.

HIGH-SPEED TRANSPORT carries four assault boats amidships, ferries troops for short hauls on raids into enemy territory. Like the AVD's

(below) APD's have only two stacks. Armament includes standard deck guns, additional AA and depth charge gear but ship has no torpedo tubes.

beach. As high-speed transports (APD's) they carry picked troops on dangerous forays. Swift seaplane tenders ply the hazardous waters of the Southwest Pacific to keep our aerial scouts on the job.

RECOGNITION: The conversions maintain the distinctive lines of the old destroyer type with its long, low hull and flush deck. The bridge structure is well forward and rather small. The stacks—which in these conversions may number from two to four—are just forward of amidships. The unshielded stern gun is mounted

on a deckhouse aft. In the DM and DMS types—the minelayer sweepers—the ship is often distinguished by the sweeping gear, mining gear amidships, and lack of torpedo tubes. The APD's, or high-speed transports, are distinguished by the heavy assault boats slung from davits port and starboard. Destroyer seaplane tenders (AVD's) have plane-handling gear. Also one set of boilers has been removed from the AVD's, so only two stacks are necessary, and the bridge superstructure has been extended across the well.

FAST SEAPLANE TENDER is formed from World War I flushdecker. Classed as AVD's, they increase the tactical mobility of our scout planes

by providing them with a home at sea. To supply increased cargo space one set of boilers has been removed, necessitating only two visible stacks.

LOOKING LIKE A CROSS BETWEEN A DESTROYER AND A TUGBOAT, THE U.S.S. HERALD IS A STURDY, FAST MINE-

MOTOR MINESWEEPERS are the only district craft commissioned for action outside district. From a high bow the hull breaks down to a low deck. The stacks are short and straight.

ASSORTED

FULFILL MANIFOLD

Of the myriad duties incidental to running a war at sea, many fall on the small ships. Minelaying and sweeping are two of these duties that are performed by a great variety of craft: specially designed types for all classes of action, converted trawlers and fishermen, ex-pleasure yachts. Other types lay and tend the anti-submarine nets that protect Allied harbors. Small boats of all varieties, incapable of sustained service at sea, patrol the coastal waters of the U. S. Large powerful seagoing tugs set off on long lonely missions across the seas towing barges, dredges, derricks, small floating drydocks and other equipment for our outlying bases.

Though many of these types are now being built to Navy designs, many of those currently in service have been adapted from their peacetime duties. Most of the district patrol vessels, for example, are converted

OCEANGOING TUG, the U.S.S. Cree, is longer than usual harbor tug. Superstructure forms mass around stack. Large crane rises from rear of deckhouse, supported by a tripod mast.

DISTRICT PATROL VESSEL (YP) is a converted trawler commissioned to patrol waters within one naval district. Superstructure is aft, well deck between the bridge and high bow.

TENDING THE NETS which protect our harbors from submarines is the duty of ships like the YN 22. Chief distinction of net tender are the net-handling ramps projecting from bow.

ONE VARIATION of AT design is ASR or submarine rescue vessel. Chief distinction from AT is separated stack and superstructure. ASR may have clutter of rescue gear on after deck.

SWEEPER FOR GENERAL SERVICE

VESSELS
DUTIES FOR NAVY

trawlers and, despite the additions of guns, they still look like fishing craft. The oceangoing tugs, with sisters serving as submarine rescue vessels, salvage vessels and small seaplane tenders, are in many cases similar to those used in peacetime ocean towing service. Many of the craft used to check the papers of ships engaged in coastal traffic are the former luxury yachts of American millionaires.

RECOGNITION: AM minesweepers of the Auk Class (*above*) are sturdy ships of moderate beam having a prominent bridge, tall foremast and two squat, widely separated stacks. The oceangoing tugs (AT's) are longer, more racy-looking craft than the usual harbor tug. The net tenders are small coastal craft distinguished by the net-handling gear projecting from the bow. Motor minesweepers (YMS's) may have either one or two short straight stacks amidships.

LOOK DIFFERENTS

P-47's HUMPBACKED FUSELAGE MEETS STRAIGHT-EDGED FIN IN SHARP ANGLE. BELLY CURVE IS BROKEN BY SUPERCHARGER IN VIEW ABOVE

OUTSTANDING DIFFERENCES between Thunderbolt and FW-190 are evident in plan view; especially unmistakable is the graceful P-47 wing.

FOCKE-WULF VERSUS P-47

Tangling daily in Europe's skies they must be quickly told apart

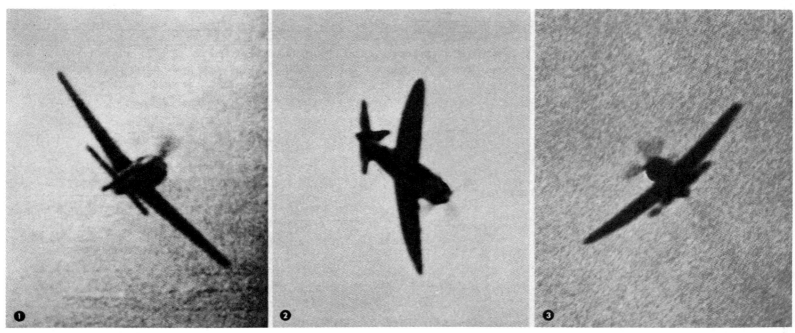

❶ ❷ ❸

THUNDERBOLT AND FOCKE-WULF 190 OPERATE AT SAME ALTITUDES AT SAME TIME. IT IS ESSENTIAL THAT AIR GUNNERS AND PILOTS RECOGNIZE

ROUND BLUNT NOSE OF FOCKE-WULF 190 IS EMPHASIZED BY UNUSUALLY LARGE SPINNER. FIN FAIRS INTO SLENDER STRAIGHT-BELLIED FUSELAGE

In the air battle now raging over Europe, two powerful high-altitude fighters are a prime recognition problem: the Focke-Wulf 190 and Republic's P-47. Both are land-based fighter planes with single radial air-cooled engines. Outside this basic resemblance they differ in many respects. FW-190's wing tapers equally and its slender fuselage tapers sharply to a point which extends well aft of the tailplane. P-47 has a very distinctive semi-elliptical wing; its fuselage is deeper, curves evenly into tail. Tailplane has a sharply tapered leading edge, and a rounded trailing edge, with cutout, in contrast to the boxy, rectangular tailplane of the Focke-Wulf.

The nose of the FW-190 is short, the cowling is a perfect circle and has a large spinner while the Thunderbolt has a long nose, a deep oval, inverted egg-shaped cowling, and a small propeller hub. The FW-190 is a low-wing plane with moderate dihedral and the P-47 is low mid-wing with marked dihedral. At the bottom of these pages are unidentified views of both planes. Answers are on p. 50.

THIN FUSELAGE of the FW-190 comes to a point, extends well beyond tailplane. Its squarish wing and tailplane are obvious recognition points.

THEM INSTANTLY IN COMBAT LEST OUR OWN PLANES BE SHOT DOWN THROUGH CARELESSNESS, OR ENEMY PLANES SLIP THROUGH OUR DEFENSES

CAMOUFLAGED M-3 MOVES ACROSS IDEAL TERRAIN IN ENFILADING ACTION. THE HALF-TRACK MOUNT OF THIS SELF-PROPELLED GUN BOGS DOWN IN

AMERICAN WEAPONS

U. S. develops fine self-propelled artillery for fast mobile warfare

German blitz tactics are largely responsible for the development of the self-propelled gun in this war. The Allies adopting the new weapon did so not in imitation of the Wehrmacht but in response to a real need for increased armored mobility to cope with the rapid German advance. Now that the German Army is on the defensive and blitz warfare is on the decline, self-propelled guns have lost some of their initial operational value. In numbers they are far less important than towed artillery. They are more vulnerable in size and weight and on long runs their complicated track gear wears out more quickly. But the self-propelled gun still remains a dangerous special-purpose weapon because it can get into firing position almost immediately, without emplacement.

Convinced that the self-propelled artillery weapons with their mobility, armor protection and firepower were necessary adjuncts to towed artillery in modern warfare, the U. S. Army started early to develop such mounts and now has a series ranging from the small 75-mm. howitzer to the huge 155-mm. gun. Our earliest tank

NEAR SALERNO M-3's came to relieve a handful of weary Rangers who were fighting to hold the Chiunzi mountain pass. This M-3 is firing on camouflaged German machine-gun positions just beyond the pass.

MARINES ON BOUGAINVILLE used the M-3 to shatter Jap pillbox strongholds. In the early stages of amphibious operations self-propelled guns can drive right out of landing craft, firing their big guns on the way.

SOFT GROUND, IS GRADUALLY BEING REPLACED BY FULL-TRACK MOUNTS

destroyer was the standard American half-track with the old field artillery 75-mm. gun mounted on it. The M-3 shown on these two pages is just such a weapon, a 75-mm. gun on a half-track. The 75-mm. howitzer on a half-track, the T-30, and the 105-mm. howitzer on the same mount, the T-19, were other early U. S. self-propelled artillery. Our fast half-track mount has been a useful expedient but it cannot carry the armor protection necessary to do battle with tanks, nor can it keep up with full-track vehicles in bad terrain. Gradually the half-track M-3 has given way to the M-10 (page 44), a full-track medium-tank chassis with 3-inch gun. The T-30 has become the M-8 (page 46); The T-19, the M-7 Priest (page 43).

These early half-track weapons have piled up good battle records in the Pacific and in Africa. Many are still in use. Some time before Pearl Harbor a consignment of M-3's was shipped to the Philippines, not put into operation until the Jap attack. Green gun crews hastily assigned found them easy to manipulate, repulsed wave after wave of Jap tank attacks in the delaying action north of Manila.

M-3'S 75-MM. WEAPON has long gun slide beneath barrel. Its armor is slight. The gun shield, a simple affair, is not much more than a flat forward wall. The gross weight of the gun and chassis is only 19,000 lb.

Battle-line hitch-hikers ride to front on sturdy M-7 Priest

SHORT, HEAVY-BARRELED GUN has over-and-under recoil mechanism visible in most views. Frontal shield protects crew from ground fire.

PRIEST'S PULPIT forms mount for a .50-cal. AA gun, is prominent feature of design. Tandem bogies are typical of most U. S. tracked vehicles.

ROMMEL WRECKER

U. S. 105-mm. howitzer nullified Nazi 88-mm. all-purpose gun in Tunisia

One of the first American self-propelled weapons to go into action, the M-7 has more than proven its worth in the field. Used at El Alamein and throughout the Tunisian campaign, it sparred effectively with Rommel's famous 88-mm. piece. A group of Priests would lob HE over miles of Axis-held lines with the shells fused to explode just off the ground. This would force the 88's to open up in an attempt to silence the attack. As soon as the German gun positions were disclosed, our heavy artillery would wipe them out as our tanks advanced or detoured through their known positions.

RECOGNITION: The M-7 is a 105-mm. howitzer mounted on the typically American chassis of the M-3 General Grant tank. Each track runs on three pairs of small tandem bogies with drive sprocket forward, idler at rear. The gun fires through the front shield slightly to the right of center. A circular AA pulpit, which gives the weapon its name, is mounted at the right forward and dominates most views of the weapon. Gun platform is open rectangle.

IN PLAN VIEW, M-7 is almost perfect rectangle, with its gun platform a smaller rectangle forward. Gun barrel ends flush with forward hull edge.

BUILT-UP SHIELD, heavy appearance forward, contrast with low boxy rear. Gun is field howitzer (minus trails, wheels), bolted to tank chassis.

M-10'S AWAITING SHIPMENT HAVE 3-INCH GUNS POINTING BACKWARDS. WEDGES FASTENED TO REAR OF TURRET GIVE IT WINGLIKE SILHOUETTE

M-10 & T-70

One self-propelled gun is seasoned campaigner. The other is brand new

Firing projectiles with delayed-action fuses that pierced Nazi tank armor and detonated inside, U. S. M-10 tank destroyers in Tunisia tore the much-vaunted German Mark VI's wide apart. The M-10 is one of our heaviest self-propelled guns, sturdily armored and designed to be more than a match for any kind of tank the Germans can put into combat. It is mounted on our most successful tank chassis, M-4 General Sherman, and its 3-inch gun is effective against any enemy tank armor. Altogether 36 M-10's ride in a tank destroyer battalion, each equipped with a .50-cal. anti-aircraft machine gun, in addition to the 3-inch main weapon.

For those who think that a tank destroyer should be the fastest

M-10 FROM ABOVE has long unbroken rectangular lines, squares off abruptly at rear. Its long, thin-barreled gun projects well beyond bow and the open-topped turret has an odd pentagonal shape.

SIDE BY SIDE M-10 and T-70 look different. Taller M-10 (*left*) has deep, rounded

44

T-70 HAS LONG 76-MM. GUN AND CHRISTIE-TYPE SUSPENSION SYSTEM OF LARGE DOUBLE EVENLY SPACED BOGIES, FIVE ON EACH SIDE OF CHASSIS

thing on a battlefield, the M-10's speed of 22 miles per hour is a little slow. Tank destroyers must be able to play a deadly game of hide-and-seek, spotting their target, moving to prepared positions, waiting, and firing at short, sure ranges. The 8-ft. silhouette of the M-10 is pretty high for successful hiding. Best protective feature is the slope of hull and turret surfaces which show distinct advance in design and welding for deflecting of enemy projectiles.

The T-70 (*above*) is our latest tank destroyer. So far it has had no combat experience in which to prove itself, but it promises to be a fast, hard-hitting anti-tank gun that may supersede the M-10. Compared with the latter, the T-70 is almost a foot shorter in height,

is 20,000 lb. lighter when fully equipped, and has twice the speed of the older mount. Its 76-mm. weapon has a higher velocity and flatter trajectory than earlier guns, and although longer and heavier than its predecessors it is so mounted that its turret moves smoothly and easily in a 360° traverse.

RECOGNITION: The M-10's tandem bogie wheels are typical of most U. S. mounts. First of our armored vehicles to deviate from this pattern is the T-70 with its Christie-type suspension system of five double evenly spaced bogies and four double return rollers on each side of the chassis. This originally American-designed suspension system is an old favorite with the Russians and Germans.

bow, jutting gun mantlet. T-70's bow slants, is boxlike. Its mantlet is round and bulbous.

RECTANGULAR LINES of T-70 chassis contrast with open pear-shaped turret, roundest at barrel base. Ring mount of .50-cal. anti-aircraft machine gun breaks curve of turret at left rear.

M-8 & M-12

New and old gun mounts complete U. S. line-up

The two guns shown on these pages illustrate the marked differences between a weapon designed for its specific task and a quick wartime expedient. The M-8 (*left*) is one of the newest of our self-propelled mounts. It is now in quantity production and has been landed in Italy. It was designed as a mobile weapon to go forward with the armored force for reconnaissance and close support. From an advanced position the M-8 can throw ammunition at the enemy lines to flush targets, then use its high speed to get away. The stubby 75-mm. howitzer is also a fine weapon for searching the invisible far side of hills.

The M-12, on the opposite page, is one of the largest self-propelled guns in operational use. It had considerable success against enemy strong points in Tunisia. Essentially, the weapon is a 155-mm. gun originally built as a towed gun in World War I, mounted on an M-3 chassis. There is no turret and the gun platform has only a light armor shield. In service, the M-12 is often dug in before firing. The tailspade is dropped to absorb recoil shock. Ammunition for the gun is in separate components, projectile and powder bags, and is carried on a separate motor carriage. The M-12 is not fired in motion and is used primarily against enemy artillery and installations, not against personnel.

RECOGNITION: The M-8 is a four-place weapon on an M-5 light tank chassis having two pairs of tandem bogies. The turret is a long oval covering most of hull. It is open-topped and has a ring mount for a .50-cal. AA gun at right rear. Hull is angular and projects over the tracks. The motor carriage of the M-12 is long and flat with a light armor shield above the tracks. In motion, the tailspade is retracted, while in action the breech end of the gun extends behind hull.

M-8'S DESIGN IS CLEAN, WELL-INTEGRATED. SLOPE-SIDED TURRET HAS A BULGING GUN MANTLET

FROM THE REAR the M-8 looks high and light. Track suspension has a small drive sprocket forward, two pairs of bogies and large cartwheel idler.

OVAL TURRET of M-8 is square at rear, has stubby howitzer forward. Mantlet serves as blast shield, protects crew from blindness in night firing.

HUGE TUBE OF 155-MM. GUN IS LONGER THAN MOTOR CARRIAGE. IN THE VIEW ABOVE, TAILSPADE IS DOWN TO ABSORB RECOIL AS GUN IS FIRED

M-12 IN MOTION looks like what it is, a very big gun mounted on a tank chassis. Only apparent addition to major elements is light armor shield.

MOTORIZED CARGO CARRIER accompanies M-12. Separate caisson looks like M-12 without gun, has truck-like body to hold shells, powder.

QUIZ NO. 3: SPOT THESE WARSHIPS

For answers, see p. 50

NEWEST GERMAN TANK IS 45-TON PzKw V PANTHER. PzKw VI-TYPE SUSPENSION GIVES SPEEDS UP TO 31 M.P.H. GUN IS LONG, THIN 75-MM. WEAPON

RECOGNITION TRAINING LIST

JANUARY, 1944

The lists below include the armored vehicles of various combatant nations which are considered important enough at present to be included in recognition instruction. Vehicles almost identical in appearance are grouped together, and only one of such a group need be taught. For example, all U. S. half-tracks look very much alike, and only one need be taught in detail. However, pictures of the others can be introduced for interest.

The most important vehicles are indicated by an asterisk (*). The importance of each vehicle may change with time and area of combat. The *Journal* will print timely amendments to this list.

UNITED STATES VEHICLES

SCOUT CAR, M-3A1
*LIGHT ARMORED CAR, M-8
ARMORED UTILITY CAR, M-20
*HALF-TRACK CAR, M-3 (M-2, M-4, M-5, M-9A1)
MULTIPLE GUN MOTOR CARRIAGE, M-15
MULTIPLE GUN MOTOR CARRIAGE, M-16 (M-13, M-14, M-17)
*LIGHT TANK, M-5A1 (M-5)
LIGHT TANK, T-9E1
MEDIUM TANK, M-3 (M-3A1, M-3A2, M-3A3, M-3A4, M-3A5)
*MEDIUM TANK, M-4 (M-4A2, M-4A3, M-4A4)
MEDIUM TANK, M-4A1
*75-MM. HOWITZER MOTOR CARRIAGE, M-8
*105-MM. HOWITZER MOTOR CARRIAGE, M-7
3-INCH GUN MOTOR CARRIAGE, M-10 (M-10A1)
76-MM. GUN MOTOR CARRIAGE, T-70
155-MM. GUN MOTOR CARRIAGE, M-12

BRITISH VEHICLES

HUMBER ARMORED CAR
DAIMLER ARMORED CAR
A. E. C. ARMORED CAR
ARMORED CAR, T-17E1
OTTER ARMORED CAR
LYNX ARMORED CAR
UNIVERSAL CARRIER
*CROMWELL TANK
*CHURCHILL INFANTRY TANK
SP 25 PDR. (SEXTON)

RUSSIAN VEHICLES

ARMORED CARRIER AND PRIME MOVER (STZ)
LIGHT TANKS (T-40, T-50, T-60, T-70)
VALENTINE TANK
MEDIUM TANK, T-34
HEAVY TANK, KV-I
HEAVY TANK, KV-II

GERMAN VEHICLES

4-WHEELED ARMORED CAR, SD KFZ 222 (SD KFZ 221)
6-WHEELED ARMORED CAR
*8-WHEELED ARMORED CAR
ARMORED HALF-TRACK VEHICLES
HALF-TRACK VEHICLES
*PzKw III TANK
*PzKw IV TANK
PzKw V TANK (PANTHER)
*PzKw VI TANK (TIGER)
76-MM. OR 75-MM. SP GUN (ON PzKw 38 TANK CHASSIS)
75-MM. SP GUN (ON PzKw III TANK CHASSIS)

ITALIAN VEHICLES

4-WHEELED ARMORED CAR
L-3 TANK
L-6 TANK
M-14 TANK
75-MM. SP GUN (ON M-14 TANK CHASSIS)

JAPANESE VEHICLES

LIGHT ARMORED CAR, 2597 (ACTUALLY A VERY SMALL TANK)
LIGHT TANK, 2595
MEDIUM TANK, 2597

NEWS & MISCELLANY

NEWS

Judy, type 2 carrier-based reconnaissance plane, built by Aichi was examined at Rekata Bay. It has 12-cylinder inverted-V inline engine.

LETTERS

Bismarck Spotter

In your December 1943 issue there is an article on British Fleet Carriers which contains this statement: "It was planes from the *Victorious* which located the *Bismarck* and planes from the *Illustrious* which stopped her."

The actual facts on the spotting of the *Bismarck* are these: she was located by Ensign (now Lieutenant) L. B. Smith, an American Naval flier in command of a British patrol plane. On May 26, 1941, before America entered the war, Smith was serving aboard a PBY as a volunteer observer with 209 Squadron of the R.A.F. Although technically a non-participant, Smith was in fact Patrol Plane Commander because of his experience with Catalinas. After seven hours' search, Smith and his copilot, Flying Officer Briggs, spotted the *Prinz Eugen* and Briggs left his post to prepare a contact report. Smith started to climb for cloud protection when he was taken under fire by the *Bismarck*. The plane suffered many shrapnel hits but continued to track the *Bismarck* for four hours. Two other planes continued the tracking after fuel considerations forced Smith to return to base.

G. T. MUNDORFF Jr.,
Commander, U. S. N.

●

Permission Granted

The silhouettes of naval vessels on pages 26 and 27 of the September 1943 issue of the *U. S. Army-Navy Journal of Recognition* are excellent training aids.

It is hereby requested that reproduction of these two pages be authorized.

Lt. Col. A. H. Parker,
Headquarters Harbor Defenses of New York,
Fort Hancock, N. J.

Any material published herein may be reproduced in any restricted publication of limited distribution as sponsored by any activity of the United States Army or Navy provided the private source of any material taken from the *Journal*, as indicated under "credits" in the *Journal*, is acknowledged under an appropriate credit in such publication.

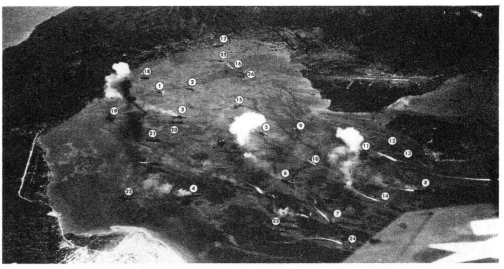

JAPANESE SHIPS IN RABAUL HARBOR PHOTOGRAPH

WARSHIPS		
1 SENDAI CLASS CL	8 MOGAMI CLASS CA	GO VESSEL 8,000 G.T.
2 NATORI CLASS CL	9 DD	16 HOSPITAL SHIP (PAINTED WHITE) 6,000 G.T.
3 ATAGO CLASS CA	10 DD	17 CARGO VESSEL 6,000 G.T.
4 TONE CLASS CA	11 DD	18 CARGO VESSEL 6,000 G.T.
5 ATAGO CLASS CA	12 DD	19 PASSENGER SHIP (KEIHUKU
ATAGO-TAKAO GROUP	13 DD	MARU CLASS) 3,500 G.T.
6 ATAGO CLASS CA	14 DD	20 MODERN TANKER, 10,000 G.T.
ATAGO-TAKAO GROUP		21-26 INCL.—SMALL CARGO VES-
7 TERUTSUKI CLASS DD	MERCHANT SHIPS	SELS 3,000 G.T.
	15 MODERN COMBINATION CAR-	

Double-Header

In the October issue of *U. S. Army-Navy Journal of Recognition* on page 32 is shown a picture of the *Kumano*, Mogami Class of Japanese heavy cruiser. The caption states, "Three triple 8-in. turrets forward and two aft give the cruiser heavy firepower." Does this information supersede the data found in ONI 41–42 and ONI 222 regarding this Class which states, "10—8 in. 50-cal. twin turrets"?

(see name, letter below)

The picture on page 32 is one of the Mogami Class taken prior to re-arming. Triples are now replaced by twins as shown in ONI 41–42.

In the article "Bumps" in the November issue of the *Journal*, the picture shown at the top of page 23 appears to be the Mauritius Class of British light cruisers, rather than the London Class of British heavy cruisers as shown. May I refer you to page 32 of Jane's Fighting Ships of 1942.

Sgt. John L. Parcels,
Recognition Department,
Ground School, AAFPS (ATE),
Moody Field, Ga.

By referring to the center spread of the December issue of the *Journal* and to the generalized silhouettes of the United Kingdom naval vessels in the Recognition Pictorial Manual of Naval Vessels (FM 30–50, Navaer, 00–80V–57), it is evident that the "Bump" representation noted in the above letter is actually the London of Devonshire Class. The Mauritius, which is one of the six units of the Fiji Class of light cruisers, is very similar to the London.

DISTRIBUTION:

The U. S. Army-Navy Journal of Recognition is published by the U. S. War and Navy Departments. It is distributed to particular activities in all the armed services. Limited numbers of additional copies may be requested through channels from:

Army:
Air Activities—Training Aids Division of the Army Air Forces
1 Park Avenue, New York, N. Y.
Ground Forces—Adjutant General Depots
Navy:
Air Activities—Office of the Chief of Naval Operations
All Others—Chief of Naval Personnel

QUIZ ANSWERS

QUIZ No. 1

1 SBD's (Ships —Old Porter Mahan (2)
2 Dave
3 Kate
4 Val
5 Lily
6 F4F
7 Beaufighter
8 Hurricane
9 F6F
10 SB2C
11 Nell
12 Tony
13 B-25

QUIZ No. 2

Plane:	Range	In or Out of Range
1 Ju-88	300 ft.	In
2 A-20	1500 ft.	Out
3 Rufe	250 ft.	In
4 Me-110	1000 ft.	In
5 Zeke	1000 ft.	In
6 Hamp	750 ft.	In
7 Nell	1200 ft.	Out
8 Fw-200K	800 ft.	In
9 Sally	1500 ft.	Out
10 Oscar Mk I	500 ft.	In
11 Betty	2250 ft.	Out
12 He-115	1500 ft.	Out

Answers for pp. 38-39: P-47-2, 3, 5; FW-190—1, 4, 6.

QUIZ No. 3

1 U.S. DD Benson-Livermore Class
2 U.S. DD Gridley Class
U.S. CA Northampton Class
3 U.S. CA Cleveland Class
U.S. CV Saratoga
U.S. CA Cleveland Class
U.S. DD Fletcher Class
4 Jap CA Atago
5 U.S. CL Atlanta Class
Br. CV H.M.S. Victorious

6 U.S. CL Atlanta Class
7 U.S. BB New Mexico Class
U.S. BB New Mexico Class
U.S. CA Portland
8 U.S. CV Enterprise
U.S. DD Mahan Class
9 Br. CA London Class
10 U.S. CVL Independence Class
11 Center of photo—LCI's
Right—U.S. CL Cleveland Class
Left—LCI, Br. DD

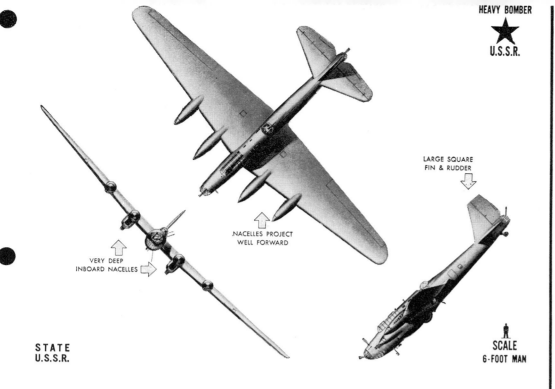

TB-7

LARGE SQUARE
FIN & RUDDER

NACELLES PROJECT
WELL FORWARD

VERY DEEP
INBOARD NACELLES

STATE
U.S.S.R.

SCALE
6-FOOT MAN

DISTINGUISHING FEATURES: Four inline engine, mid-wing monoplane. Wings are tapered on both edges with rounded tips. Outboard nacelles small and round. Inboard nacelles deep with large radiator under engine and gun position in rear. Raised greenhouse with rear portion covered. Top gun turret. Tailplane tapers to round tips, while fin and rudder is tall and angular.
INTEREST: This is the best-known Soviet long-range bomber. These planes have made effective raids on Berlin, Danzig and Balkan cities. It is now in large-scale production and is in service with the new bomber command of the Red Air Force. The TB-6B, from which the TB-7 was redesigned, was used in Soviet Polar expeditions before the war. The TB-7 carries a crew of about nine men. Gun positions in the large underslung inboard nacelles are interesting feature of this aircraft.

SPAN: 131 ft. 2 in.   **SERVICE CEILING:** 26,000 ft.
LENGTH: 73 ft. 10 in.
MAX. SPEED: 276 m p.h. at 21,000 ft.

DECEMBER, 1943
FROM DATA CURRENTLY AVAILABLE

WAR DEPARTMENT FM 30-30
NAVY DEPARTMENT BUAER 3

RESTRICTED

NOTE: This page is to be cut along dotted lines (*above* and *below*), added to the proper nation's section in the Recognition Pictorial Manual. The dots indicate perforations.

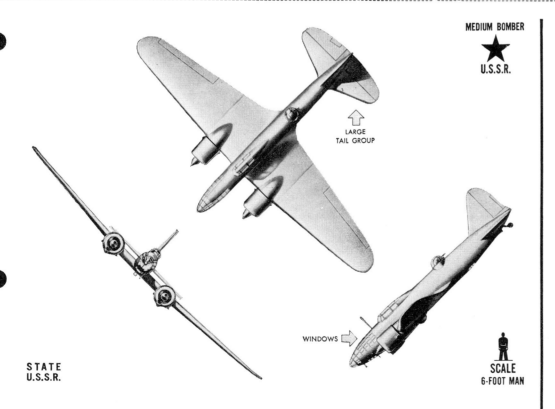

DB-3F

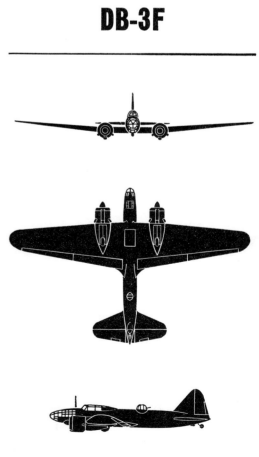

LARGE
TAIL GROUP

STATE
U.S.S.R.

WINDOWS

SCALE
6-FOOT MAN

DISTINGUISHING FEATURES: Twin radial engine, low-wing monoplane. Trailing edge has taper and fairs into fuselage. Transparent nose. Raised cockpit canopy. Round turret centered between fin and cockpit. Fin tapers forward. Tapered tailplane with rounded tips.
INTEREST: The DB-3 and DB-3F were developed from the ZKB-26 which flew from Moscow to Miscou Island, New Brunswick in April 1939. The DB-3F has a streamlined pointed nose instead of a turret and slightly different engine cowlings; otherwise it is identical to the DB-3. The large wing-root fillets are characteristic of most Soviet types. The M-88 radial engines give about 1,100 h.p. and are fitted with two speed superchargers. Other equipment consists of variable pitch propellers and three 7.6-mm. or 12.7-mm. free machine guns. The DB-3F is slightly faster than the DB-3 and when fitted with extra gas tanks it can be used for long range photographic reconnaissance.

SPAN: 70 ft. 2 in.   **SERVICE CEILING:** 30,700 ft.
LENGTH: 47 ft. 7 in.
APPROX. SPEED: 300 m.p.h. at 21,000 ft.

DECEMBER, 1943
FROM DATA CURRENTLY AVAILABLE

WAR DEPARTMENT FM 30-30
NAVY DEPARTMENT BUAER 3

RESTRICTED

A

B

C

TB-7, standard heavy bomber of Red Air Force, has also been used as a transport for Soviet officials. With a wing span greater than that of the B-24 Liberator, the TB-7 is a big plane, fast and well armed. Carrying 2 to 4 tons of bombs, it has a range of 2,500 miles.

DB-3F has been compared in size and performance to the B-25 Mitchell, although recognitionally they are quite different. The first Soviet plane to bomb Berlin, the DB-3F is a long-range ship. Its 2 tons of bombs are carried partly internally and partly externally.

A

C

B

D

U. S. ARMY-NAVY JOURNAL OF
RECOGNITION

A-2, 2 AF N 901

ACIFIC BEACHHEAD

FEBRUARY, 1944
NUMBER 6

RESTRICTED

SHARE THIS COPY

QUIZ NO. 1: THESE ARE SILLOGRAPHS

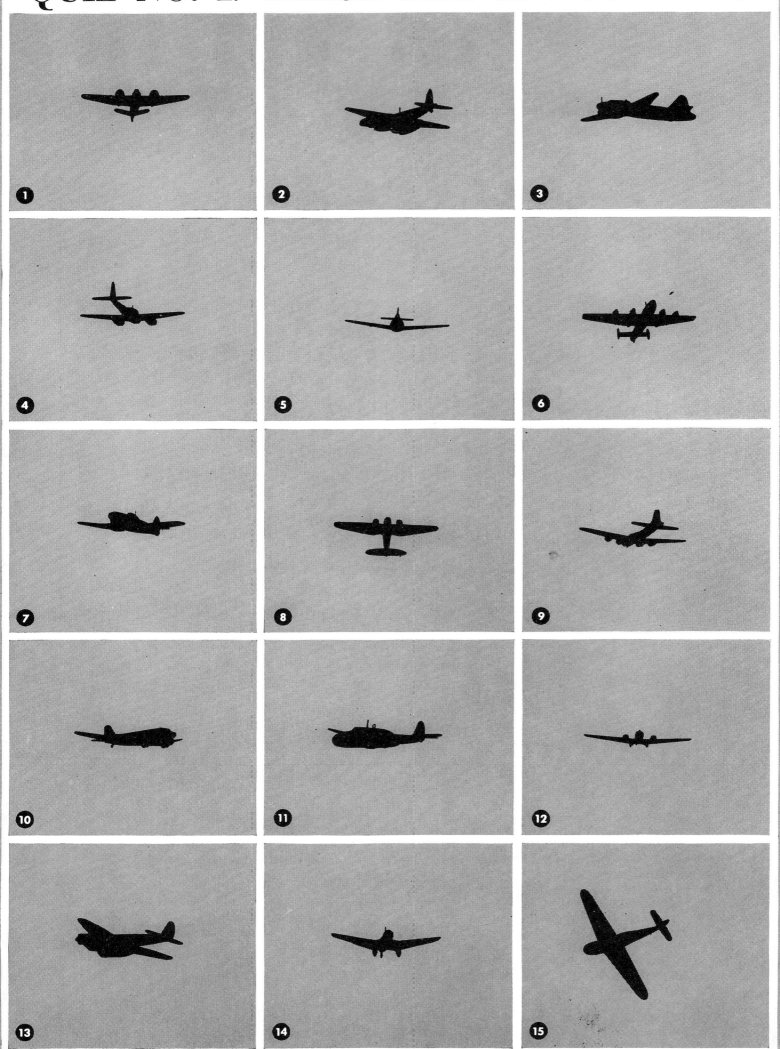

For answers, see p. 50

U. S. ARMY-NAVY JOURNAL OF

RECOGNITION

FEBRUARY, 1944

NUMBER 6

PUBLISHED BY THE U.S. WAR AND NAVY DEPARTMENTS

COPYRIGHT 1944 BY STEPHEN R. CONNOLLY, IST LT., AIR CORPS

TRAINING AIDS

Since it got underway in September 1943, the *Journal* has tried to present the latest information and best available pictures on various forms of operationally important matériel, both friendly and enemy. With this article, the *Journal* is venturing into a new field—the methods and devices for presenting recognition instruction.

Many synthetic methods of duplicating actual visual conditions have been devised. In most distant views of aircraft, for example, the interesting details of construction disappear and the plane appears to the eye as a dark gray silhouette. The sillographs on the facing page are an attempt to reproduce this condition in print. The detail has been removed; engine nacelles, turrets, and other features are seen only in relief against the gray sky. Since the images are made from flying photographs, they are presented in the same attitudes as they would be to the eye. And they give a large image for printing or magic-lantern projection.

But sillographs have one major weakness. Like all pictures, they are static. The actual spotting of airplanes consists of recognizing a moving, constantly altering shape.

Better than the sillograph, is the shadowgraph presented on the following two pages. This is an excellent recognition training aid. It is simple to construct, easy to operate. The aircraft can be presented realistically and in motion; contrasts and comparisons may be made between types. A number of people can see the screen at once and all see the same view at the same time. By superimposing a ringsight on the screen, the device can be used to teach and test range estimation. And, finally, an almost unlimited variety of views can be shown.

The shadowgraph operates on the same principle as the shadowplays frequently presented in church and school auditoriums. A light source is placed behind a translucent screen (a taut bed sheet or tracing paper will do), and a scale model of the airplane is introduced between the light and screen. The light should be small and concentrated and should be at least eight feet from the screen. The audience should be about the same distance on the other side of the screen. For a sharp silhouette and to reduce distortion, the model should be as close to the screen as possible.

In using the shadowgraph it is important to remember that the model has the same relation to the light as the shadow has to the audience. Thus, when the model is held with its nose pointed at the light, the shadow is the silhouette of the airplane as it would look coming at the viewer. If the light shines on the bottom of the model, the shadow is that of an aircraft seen from below. If it shines on top, the plane is seen from above, irrespective of where the students are sitting.

After the plane is shown from several angles, as a form of review the model can be moved to simulate flight. For an approach view, the model should be brought down on to the screen in a head-on view. Then, by gradually tilting the nose and moving the model upwards and towards the light, the effect of a plane approaching and passing overhead may be reproduced. By lowering the nose the plane can be made to appear to pass beneath the observer. Reversing these conditions, the plane can be made to fly away from the student. From a side view, the plane can be made to bank and sweep across the field of view in varied maneuvers.

Perspective distorts plane shape

One of the most disturbing factors in recognition which the shadowgraph can do much to clear up, is the illusion created by perspective and dihedral. Take for example the Army's chief transport, the C-47. This plane has a wing with marked dihedral, a very pronounced taper on the leading edge, a straight trailing edge. In plan view, this wing is one of the chief recognition points for the airplane. However, when the C-47 is seen from below coming at you, perspective causes the wing to appear swept forward; the leading edge seems almost straight, while the taper seems to be on the trailing edge. Thus the plan form of the wing is just reversed. By using the shadowgraph, the effect of this distortion on a particular plane can be easily demonstrated. By rule, when seen from above, front or rear, a wing with marked dihedral will appear to be swept away from you; when seen from below, the wings will be bent toward you (*see diagram, lower right, page 5*).

With the shadowgraph, two or more planes may be shown at the same time so that differences between similar craft may be pointed out in identical views. This is a great advantage when considering planes which have had limited photographic coverage. Not only can identical views be shown, but models built to the same scale (usually 1:72) can be used and their size compared exactly.

On next two pages the *Journal* presents photographs of the shadowgraph set-up at the AAF Air Intelligence School at Harrisburg, Pa., and schematic diagrams showing the arrangement and use of a typical shadowgraph.

LIGHT SOURCE FOR SHADOWGRAPH used at Harrisburg school is demonstrated by an instructor on the school staff. Baffle plates held by the instructor allow heat to escape from lamp, control the flow of light.

SCALE MODEL OF C-47, 1:72 true size, is held on wand formed of ten-gauge wire. Sharp point of wire fits in hole in model. The instructor can remain hidden behind framework of screen, move model about to simulate flight conditions.

IMAGE APPEARS on the screen as the instructor holds model behind it. Plane appears to be coming toward audience if model is pointed at light source. As the instructor moves the plane toward light, it appears to fly over heads of onlookers, disappear. Wooden framework holding screen prevents audience from seeing which model is selected. Student seated about 30 ft. from screen sees plane at about 700 yd. range.

TYPICAL CLASSROOM ARRANGEMENT for shadowgraph instruction is shown in the picture above. Translucent screen is set up approximately 8 ft. from the source of light, in this case a standard slide projector such as is avail-able for field use. Instructor holds model on thin wire wand very close to screen. The students sit in half dusk of semi-darkened room. For best results they should not be closer to the screen than the source of light.

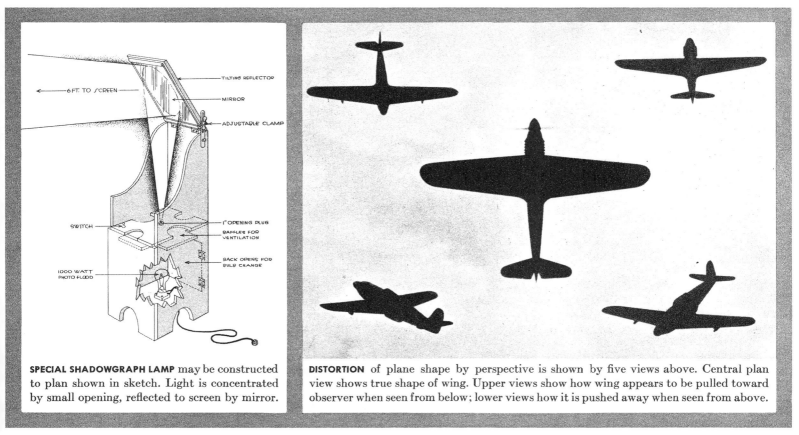

SPECIAL SHADOWGRAPH LAMP may be constructed to plan shown in sketch. Light is concentrated by small opening, reflected to screen by mirror.

DISTORTION of plane shape by perspective is shown by five views above. Central plan view shows true shape of wing. Upper views show how wing appears to be pulled toward observer when seen from below; lower views how it is pushed away when seen from above.

THESE LISTS ARE DESIGNED MERELY TO GUIDE RECOGNITION TRAINING IN AIRCRAFT AND ARE NOT TO BE CONSTRUED AS SUPERSEDING ANY PREVIOUSLY ISSUED DIRECTIVE. CLASS A COMPRISES AIRCRAFT THAT ARE OPERATIONALLY MOST IMPORTANT. CLASS B COMPRISES AIRCRAFT THAT ARE OPERATIONALLY IMPORTANT IN SOME AREAS AND/OR ARE NUMERICALLY LESS IMPORTANT THAN CLASS A, AND ALSO AIRCRAFT WHICH, THOUGH NUMERICALLY IMPORTANT, ARE BEING GRADUALLY REPLACED. EMPHASIS SHOULD BE PLACED ON AIRPLANES IN CLASS A.

U. S. NAVY

CLASS A

DESIGNATION	COMMON NAME	TYPE
F4F	WILDCAT	1E-SSF
F6F	HELLCAT	1E-SSF
F4U	CORSAIR	1E-SSF
OS2U	KINGFISHER	1E-S/O
SBD	DAUNTLESS	1E-S/B
SB2C	HELLDIVER	1E-S/B
TBF	AVENGER	1E-T/B
PBY-5 & 5A	CATALINA	2E-P/B
PV	VENTURA	2E-P/B
PBM-3C	MARINER	2E-P/B

CLASS B

SO3C	SEAGULL	1E-S/O
SOC		1E-S/O
SNJ	TEXAN	1E-S/N
J2F	DUCK	1E-J
PB2Y	CORONADO	4E-P/B

U. S. ARMY

CLASS A

P-38	LIGHTNING	2E-SSF, R
P-39	AIRACOBRA	1E-SSF
P-40	WARHAWK	1E-SSF
P-47	THUNDERBOLT	1E-SSF
P-51	MUSTANG	1E-SSF
A-20	HAVOC	2E-LB, 2SF
B-17	FORTRESS	4E-HB
B-24	LIBERATOR	4E-HB
B-25	MITCHELL	2E-MB
B-26	MARAUDER	2E-MB
C-46	COMMANDO	2E-C
C-47	SKYTRAIN	2E-C
C-54	SKYMASTER	4E-C

CLASS B

C-60	LODESTAR	2E-C
A-29	HUDSON	2E-LB
A-30	BALTIMORE	2E-LB
A-31 (A-35)	VENGEANCE	1E-DB
L-4*	PIPER GRASSHOPPER	1E-L
L-5*	SENTINEL	1E-L

*NOTE: THESE TWO AIRCRAFT ARE REPRESENTATIVE OF THE L-TYPE.

BRITISH—R. A. F.

CLASS A

SPITFIRE		1E-SSF
HURRICANE		1E-SSF
TYPHOON		1E-SSF
MOSQUITO		2E-2SF, LB
BEAUFIGHTER		2E-2SF
WELLINGTON		2E-MB, T/B
BLENHEIM		2E-MB
BEAUFORT		2E-T/B, R
LANCASTER		4E-HB
HALIFAX		4E-HB
STIRLING		4E-HB
SUNDERLAND		4E-P/B

CLASS B

WHITLEY	2E-MB
HAMPDEN	2E-MB, T/B
WHIRLWIND (WELKIN)	2E-SSF
MASTER	1E-N

AMERICAN AIRCRAFT USED BY R.A.F.

DESIGNATION	COMMON NAME	TYPE
P-51	MUSTANG	
A-20	BOSTON	
A-29	HUDSON	
A-30	BALTIMORE	
B-25	MITCHELL	
PV	VENTURA	
B-24	LIBERATOR	
PBY-5	CATALINA	
P-40	KITTYHAWK	
A-31	VENGEANCE	

BRITISH FLEET AIR ARM

CLASS A

SWORDFISH	1E-T/B, R
BARRACUDA	1E-T/B

CLASS B

FULMAR	1E-SSF
ALBACORE	1E-T/B, R
WALRUS	1E-R

OTHER AIRCRAFT USED BY FLEET AIR ARM (ON U. S. AND R. A. F. LISTS)

	SEAFIRE	1E-SSF
	SEA HURRICANE	1E-SSF
F4F	WILDCAT	1E-SSF
TBF	AVENGER	1E-T/B
F6F	HELLCAT	1E-SSF
F4U	CORSAIR	1E-SSF

RUSSIAN

CLASS A

LA-5		1E-SSF
LAGG 3		1E-SSF
IL-2 & IL-3	STORMOVIK	1E-LB
PE-2		2E-DB
SB-3		2E-MB
PE-2B (PE-3)		2E-LB
DB-3F (IL-4)		2E-MB, T/B
TB-7		4E-HB
YAK-4 (BB-22)		2E-LB, R

CLASS B

YAK-1 (I-26)	1E-SSF
MIG-3 (I-18)	1E-SSF
I-16	1E-SSF
SU-2	1E-LB, R
ER-2	2E-MB
AR-2 (improved SB)	2E-DB
DB-3	2E-MB, T/B

AMERICAN AIRCRAFT USED BY RUSSIANS (ON U. S. ARMY AND NAVY LISTS)

P-39	AIRACOBRA	1E-SSF
P-40	WARHAWK	1E-SSF
A-20	HAVOC	2E-LB
B-25	MITCHELL	2E-MB
PBY (GST)	CATALINA	2E-P/B
C-47 (PS-84)	SKYTRAIN	2E-C

GERMAN

CLASS A

DESIGNATION	COMMON NAME	TYPE
ME-109 F & G		1E-B, SSF
ME-110 F & G		2E-B, 2SF
ME-410*		2E-B, 2SF
FW-190A		1E-B, SSF
JU-87D	STUKA	1E-DB
JU-88A, C & S		2E-MB, DB
HE-111H		2E-MB, T/B
JU-188		2E-MB, DB
DO-217E, K & M**		2E-MB, DB
HE-177		2E-HB, R
JU-52		3E-C, GT
JU-290		4E-C, HB, R
ME-323		6E-C

CLASS B

ME-210*		2E-B, 2SF
AR-196		1E-R, FP
BV-138		3E-P/B
BV-222		6E-P/B
HS-129		2E-LB, GA
HE-115		2E-R, FP, T/B
FW-189		2E-LB, R
HS-126		1E-R
FI-156		1E-L
JU-90		4E-C
JU-86P		2E-LB, R
FW-200C	KURIER	4E-HB
DFS-230		G
GO-242 & GO-244		G and 2E-C

*NOTE: RECOGNITIONALLY THE SAME.
**NOTE: DIFFERENCES IN THESE MODELS SHOULD BE NOTED IN INSTRUCTION.

JAPANESE

CLASS A

T-3		TONY	1E-SSF
T-2		TOJO	1E-SSF
T-2		NICK	2E-2SF
T-1, MARK 1, 2		OSCAR	1E-SSF
T-O, MARK 1, 2*		ZEKE	1E-SSF
T-O, MARK 2		HAMP	1E-SSF
T-O or T-2		RUFE	1E-SSF, FP
T-O		PETE	1E-R, FP
T-O		JAKE	1E-FP, DB
T-100, MARK 1, 2		DINAH	2E-R
T-99, MARK 1, 2		VAL	1E-DB
T-97		KATE	1E-T/B
T-1		BETTY	2E-MB, T/B
T-100		HELEN	2E-MB
T-99		LILY	2E-LB
T-97, MARK 1, 2, 3		SALLY	2E-MB, T/B
T-96		NELL	2E-MB, T/B
T-2		EMILY	4E-P/B
T-97		MAVIS	4E-P/B

CLASS B

T-97		NATE	1E-SSF
T-95		DAVE	1E-R, FP
T-99		SONIA	1E-R
T-99		CHERRY	2E-FB
T-MC-20		TOPSY	2E-C
T-DC-2		TESS	2E-C
T-LOCKHEED		THELMA	2E-C

*NOTE: ZEKE 2 HAS A HAMP FUSELAGE AND ENGINE WITH ZEKE WINGS, BOMB RACKS.

◄ **ABBREVIATIONS** ►

B..............BOMBER	L..............LIAISON	GT............GLIDER TUG	S/N..SCOUTING, TRAINING	1E..........SINGLE-ENGINE
C..............CARGO	N..............TRAINER	HB.........HEAVY BOMBER	S/O............SCOUTING	2E............TWIN-ENGINE
F..............FIGHTER	R.......RECONNAISSANCE	LB.......LIGHT BOMBER	S/O.......OBSERVATION	3E........THREE-ENGINE
G..............GLIDER	DB..........DIVEBOMBER	MB......MEDIUM BOMBER	T/B.....TORPEDO BOMBER	4E..........FOUR-ENGINE
J..............UTILITY	FP..........FLOATPLANE	P/B........PATROL BOMBER	SSF SINGLE-SEAT FIGHTER	6E..............SIX-ENGINE
	GA.......GROUND ATTACK	S/B........SCOUT BOMBER	2SF...TWO-SEAT FIGHTER	

ARMY'S NEWEST PURSUIT IS TWIN-ENGINE, TWIN-BOOM JOB WITH TRICYCLE LANDING GEAR, HAS LARGE GLASSED-IN GONDOLA TO HOUSE CREW OF THREE

USAAF'S FAST NEW PURSUIT

About to go into action with the Army Air Forces is the P-61, a new plane built by Northrop to serve as a night interceptor-fighter. It is in the high-speed class at medium altitudes, and has already acquired the nickname "Black Widow."

RECOGNITION: P-61 is a three-place, high-wing monoplane with a tailboom running aft from each fat radial-engine nacelle. Each boom is smoothly streamlined with slight bulge on under side for landing wheel. The pilot's nacelle is long nosed, is deepest opposite wing. It is pointed aft. Wing has straight leading, tapered trailing edge. Span, 66 ft.; length, 49 ft.

WHEELS FOLD INTO BOOMS as Black Widow takes off. Though similar to the P-38, P-61 has much larger gondola to house bigger crew. Glassed-in rear section provides good visibility for gunner.

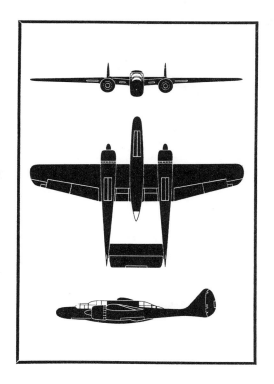

P-61'S WING has slight gull effect because of dihedral on the inboard panels. Tailplane is straight with cutouts at end for rudder clearance. Lines of the tailbooms are unbroken in the plan view.

The winner in its battles over Britain, the RAF now sends its fighters winging against Reich

ROYAL AIR FORCE

Greatest air force of the First World War, it has reaffirmed its position in the Second

The Royal Air Force was created on April 1, 1918. Its first communique, issued a few days later, reported that No. 20 Squadron dropped sixteen 20-lb. bombs; No. 1 Squadron thirteen 25-lb. bombs; and No. 206 Squadron seventy-four 25-lb. bombs. In addition, four 40-lb. phosphorous bombs were dropped. In terms of this war's 8,000-lb. blockbusters, this may not seem like a very auspicious start, but within three months the RAF had command of the air over Europe. Against the Germans' 340 planes, Britain could rank 1,390 better machines better manned. By the end of the war, when the rout of the first Luftwaffe was complete, the RAF had 22,647 airplanes, 103 airships, 291,000 officers and men plus 25,-000 women in the WRAF. In the short eight months of its wartime life, it had become the world's first great air force.

Many of the men who are leading the RAF to victory in its second great trial gained their first experience with the infant RAF and its immediate predecessors, the Royal Flying Corps and Royal Naval Air Service. Sir Charles Portal, Marshal of the RAF and Chief of Air Staff, flew as an observer in the RFC as early as 1915, once pot-shotted the German ace Immelmann with a rifle. Air Chief Marshal Sir Arthur Tedder, Deputy Allied Commander in Europe, flew with the RFC in 1916, was squadron leader in the RAF by 1919. Air Marshal Sir Arthur Harris commanded the first experimental night-flying detachment in World War I for defense against Zeppelin attacks on London.

Chief of Air Staff from the beginning was Sir Hugh Trenchard, England's Billy Mitchell. Just after the war, he had the great task of transforming the war-created RAF into a vital peacetime military arm, of keeping morale at a high pitch, of establishing a thorough training program and maintaining experimental work on military aircraft. During his tenure Capt. John Alcock and Lieut. Arthur Whitten Brown made the first transatlantic flight, the dirigible R-34 flew to America and back, and other flights were made to India and Australia. Perhaps most important of all, the series of Schneider Cup racers that culminated in the Spitfire got underway. When "Boom" Trenchard retired in 1929 with the rank of Marshal of the Royal Air Force, he remarked truthfully that he had laid the foundations for a castle but if nobody wanted to build anything bigger than a cottage on them, they would still have a jolly good cottage.

When the Second World War broke out, Trenchard's foundations stood fast. In the months of August and September 1940, when Britain's Spitfires and Hurricanes broke the legend of the Luftwaffe's invincibility, the RAF took its place among the great military or-

ganizations of all time. For the next year the war was bitter. Foiled in the daytime, the Germans took to night bombing. But after the first few thunderous assaults, the RAF came back with radar-equipped Beaufighter and Havoc nightfighters. On May 10, 1941, 33 of the raiders failed to return home.

Meanwhile, the RAF's Coastal Command had been insuring the flow of lend-leased supplies to the island kingdom. To the Coastal Command falls the job of patrolling all British waters. Flying far beyond the range of fighter escorts, RAF's patrol bombers must rely on their own limited armament or their pilots' skill. Smaller anti-ship planes, like the torpedo-carrying versions of the Beaufighter and Beaufort, carry on a constant harrying of Axis supply lines in the Mediterranean while England-based craft blast German E-boats and other Channel craft (*see pages 22–25*). It is a tough job which will not end until the peace.

Throughout Allied lands the stations of the Training Command have maintained a steady flow of new, fully prepared men to crew British aircraft. And wherever the British Army has gone, the Mustangs and Typhoons of the Army Cooperation Command have been in there slugging. But the chief glory of the RAF today is the Bomber Command. Nightly ferrying the war to Hitler and his minions, the huge Halifaxes, Stirlings and Lancasters carrying $5\frac{1}{2}$ to 8 tons of bombs apiece have blasted all the Reich's chief ports, pulverized the Ruhr and made a smoking hell of the Nazis' capital. Direct damage to steel works in the Ruhr area alone have caused a loss of 1,250,000 tons of steel and the total loss of steel must be much greater. In three months of 1942, the daily output of coal in the Ruhr fell 20%. In Turin, 70 factories have been damaged including ten of the Fiat factories. In Genoa, acres of docks have been left waste. This constant attack has meant that the enemy has been compelled to keep his finest fighters and pilots away from the Russian front. Little more than one-quarter of the German fighter force has been strung out from the White to the Black Sea, while nearly double that number have been held in Western Europe. In all, the Bomber Command has destroyed or seriously damaged close to 3,000 factories and industrial works in Axis-held Europe.

The planes which have carried democracy's banners throughout the European theater since the first gun was fired are pictured on the following pages. Though Americans can be proud of the USAAF as the biggest and strongest assemblage of planes in the world, the airplanes of the Royal Air Force rate close to the top in every category. They have done the war's greatest job.

SIR CHARLES F. A. PORTAL, G. C. B., D. S. O., M. C., Marshal of Royal Air Force.

HURRICANE

TALL OVAL FUSELAGE and almost straight wing mark Hurricane in head-on views. High-set tailplane may be visible above the wing. Three-bladed prop cannot be seen by the eye, is not recognition feature.

BOMBS OR FUEL TANKS may be suspended from Hurricane's wing (*above, below*). Thickset fuselage and broad fin and rudder contrast with sharply pointed nose, make plane appear to have tail-heavy sit.

HURRICANE

Have retained superiority

From the chaos of air war which has since been named the Battle of Britain, two great airplanes arose. These were the RAF's famed single-engine fighters, the Hawker Hurricane and the Supermarine Spitfire. Between them they accounted for well over 2,000 enemy craft during the first year of war. The Hurricane was first of the pair to go into production and outnumbered the Spit almost two to one. For this reason it bore the brunt of the early fighting. However, Spitfire's performance was slightly better—it had more speed and climb and operated at higher altitudes—so that in the later days of the battle its percentage of kills per plane was higher.

As the war progressed and the need for specialized aircraft became obvious, the Hurricane took over many jobs which were undreamed of at the time of its original design. To protect hard-pressed convoys, it was catapulted from merchantmen as an expendable interceptor of German bombers. At Narvik, a squadron of Hurricanes flew from the carrier H. M. S. Glorious. In November 1941, others were equipped with bomb racks and used as one of the first fighter-bombers. The Hurricane has also been used as a fighter and ground-attack plane in the African desert and Burmese jungles. Most recently, the Hurricane IID with two 40-mm. cannon in the wing has been used as a tank-buster. Though these adaptations have changed the airplane's appearance in detail, they have not fundamentally altered its personality.

The Spitfire, which still remains one of the greatest fighters in the air, has also undergone a number of alterations (*see Journal, Oct. issue*). As with the Hurri-

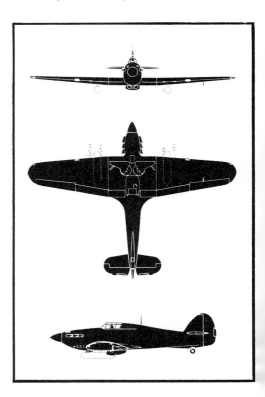

& SPITFIRE

since the Battle of Britain

cane, many of the early changes were in the power plant to boost speed and altitude. From the original two-bladed fixed-pitch propeller, it changed first to a three-bladed variable-pitch prop and then to a three or four-bladed constant-speed propeller. Changes in the airframe to accommodate refinements have materially altered the appearance of the Spit from its prototype. The Marks XII and some Mark V's have had the typical elliptical wing clipped to provide greater speed and maneuverability at low altitudes. This reduces the span by 5 ft.

Marks VI and VII, on the other hand, had very pointed wings. The new Mark XII is clip-winged and has a new Rolls-Royce Griffon engine. A large spinner which fairs into the belly-line of the fuselage gives this model a nose-low appearance and a markedly different sit in the air. The Mark IX, most important operational version, has a slightly longer nose and a foot more of overall length and has radiator intakes at the root of each wing. Fin and rudder is more pointed.

RECOGNITION: Hurricane has wing and tailplane which taper evenly to rounded tips. Wing has slight dihedral from a straight inboard section. Nose is pointed. Fuselage has straight lower line, humped upper surface. Fin and rudder is broad and rounded. Span, 40 ft.; length, 31 ft.

The basic Spitfire, subject to variations above, has distinctive elliptical wing and tailplane. Fuselage belly curves down from high spinner and up to high-set tail. Upper surface of fuselage runs level from cockpit fairing to tail. Fin and rudder is tall, narrow, rounded. Span, 37 ft.; length, 30 ft.

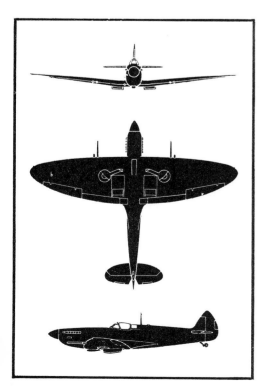

SPITFIRE FOUGHT AT NIGHT in Battle of Britain. Silhouetted Mark IX's (*above*) are now used chiefly for high-altitude fighting. Wing form and straight sit in the air are best clues in such difficult views.

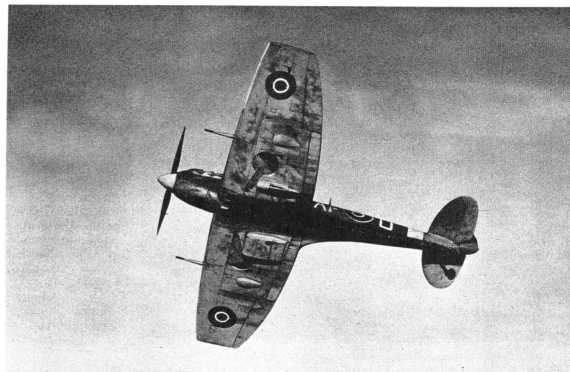

CLIP-WINGED MARK V (*above*) has single radiator intake on starboard wing. Mark IX (*below*) shows two intakes at wing roots. Dihedral is very clear; wing tapers from thick chord at root to thin wingtips.

TYPHOON BOMBER AND BEAUFIGHTER

Constantly harass Axis outskirts of Europe

Both the Beaufighter and the Typhoon were designed as fighters, but have scored more outstanding successes in other capacities. The Beaufighter is the more versatile, continuing as day, night, and long-range fighter, while it has added strafing, tank-busting and land-based torpedo-carrying to its occupational list. The Typhoon with a bomb load of 1,000 lb. and mounting four cannon in the wings, is now more commonly seen than the original type with twelve machine guns.

The Typhoon was built around the 2,400-h.p. Napier Sabre engine, and was intended as a bomber-destroyer, which accounts for its big size. The Napier motor gives the Typhoon a speed of more than 400 m.p.h. so that the Typhoon is very difficult to recognize when flying high, and hard to hit during its bombing dives.

Although the U. S. classification does not exist in the RAF, the Beaufighter is an attack plane, used against all targets. It is the most powerfully armed fighting plane in service, with a 765-lb. weight of fire per minute, coming from four machine guns mounted in the starboard wing, two in the port wing, one in the observer's cockpit, and four 20-mm. cannon in the nose. Descended from the Beaufort, from which it derives its range and structural strength, the Bristol plane is usually seen with two Hercules radial engines, although one model is powered with Merlin inlines.

RECOGNITION: Deep radiator intake under the nose distinguishes the Typhoon. It is a low-wing airplane, with a dihedral on the outer panels only. Wings are equally tapered with rounding edges, the shape being repeated in the tailplane. Fin and rudder is rounded, and extends below fuselage. Span, 41 ft.; length, 32 ft.

The Beaufighter is a midwing monoplane. The fin and rudder is broad and triangular. Engine nacelles are underslung, extend slightly beyond the stubby nose. The tailplane is broad, rounded, has a sharp dihedral and V cutout. Span, 58 ft.; length, 41 ft.

TYPHOON BOMBING RAIDS are usually connected with Fortress raids on Western Europe, and diversionary sweeps. Typhoon rate of climb is phenomenal.

DEEP UNDER-COWLING which houses the oil-cooling system of the high-powered Sabre engine shows in head-on view. The Typhoon is very maneuverable, and can turn inside the FW-190 even when loaded.

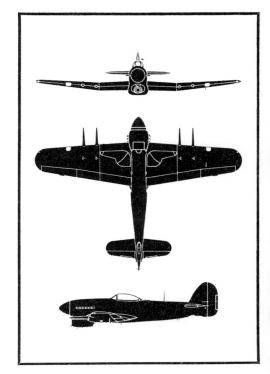

REAR VIEW SHOWS dihedral of the Beaufighter's tailplane, a feature added to counteract swing during take-offs and so avoid damage resulting from slips off the runway at night. Torpedoes are carried externally, reducing speed below usual 335 m.p.h., but making changes in the fuselage unnecessary.

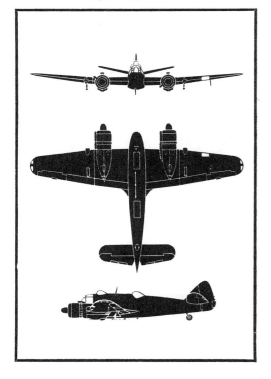

BEAUFIGHTER IS SCOURGE to Axis shipping, also protects Coastal Command bombers on anti-sub patrol. Japs name it "Whispering Death" because of swift, silent approach at low level over the jungle.

MOSQUITO'S GREAT SPEED MAKES DEFENSIVE ARMAMENT UNNECESSARY, GIVES AIRPLANE CLEAN LINES FREE OF GUN TURRETS AND OTHER LARGE PROTUBERANCES

LETHAL MOSQUITO

Fast nightfighter, intruder bomber, reconnaissance plane is world's most versatile aircraft

Since entering operations as an unarmed high-speed bomber late in 1941, the De Havilland Mosquito has performed about every job in the book. With four 20-mm. cannon and four .303 machine guns mounted in a solid nose, the Mosquito is one of the world's best nightfighters and tank-busters. With a glassed-in nose, it has been a superlative light bomber, spot-bombing Party headquarters and Nazi demonstrations when least expected, flying in at roof level to avoid the radar. In a sub-stratosphere version with modified engines, extra wing tanks and low-drag finish, it has been the RAF's best photo-reconnaissance plane. In every use, its twin en-

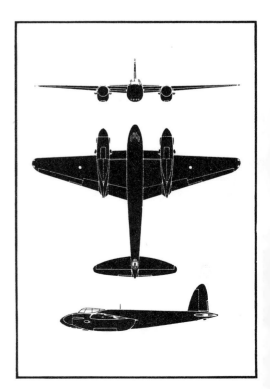

WING RADIATOR INTAKES project between the Mosquito's engine nacelles, break straight leading edge of the wing. Nacelles and nose project evenly. Long elliptical tailplane repeats curved lines of fuselage.

MOSQUITO FIGHTERS FLY FORMATION ON WAY TO CONTINENT. THIS TYPE IS DISTINGUISHED BY SOLID NOSE AND PROJECTIONS OF FOUR .303-CAL. MACHINE GUNS

gines have given it a speed of over 400 m.p.h., enabling it to get in its blows before being discovered and to outrun interceptors on the way home.

The all-wood construction of the Mosquito's airframe has been a production godsend. In this war of metals, there has been a less pronounced shortage of wood. Woodworkers in England were an untapped source of skilled labor. Basic components of the Mosquito's production could be distributed among over 400 subcontractors. With these advantages the Mosquito was in operational use only 22 months after its original design. In combat, the wood skin gives a low-drag surface, does not splinter when struck. It can be quickly and easily repaired and will stand up even under the shock of belly landings.

RECOGNITION: The design is aerodynamically clean. The fuselage tapers from a rather pointed nose; only the glazed cockpit breaks the contours. The wing has a straight leading edge, pronounced taper on trailing edge. Tailplane is smooth ellipse; fin and rudder is tall and elliptical. Wing radiators cause leading edge to extend forward between twin nacelles. Nacelles project evenly with nose, slightly beyond trailing edge. Span, 54 ft.; length, 41 ft.

TWO INLINE ENGINE NACELLES are slung under Mosquito's high midwing. The two Rolls-Royce Merlin 21 engines drive airplane through the air at over 400 m.p.h., make the Mosquito the fastest light bomber in the world and one of the fastest aircraft in service. It can outrun most interceptors.

WELLINGTON'S FUSELAGE IS VERY DISTINCTIVE, WITH BLUNT NOSE AND TAIL, STRAIGHT BACK AND CURVED BELLY-LINE. FIN AND RUDDER IS TALL AND TRIANGULAR

WELLINGTON, SUNDERLAND

Have fought since beginning

Among the RAF's oldest planes are the Bomber Command's medium, the Wellington, and Coastal Command's flying boat, the Sunderland. Both were in service at the outbreak of war. The Wellington, in fact, made the first bombing raid of the war, an attack on Wilhelmshaven, Sept. 4, 1939. Both are doing a good job today.

Originally, the Wellington was mainstay of the small RAF bombing force. Performance in Mediterranean has been exceptional. In Sicily it has been a fine ground-support plane, spotting targets with great precision in advance of the troops. Prior to the invasion it helped clear land and water areas, bomb ground objectives, torpedo ships. It has worked both as a mine-layer and minesweeper. In the latter use, known as "Wedding Ring Wimpy," it carried a cumbersome ring about two-thirds the wingspan in diameter which, being charged, set off magnetic mines when the plane flew low over them.

Like most of the older RAF planes the Wellington has gone through a number of variations. Different models have been powered by radial Bristol Pegasus or Her-

ENGINE NACELLES of Wellington are bulky, are set midwing. This particular model has Merlin engines. Basket-weave structure that forms Wellington's peculiar geodetic airframe is visible through windows.

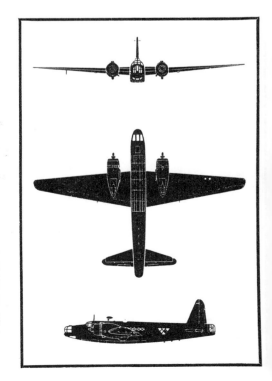

SUNDERLAND HAS CLOSE RESEMBLANCE TO JAP PATROL BOMBER EMILY.   CHIEF DISTINCTIONS ARE SUNDERLAND'S STUBBIER WING, DEEPER BLUNTER HULL, TALLER FIN

cules engines, Pratt & Whitney Wasps or inline Rolls-Royce Merlins. One newer version has a solid rather than a turret nose. In this version the fuselage comes to a high point forward.

The Sunderland is an outgrowth of the flying boats built by Short Bros. for British Overseas Airways. It is a big plane with great carrying capacity. During the fight for Crete, one Sunderland brought out 80 men in a single trip. When the Kensington Court was sunk in 1940, a Sunderland rescued the entire crew. The Sunderland has two nose guns, four in the tail turret and two amidships or in a dorsal turret.

RECOGNITION: Wellington has thick fuselage with blunt nose, blunt tail. Long tapered wing and tailplane. Fat engine nacelles set close to fuselage. Tall fin and rudder set high on fuselage. Span, 86 ft.; length, 61 ft.

Sunderland is deep, broad-hulled flying boat. Four engines are mounted midwing in high double-tapered wing. Fin and rudder is very tall, set high above upswept tail. The nose turret gives the hull a bulldog snout. Span, 112 ft.; length, 85 ft.

SUNDERLAND'S BROAD WING tapers to rounded tips. Deep flying-boat hull is impressive from below.

GREAT SIZE of British flying boat is shown by crew members watching camera plane from top gunner's position. Despite its bulk, four engines get airplane through the air at speeds over 200 m.p.h.

FIRST VERSION OF HALIFAX II HAD NEW GLASSED-IN NOSE AND SEMI-RETRACTABLE TAIL WHEEL, BUT KEPT ORIGINAL TRIANGULAR FINS AND RUDDERS, RADIO ANTENNA

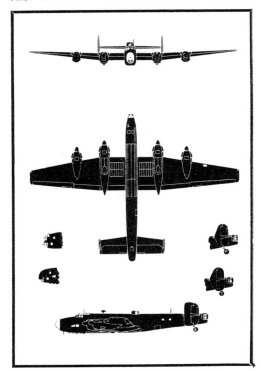

HALIFAX AND STIRLING

Britain gets revenge as heavies pour weight on Germany

For the first year and a half of air war, Great Britain was on the defensive. Her fine fighting planes battled against almost overwhelming odds and, in the end, battled successfully. During the summer of 1940 the names Spitfire and Hurricane became household words throughout the world. But in the spring of 1941, heavy bombers, the weapons of offense, began to come off British production lines. The Short Stirling made its first sorties the night of Feb. 10, 1941. The Handley-Page Halifax went on its first mission—raids on Kiel and Le Havre—on

March 11, 1941. Since that time, these craft and the newer Lancaster have stolen the headlines from their swift fighter defenders.

The Halifax has gone through a number of variations since it first appeared. Some changes in nose and tail are included in the silhouettes at the left. The original "Hali-bag" was of full monocoque construction, powered by four Merlin 10 engines. Its wingspread was limited to less than 100 ft. by the available hangars. Trailing-edge flaps extended from wing root to the ailerons to permit take-offs from small fields under

HALIFAX I HAS NOSE, TAIL AND DORSAL TURRETS, TRIANGULAR FINS

PRODUCTION MODEL OF HALIFAX II IS IDENTIFIED BY ROUNDED, RECTANGULAR TWIN TAILS

LONG BULKY FUSELAGE OF SHORT STIRLING MADE IT FIRST FLYING "BOXCAR." ANGULAR SNOUT AND TALL, HIGH-SET FIN AND RUDDER DISTINGUISH IT IN SIDE VIEW

heavy load. The original nose had a bulbous turret at the top, a prominent chin for the bombardier's position below. The twin fins came to a point at the tailplane while the rudders were broad and rounded. The Halifax II has a smooth glassed-in nose and more rectangular fins and rudders. Defensive armament is concentrated in four-gun turrets in the tail and on top of the fuselage. An intermediate stage had the new nose and the old tail assembly (*see left*). In its newest form, the performance of the Halifax compares with that of the Lancaster.

The Stirling, which is now being superseded by the Halifax and Lancaster, was once the biggest weight-lifter in the RAF's line-up, carrying a bomb load of over eight tons. Like the Halifax, its wingspan was limited by the available hangar space. Because of this and its great weight, the Stirling lands at high speed and cannot climb until its landing gear is retracted. The plane

carries more armor than any other craft in the air, even its leading edge is armored.

RECOGNITION: Despite nose and tail changes, the Halifax has a distinct character. The fuselage is long and deep-bodied, rounded fore and aft. Midwing has straight panel inboard, then tapers evenly to square tips. All nacelles are underslung, inner ones may extend beyond trailing edge. Tailplane has slight taper on leading edge. Span, 99 ft.; length, 71 ft.

The Stirling has very long fuselage with almost straight lines top and bottom. Cockpit forms noticeable hump forward of leading edge. Wing tapers evenly from thick root chord to very thin tips, with a pronounced dihedral angle. Inboard radial engine nacelles are long and underslung; outboard nacelles short, midwing. Single fin and rudder is mounted high on the fuselage forward of gunner's position. Tailplane is long and tapering. Span, 99 ft.; length, 87 ft.

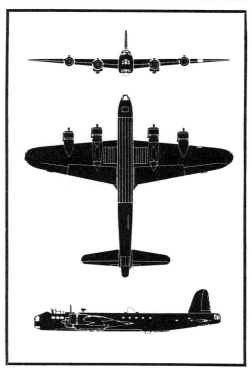

STIRLING'S THICK WING, TAPERING TO VERY THIN TIPS, AND MIXED MOUNTING OF ENGINES, TWO HIGH, TWO LOW, MAKE PLANE UNLIKE ANY OTHER SEEN HEAD-ON

LIKE ALL BRITISH HEAVIES, "LANK" HAS LONG INBOARD NACELLES, BOXCAR FUSELAGE. MOST PROMINENT DISTINCTION IS GUITAR-PICK FIN AND RUDDER

LANCASTER

RAF's fastest big bomber, it is

mainstay of Bomber Command

Since April 1942, when the Lancasters went out on their first daylight sweep, a roof-level attack on the Diesel plant at Augsburg, they have grown into the greatest strategic weapon in the European air war.

With a maximum speed of over 300 m.p.h., a maximum range of 3,000 miles, and able to carry an 8-ton load, the Lancaster has a generally high performance. It dives at 360 m.p.h. and, when fully loaded, can climb at a rate of 1,000 ft. per minute.

RECOGNITION: Long boxy fuselage has prominent turrets on nose and tail, bulbous top turret and inconspicuous remotely controlled belly turret. The wing has straight section to inboard nacelles, tapers outboard to round tips. Dihedral starts from inboard engines. Tailplane is long and narrow; fins and rudders form long ovals. "Lank" usually has four Merlin inline engines, but may have four Bristol Hercules radials. Span, 102 ft.; length, 69½ ft.

LEADING EDGE TAPER DISAPPEARS in this view of Lancaster but graceful lines of the wing remain, with straight section inboard. Inboard nacelles are longer and project farther forward. Fins are very tall.

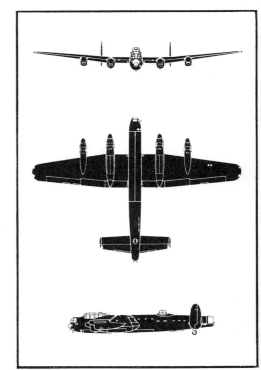

Above fire and flak of Hamburg

broad-winged Lancaster looses

tons of bombs on U-boat yards

POWERFUL NARVIK CLASS DESTROYER CAN BE RECOGNIZED BY THE HEAVY FORESTACK, TRIPOD MAST AND CLIPPER BOW. SOME UNITS HAVE TWIN MOUNTS FORWARD

CHANNEL CRAFT

With heavier classes crippled, German Fleet's sting depends on smaller types

Two sharp displays of naval action coming within a few days of each other brought out clearly the situation of German sea might. The Scharnhorst, a fast but undergunned battleship of 26,000 tons, was sunk off North Cape, leaving the Nazi Navy without a single battleship in fighting trim. Three days later eleven Narvik and Elbing Class destroyers were sighted west of the Bay of Biscay, evidently seeking to contact an important blockade runner. Aircraft of RAF's Coastal Command had already accounted for the merchantman, and a U. S. Navy Liberator sighted the destroyer squadron in time to call in the British cruisers Glasgow and Enterprise. Expert British gunnery sank three of the German destroyers and damaged several others.

But these losses are no indication that the coastal sniping between German and Anglo-American sea and air forces will subside. As long as Nazi convoys slink from port to port in the English Channel and North Sea, planes of the RAF and ships of the Royal Navy's coastal forces will be out to attack them.

Most powerful destroyers of the German Fleet are the Narvik Class. Their four 5.9-in. guns enable them to engage light cruisers, have caused the Germans to call them convoy destroyers. They were laid down in 1939 and were first seen off Narvik. Newer than the Narviks but less heavily armed are the flushdeck Elbings (*see grid, pages 26–27*). They were laid down in 1942, got provisional class name when they were first identified off the East Prussian coast near Elbing. Except for the Karl Galster, lone survivor of the Roeder Class virtually wiped out at Narvik, the remaining German-built DD's belong to the Maasz Class laid down in 1935. Displacing 1,625 tons, and 381 ft. long, they are less formidable than the Narviks which measure 410 ft. in length, displace 1,870 tons.

Although destroyers have largely replaced torpedo boats in other navies, the Germans in the 1920's built the Möwe and Wolf Classes (*see opposite*). Since the Narvik, Roeder, Maasz, Wolf and Möwe Classes are somewhat similar in appearance, they appear on the training list as one group. Another class of torpedo boat, T-1's, were completed between 1938–40.

The balance of German minor combatant types and auxiliaries follow the conventional pattern of PT boats (S-boats), various types of minesweeping, minelaying craft, patrol boats, trawlers. The more important types are pictured on pages 24–25, while the German Navy as a whole, including seizures, is shown to scale on the grid which follows.

MAASZ was typical prewar Nazi destroyer. Note how widely-spaced stacks, with heavier one forward, break in deckline correspond with similar features on the Narvik Class DD shown above. Maasz's bow differs, however.

WOLF CLASS TORPEDO BOATS Jaguar and Tiger cross the T of old battleships Hessen and Schleswig-Holstein during Baltic maneuvers. Built as destroyers under limitations of the Versailles Treaty, these 800-ton ships are seaworthy enough for high seas duty with the Fleet. Their speed is 34 knots; armament includes three 4.1-in. guns, six 21-in. torpedo tubes in triple mounts. All of the Wolf Class ships are named for animals of prey.

MÖWE CLASS TB SEEADLER (Sea Eagle) follows Leopard of Wolf Class in reviews at Kiel. Laid down in 1925, two years earlier than Wolf Class ships, the Möwes are slightly shorter (288 ft. vs. 304 ft.), displace same tonnage. Möwe means gull, and all ships in this class are named for birds. Distinguishing Möwe and Wolf ships from each other is difficult; Möwe's stack is set close to the bridge, both have raked rather than clipper bows.

TB'S OF MÖWE CLASS show typical German torpedo-boat and destroyer design. They carry two stacks widely spaced with the heavier one forward. Break in deckline comes abreast of the forestack (*see Narvik and Maasz opposite*). As is the case with German light cruisers, armament of TB's is concentrated at the rear, indicating use of hit-and-run tactics. T-1 Class (*see grid*) is smaller, faster, less heavily armed than Wolf and Möwe.

23

R-BOATS ARE USED in the German Navy as minesweepers, minelayers and patrol craft. In the U. S. Navy their classification would be coastal minesweeper (AMc). Length of R-boats varies from 85 to 121 ft.; speed is 17 to 18 knots; armament consists of single AA guns fore and aft. Flushdeck craft, with no visible stacks, they sometimes appear with small center island (*above*), also with additional superstructure extending far aft of bridge.

OFFENSIVE THREAT in the English Channel is supplied by torpedo-carrying S-boats which frequently attack British forces. The known types have lengths of 92, 106, and 115 ft. They are bigger than U. S. PT's, though they are slower. The longest S-boat Class carries mines in addition to its two torpedo tubes. The tubes can be seen externally on the type shown above; on other S types they are built into the top of the hull near bow.

MINELAYING GUNBOATS, units of F-1 Class, have seen but little service to date. Their armament consists of single 4.1-in. guns fore and aft, also four 1.460-in. AA guns. Except for flushdeck Königin Luise (F-3), ships of F-1 Class have two breaks in deckline, one just fore, the other just aft of forestack. Length of the F-1's is approximately 250 ft., displacement 600 tons. Widely-spaced stacks and high freeboard forward aid identification.

STANDARD MINESWEEPERS of German Navy are the 215-ft. ships of M-1 Class. Escorting convoys and subs in Bay of Biscay, they seek to counteract minelaying campaign of RAF's Coastal Command. Class included 40 units, has been cut sharply through war losses. Tonnage and armament are approximately same as F-1's. Outstanding recognition features are barge-like stern, high boat davits amidships (*here shown lowered*), and single stack.

The 38 classes of fighting ships which make up the substance of the German Navy are portrayed to scale in the silhouettes on this spread. Ships which have never been completed, or which are being rebuilt after heavy damage, are shown in black. Just how these will look when and if they appear is uncertain.

Offensive strength of the German Fleet has been dissipated by individual defeats at the hands of Allied vessels and planes but certain large ships and numerous small ones remain as threats to Allied movements in northern waters.

SCALE: EACH SQUARE EQUALS 50 FT.

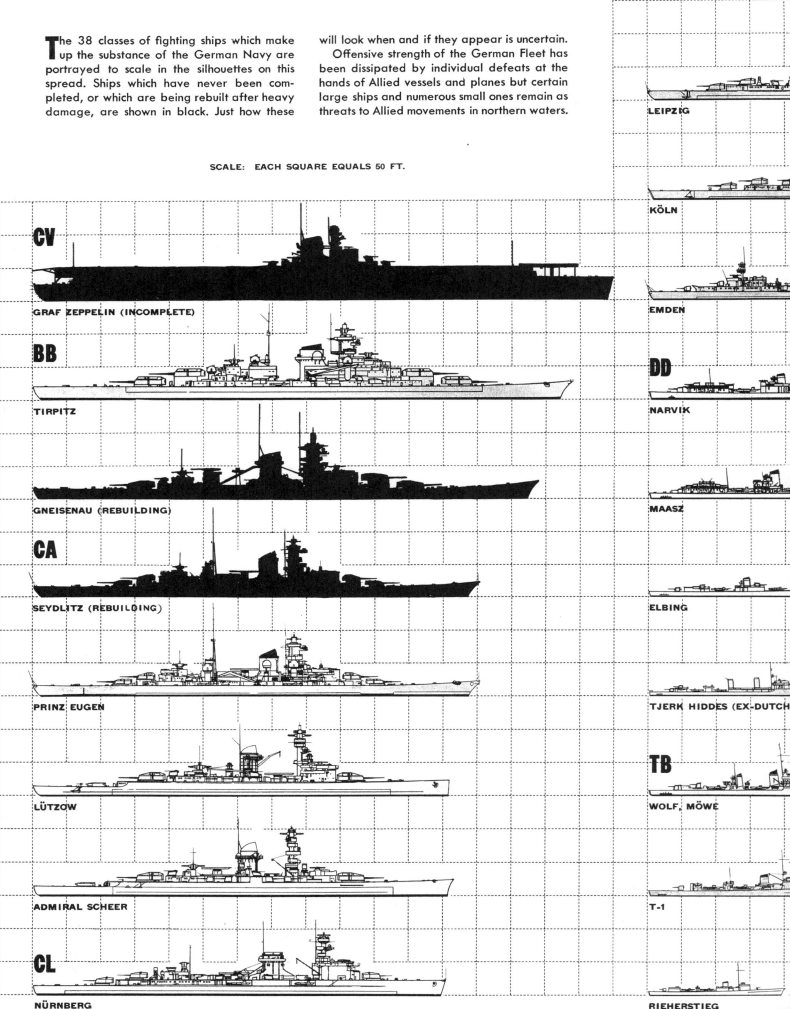

CV GRAF ZEPPELIN (INCOMPLETE)

BB TIRPITZ

GNEISENAU (REBUILDING)

CA SEYDLITZ (REBUILDING)

PRINZ EUGEN

LÜTZOW

ADMIRAL SCHEER

CL NÜRNBERG

LEIPZIG

KÖLN

EMDEN

DD NARVIK

MAASZ

ELBING

TJERK HIDDES (EX-DUTCH)

TB WOLF, MÖWE

T-1

RIEHERSTIEG

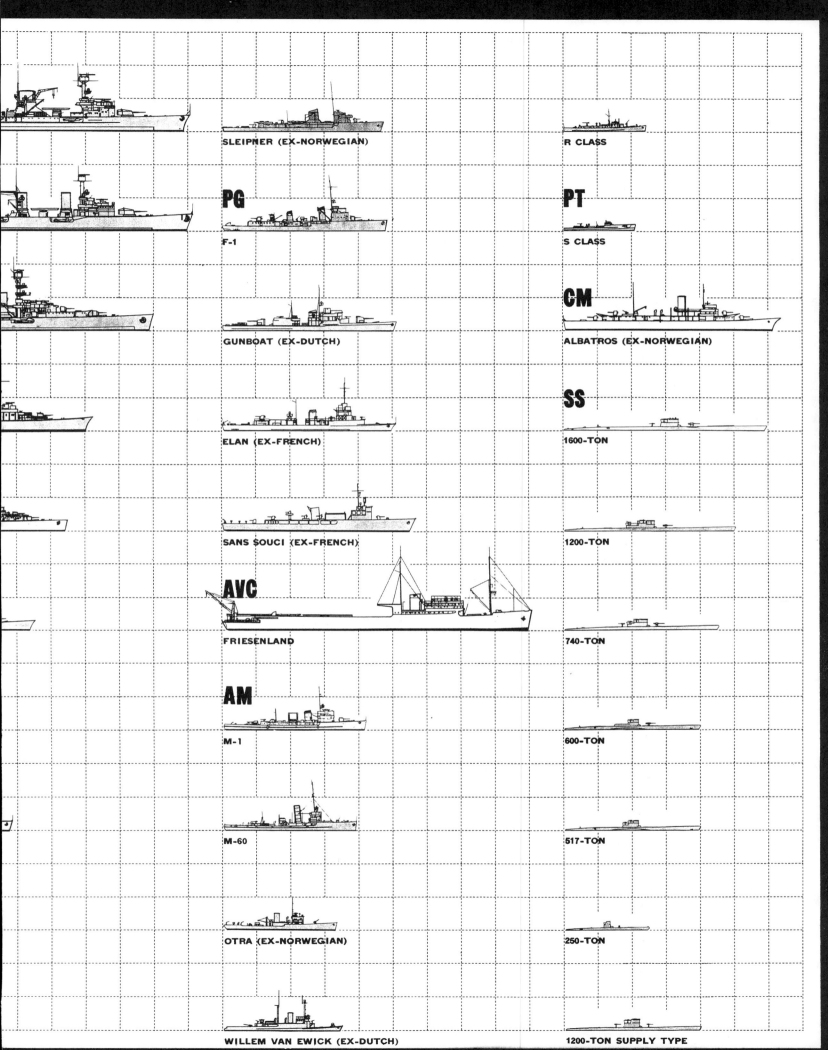

SLEIPNER (EX-NORWEGIAN)

R CLASS

PG

F-1

PT

S CLASS

GUNBOAT (EX-DUTCH)

CM

ALBATROS (EX-NORWEGIAN)

ELAN (EX-FRENCH)

SS

1600-TON

SANS SOUCI (EX-FRENCH)

1200-TON

AVC

FRIESENLAND

740-TON

AM

M-1

600-TON

M-60

517-TON

OTRA (EX-NORWEGIAN)

250-TON

WILLEM VAN EWICK (EX-DUTCH)

1200-TON SUPPLY TYPE

LACK OF RETURN ROLLERS TO TAKE UP SLACK IN TRACK GIVES MOTIVE GEAR OF FERDINAND A DILAPIDATED LOOK. CHASSIS BOW IS LONG BUT GUN BARREL LONGER

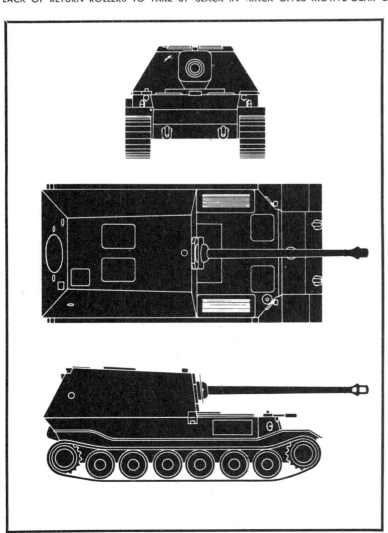

FERDINAND &

More pictures of self-propelled "88" and PzKw

The Germans have been hurling their heaviest armored equipment against the Russians. Recently silhouettes and more pictures of the two newest Nazi armored threats encountered on the Russian front, Ferdinand and the Panther (*see Journal Nov. and Dec.*), have been made available to the *Journal*, are shown on these two pages.

Ferdinand is a tremendous 70-ton self-propelled mount which carries an 88-mm. gun on a chassis built to offer maximum resistance to enemy firepower. The thickness of Ferdinand's armor plate is as much as 8 in. on the front, intended to make the mount serve as a battering ram to clear the way for lighter armored vehicles of the Nazi anti-tank battalions. There are usually 44 of these self-propelled "88's" in one heavy battalion and each one carries a crew of six. Although the mighty firepower and armor of Ferdinand make it a dangerous opponent, it has been proved to be quite vulnerable. Unwieldy and underpowered for its great size, it can travel only 12 m.p.h. on a highway and 6 to 9 m.p.h. on rough ground; to fire, it must come to a full stop. When Ferdinand is attacked by more than one opponent at a time, its fixed weapon is a great handicap. Russians concentrate their artillery attacks on Ferdinand's mobile parts which break down readily under the great weight of the chassis; also on the gun installation and on the gas tanks in the center of the hull. Grenades and Molotov cocktails hurled through a large shell-case ejection opening in the rear of the mount will blast the twin electric motors located directly inside.

A new heavy tank in the German arsenal, the 45-ton PzKw

HUGE BOW OF PANTHER SLOPES UP TO IMPOSING HEIGHT. TURRET HAS ROUNDED FORWARD WALL RESEMBLING RUSSIAN T-34. ARMOR PLATE PROTECTS SUSPENSION

THE PANTHER

Mark V reveal details of new Nazi weapons

Mark V serves to bridge the gap between the 22-ton Mark IV and the 60-ton Mark VI, Tiger. This tank, which is called the Panther, appears to be a first-class vehicle, fast, well-armored and hard-hitting. It has the advantage of being swifter and more maneuverable than the Tiger but at the same time is easier to knock out because of lighter armor protection. Its long-barreled 75-mm. gun with double-baffle muzzle brake is a new weapon which has a high velocity, considerable armor penetration, and direct sights up to a distance of 1,640 yd.

Like the Tiger, the Panther can be converted for deep stream fording. It has a speed of 31 m.p.h. and carries a crew of five. Its heaviest armor plate, on the front of the turret and the cannon shield, is about 3.94 in. thick. The top and bottom of the tank are lightly armored and are especially vulnerable to grenade fire.

RECOGNITION: The huge coffinlike gunshield of Ferdinand, set well to rear, has sloping sides and top. Hull is rectangular and straight-sided. Six large evenly-spaced bogie wheels support a track approximately 2½ ft. wide.

The Panther is built close to the ground with a low center of gravity. Its turret sides flow in sloping line into the sides of the hull. The turret is slab-sided and set slightly to the rear of center with a cupola at the back. The 75-mm. gun barrel is extremely long. From the side, the Panther's hull is sharply undercut behind. Eight overlapping bogie wheels on each side with driving sprocket in front are typical of German-designed suspension systems.

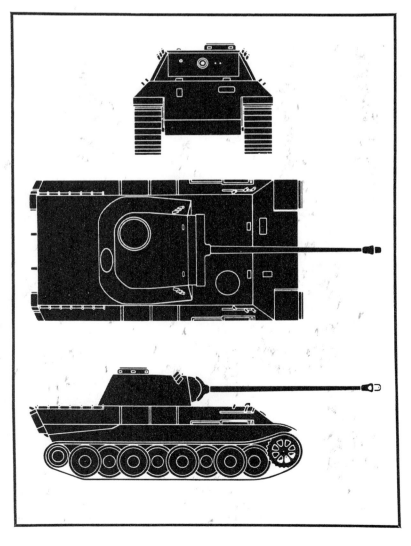

ARMY'S FIRST AIRBORNE TANK

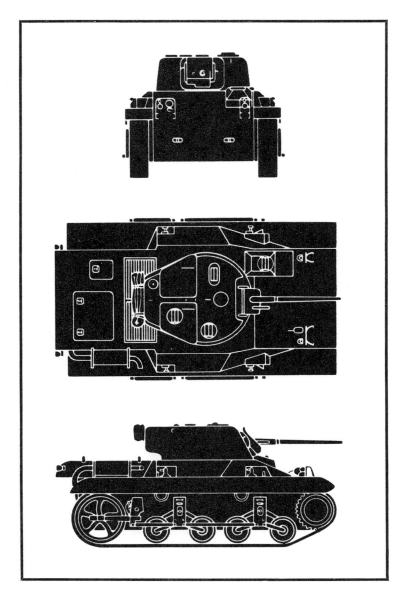

Airplanes in this war have carried all kinds of supplies, have ferried men and jeeps and field guns to the front lines. During the Papuan campaign alone the Army Air Forces Troop Carrier Command transported 12,000,000 lb. of equipment in less than 2½ months over the storm-swept ranges of the Owen-Stanley Mountains between Port Moresby and Buna Mission. One Flying Fortress ferried across a four-gun battery of 105-mm. howitzers.

Now, for the first time, the U. S. is prepared to transport armored vehicles by air. The Russians who were first to experiment with parachute-borne artillery have scarcely ever employed these tactics seriously. Even the Germans in their well-organized airborne invasions only occasionally have flown tanks to battle. But the U. S. Army's new T9E1, world's smallest four-man tank, has been specially designed to be airborne. It is a fast, light and maneuverable tank with many features in its construction which mark a departure from previous American design. Its 37-mm. gun has an angular rather than a circular mantlet. Hull sides are sloping rather than vertical and are covered with hooks and other gadgets. The usual tandem bogie wheels, in two pairs, have horizontal rods to keep them in place during transit.

The total weight of the vehicle is only 7.9 tons; height is 5 ft. 9 in. Its armor plate averages less than an inch in thickness. Maximum speed is 40 m.p.h. and the tank has a cruising range of 135 miles.

RECOGNITION: From above, cast turret of the T9E1 forms a curve at front, then gradually tapers to a straight edge in rear. Sides of hull form an almost perfect rectangle except for the rear where a rounded extension overhangs the tracks. From the side the gun turret is undercut behind, slopes into the bow in front.

A COMPACT VEHICLE, the smallest four-man tank in the world should provide new striking power to our airborne troops. From the head-on view, the T9E1 has a deep curving belly and a distinctly low squat silhouette which affords very slight ground clearance. Its 37-mm. gun reaches the complete length of the front section, has an angular mantlet. All possible deadweight has been eliminated in the T9E1's suspension system.

DIVEBOMBER

This fine, exciting picture of an SBD taken a split second after the 500-lb. bomb was released from rack was taken by a U. S. Navy photographer. Because there has been a great demand for such pictures, the *Journal* will hereafter try to publish in each issue a Plane of the Month.

QUIZ NO. 2: ARMORED COMBATANTS

(For key to numbers, see p. 50)

QUIZ NO. 3: IT TAKES ALL KINDS

(For key to numbers, see p. 50)

NOEL SICKLES' DRAWING OF INVASION SCENE SHOWS COMPLEXITY OF OPERATION, VARIETY OF EQUIPMENT USED. LST'S AT LEFT CARRY LCV'S. M-4 TANK IN LEFT FORE-

LANDING CRAFT

Driven off the continent of Europe and pushed deep into the South Pacific, the Allies in 1942 had to revive an outmoded form of warfare—landing operations. Invasion by sea, even in earliest days of an expanding and warring world, was as commonplace as war itself. However, the developments which changed war from simple infantry and cavalry fighting to an involved mechanical holocaust stacked the cards very heavily in favor of the defense.

Three factors were responsible for the assumption that defensive power held the whip hand. The first was the increasing strength of coast artillery, considered more accurate at long range than naval gunfire. The second was the question of supply; since heavy guns and tanks could not be landed without dock facilities, infantry which might force a beach could be hacked to pieces by the defender's mechanized might. The third was land-based airpower.

Between World Wars I and II, military thinkers were convinced that because of the above factors, sea-borne attackers did not stand a chance against big-league opposition. But in World War II the Germans smashed Polish resistance on the Hela Peninsula from the sea, conquered Norway and Crete by sea and air. The Japanese made repeated landings in the course of their drive down the Malay Peninsula and took the Philippines, the Netherlands East Indies and a multitude of South Pacific islands by overwater invasion. It can be argued that most of these invasions did

not come off according to the book. Coast defenses were feeble, land-based airpower was quickly crushed, treachery gave the invaders seaports intact (Bergen, Trondheim, Stavanger) enabling them, in some instances, to walk down gangplanks.

But regardless of whether Axis success in amphibious operations has proved or disproved anything, the Allied counteroffensive is based on storming the beaches. Abandoning the slow, vulnerable ship-to-shore methods of the past, the U. S. and Great Britain have developed nearly 15 types of landing craft: ships, barges, amphibious vehicles. They range in size from the ocean-going LST (Landing Ship, Tank) and LCI (Landing Craft, Infantry) to amphibian jeeps and rubber rafts. Where a short year ago patrol and escort craft had first priority in naval construction, landing vessels now have priority over all wartime construction.

Except for the recapture of Cos, Leros and Samos in the Aegean Sea, landing operations have, since the summer of 1942, become an Allied monopoly. But even before that, Combined Operations was executing swift stabs at German-held shore positions from the Lofoten Islands off the northern coast of Norway to St. Nazaire in western France. For the most part, these raids were not on a large scale, and the smaller landing craft sufficed to put the Commandos ashore.

Climax to the Commando raids from the standpoint of size was the assault on Dieppe on Aug. 19, 1942. Involving 200 ships, 10,000 men and 40-ton Churchill tanks brought in by LCT's (Landing

ROUND IS ABOUT TO BE JOINED BY SECOND M-4 EMERGING FROM LST WHICH HAS SECTIONAL FLOATS LASHED TO SIDE. IN RIGHT FOREGROUND ARE "DUCK" AND LCVP

NEW TYPES LEAD ASSAULTS

ON BEACHES HELD BY ENEMY

Craft, Tank), this landing was a severe enough laboratory test to satisfy the fussiest critic. The casualties were very heavy for the attackers, but the point that troops and tanks could be put ashore against the most rugged opposition was demonstrated.

Earlier in August U. S. Marines swarmed ashore on Guadalcanal to open the Allied attack in the Pacific. In this operation, as well as most of those in the South Pacific and the Aleutians, there was little or no Japanese resistance at the beaches, savage opposition farther inland. But at Tarawa late in November 1943, there was no chance of finding a weakly held strip of shore and the going was hellishly tough, geographically and militarily, from the start.

In November 1942, a huge United Nations convoy steamed into North African waters to seize control of Morocco and Algeria from the sea. Resistance was severe only in isolated spots, and in the military sense we got away with the easy type of invasion which marked German and Japanese conquests. However, in the summer of 1943 the Allies undertook two further invasions in the Mediterranean theater, Sicily and Italy. This time the beaches had to be stormed against experienced and well-armed defenders, had to be held while the heaviest equipment was being landed for big armies. It was here that the big landing boats, LST's and LCI's were introduced and proved their worth. How amphibious warfare in the West developed from Narvik to Salerno is shown on pages 36–39; pictures of the major types of U. S. landing craft on pages 40–47.

PROCESSION OF TRUCKS rolls ashore from LST as U.S. Marines occupy Nanumea in Ellice Islands near the Gilberts. A converted destroyer, possibly a high-speed transport (APD) or seaplane tender (AVD), is on patrol offshore.

COMRADES HELP COMMANDO WOUNDED IN VAAGSOE-MAALOY RAID TOWARD A BRITISH LCA (ASSAULT). THIS CRAFT OFFERS PROTECTION FROM MACHINE-GUN FIRE

NORWAY AND THE CHANNEL

Three purposes have been served by the countless Commando attacks against German objectives on Norwegian and French shores. Specific targets may be destroyed; defenses are tested and experience gained in amphibious warfare. The best example of a target destroyed was the demolition of the radar station at Bruneval in France. Best example of the other two was Dieppe.

As early as June 1940, scarcely more than a month after the Wehrmacht attacked in the West, raiding parties stabbed at the Nazi-held coast to study defenses, take prisoners. First sea attack in which destruction was the main object took place on March 4, 1941, in the Lofoten Islands, far up the Norwegian Coast. Just before the end of 1941 a second major raid was undertaken in the North, this time against factories and shipping at Vaagsoe and Maaloy (*above*).

Shifting attention to France, Combined Operations then attacked Bruneval in February 1942. A month later, H. M. S. Campbeltown was rammed in and blown up at St. Nazaire to wreck the only Atlantic drydock capable of handling the battleship Tirpitz. Dieppe, in August 1942, was the biggest raid of all, served as an experiment in landing tanks, knocking out gun positions.

DIEPPE CONVOY demonstrated importance of patrol and escort craft in landing operations. Pictured here are minor combatant types of the Royal Navy.

BRITISH LANDING CRAFT HEAD FOR NARVIK UNDER COVER OF HEAVY FIRE FROM ALLIED WARSHIPS. BARGES WERE EARLY TYPE, BUILT FOR USE OFF ROCKY COASTS

LANDING CRAFT (LCP'S) race for Dieppe shore under cover of smokescreen laid down by the Royal Navy. Attack marked first use of British LCT's.

COMMANDOS RE-EMBARK IN LCA'S after a successful reconnaissance raid near Boulogne in June 1942. The boats on the beach are French fishing vessels.

AMERICAN LANDING AT SURCOUF IN NORTH AFRICA SHOWS USE OF SMALL CRAFT, ABSENCE OF HEAVY EQUIPMENT. SCENE INDICATES LACK OF SERIOUS RESISTANCE

THE MEDITERRANEAN

The three great amphibious operations in the Mediterranean were the assaults on French Africa, Sicily and finally the Italian mainland. Departures from earlier landings in that they opened full-scale campaigns, they introduced supply problems which did not have to be considered in the lightning-like Commando raids in the West. Algiers and Casablanca in Africa and Augusta in Sicily fell to the Allies very quickly, giving them good harbors for unloading. Salerno, however, was a different matter, since a great

deal of heavy fighting took place before that city or the port at Naples were of any value to the invading forces. Here conditions were tough enough to satisfy military experts that a fair test of invasion strength was being made. The enemy was firmly entrenched and ready for the landing where it took place; they had airfields nearby from which they could hammer at the convoy. But carrier-based Seafires held them off while coordinated amphibian assault waves bulled their way through to take and hold the beach.

SUPPLY TRUCKS SHUTTLE TO & FRO LOADING HUGE ARMADA OF LST'S AT A NORTH AFRICAN PORT. SHIPS WERE PART OF CONVOY WHICH OPENED SALERNO ATTACK

SICILY-BOUND LCI'S carry U. S. Seventh Army to Gela where the most bitter beachhead opposition of the entire campaign was encountered. Fire from DD's finally turned the tide against Nazi tanks which threatened to drive U. S. forces into the sea. Heavy weather made the landing more difficult than was anticipated but added to the surprise element since the Italian defenders thought the sea so rough that invasion would be postponed.

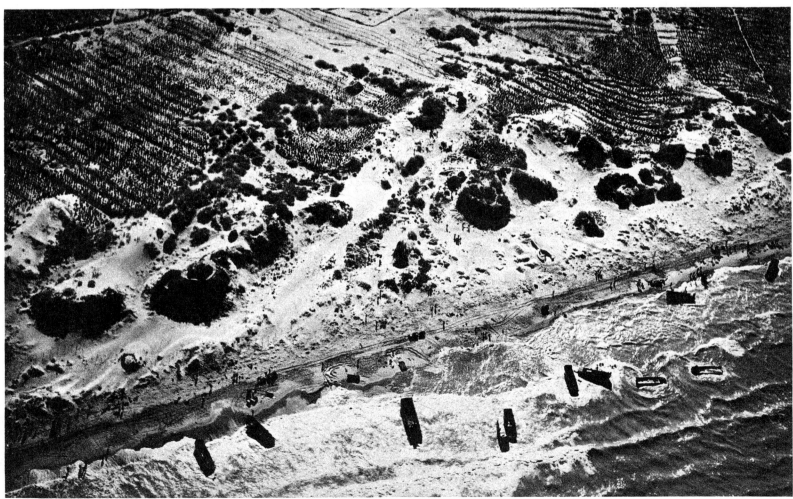

AERIAL VIEW OF SICILIAN SHORE shows an assortment of landing craft scattered along the beach. Owing to barge-like appearance, only length can aid observer in distinguishing craft from each other. Those to the right and left of center are LCV's while the larger one at the center is an LCM. When barges are close to Allied beaches, recognition is not difficult. They are, however, likely to be seen in rough water under combat conditions.

LST (LANDING SHIP, TANK)

GROUP OF LST'S steam through Pacific waters on the way to Lae in New Guinea. The backbone of modern invasion armadas, these 5,500-ton ships carry all sorts of war matériel, are the most versatile of all landing craft, serving as both hospital and repair ships on occasion. They were originally sketched in November 1941, with acceptance trial for first completed unit coming 11 months later. Sicily marked their first combat use in the Medi-

SIZE OF LST can be judged from M-4 tanks rolling up on beach. Length of these ships is 327 ft. For unloading, gates are swung outward, ramp is then lowered for tanks or other mechanized equipment. Elevator service from deck to hold enables trucks to be lowered for disembarkation. Extra ramps can be carried on sides of LST in case bow of vessel cannot come in close enough to permit the vehicles to go ashore through shallow water.

terranean. Able to cross any ocean under their own power, these long-range ships are used to carry other landing craft to the scene of operations, frequently carry trucks and bulldozers as well on their wide decks.

ENGINES AFT, HIGH FREEBOARD FORWARD and flush deck help identify LST's. Hull is straight-sided, tapers abruptly at bow and stern. Ship has short pole mast, no visible stack. Engines aft permit cargo space forward for landing.

DECKLOADS MAKE RECOGNITION of LST's a major problem since cargoes carried topside vary considerably. This LST has LCT and LCM. Vents on deck forward of load are helpful for identification, particularly from the air. Except for the 450-ft. LSD's (Landing Ship, Dock), LST is the biggest of all the invasion craft. LST's versatility makes it possible for the Navy to free more specialized ships for service in other vital operations.

LCI (LANDING CRAFT, INFANTRY)

LCI SAILS UP COAST during Allied landings near Lae. Ship in background is LST. British request in May 1942 for larger type of infantry landing craft led to LCI's development. First unit was completed in October. LCI's can cross ocean under their own power, but only carry troops just before landing operations.

LCVP'S COME ASHORE ahead of LCI at Gela in Sicily. Ammunition ship in the background explodes following hit by

SOLDIERS RUSH DOWN RAMP of LCI a few yards offshore. Ramps are carried outside forward bulwarks, provide excellent recognition feature for low-flying planes. LCI may carry more than 150 men, accommodates them in the hull.

STICK MAST ABAFT BRIDGE, flush deck help identify LCI. The unit shown here is newer class, differs from old type (*above, left*) in superstructure and AAMG position. Depth charges at stern provide anti-sub defense.

Nazi bomber. Unlike many other invasion boats, LCI looks like a ship, not a barge. Just over 155 ft. long, it has bridge amidships, no visible stack. Block tower characterizes earlier version (*left*), while newer model has round tower. Put into mass production only recently, the round-tower model is being supplied to Great Britain via lend-lease on a large scale. Appearance of LCI, as well as wake, has led to its being confused with subs.

LCI'S HEAD FOR SHORE in Salerno attack. Their low hulls may cause confusion with DD's or minor combatant types when seen from this angle, but LCI's should be distinguishable by relatively bulky outline. Devel-oped simultaneously with LST's, LCI's are the only other beaching types likely to be encountered on the high seas. They are not usually seen at the beaches during preliminary stages of assault when smaller craft are used.

LCT (LANDING CRAFT, TANK)

LCT'S, SHOWN HERE AT KISKA, are largest of the landing craft to have ramp for bow. Logical development of an early type LCM, they were first built in May 1942, were designed to bring in tanks behind first wave of assault troops. LCT's are frequently carried in three sections on cargo ships, transports or as assembled units on LST's. With sides cut away, LCT's can be lined across bow of LST when conditions prevent use of portable ramps.

BEACHED LCT gives indication of craft's length, 112 ft. for Mark V (*above*) and 105 ft. for Mark VI which differs slightly, having longer, higher off-center superstructure at stern, shorter center section. Squared-off bow, pilot house aft are important recognition details. As with LST, recognition of LCT is made more difficult owing to differing loads: tanks, trucks, personnel. Shape and wake classify LCT's and most smaller craft as barges.

LCM (LANDING CRAFT, MECHANIZED EQUIPMENT)

LCM AND LCVP race for shore near Salerno. LCM with anti-aircraft machine guns is in right foreground, can be identified by high grilled bow ramp. This type is 50 ft. long. LCV's (Landing Craft, Vehicles) double up as vehicle and personnel carriers, are called LCVP when used in the latter capacity. About 36 ft. in length, they have also been built with a small pilot house at the stern. The ramp and the sides of the LCV are armored.

VARIED LANDING CRAFT MANEUVER in Chesapeake Bay just before departure for North Africa. Grilled bow of LCM is distinguishable at the right. Craft in the foreground are 36-ft. LCP's (Landing Craft, Personnel) and LCPR's (Landing Craft, Personnel, with Ramp). LCP has a rounded bow, looks less like barge than other invasion boats (*see next page*). Towing rubber landing rafts (LCR's) is important function of LCP's and LCPR's.

LCP (LANDING CRAFT, PERSONNEL)

Y 8

B 9

SHIP UNLOADING TROOPS IN LCP'S

LCS (LANDING CRAFT, SUPPORT)

CLOSE-UP FIRE SUPPORT for landings is given by heavily armed LCS (Landing Craft, Support)

LVT (LANDING VEHICLE, TRACKED)

RIDING LOW IN THE WATER, L (Landing Vehicle, Tracked) offers a poor target to shoregun

This armored, rocket-firing boat is likely to be seen in the first wave, rendering the beaches untenable for the enemy before LCP's go ashore with the infantry. Unlike other landing craft, LCS's do not transport personnel or equipment, carry crew just large enough to man the boat controls and weapons. Armor plate can be put up to shield the crew completely from enemy small-arms fire, gives LCS the appearance of low blockhouse on a speedboat.

ers. First developed for rescue work in swamps following Florida hurricane of 1933, the versatile LVT attracted the attention of U. S. Marine Corps and was adopted by them.

LVT ROLLING UP BEACH, shows self to be genuinely amphibious vehicle. Ability to negotiate all sorts of terrain, including coral reefs which would rip tires on "duck" or amphibian "jeep," is the greatest asset of LVT or Alligator. Armored version, LVT(A), has turret with 37-mm. gun.

QUIZ NO. 4: WARPLANES IN E.T.O.

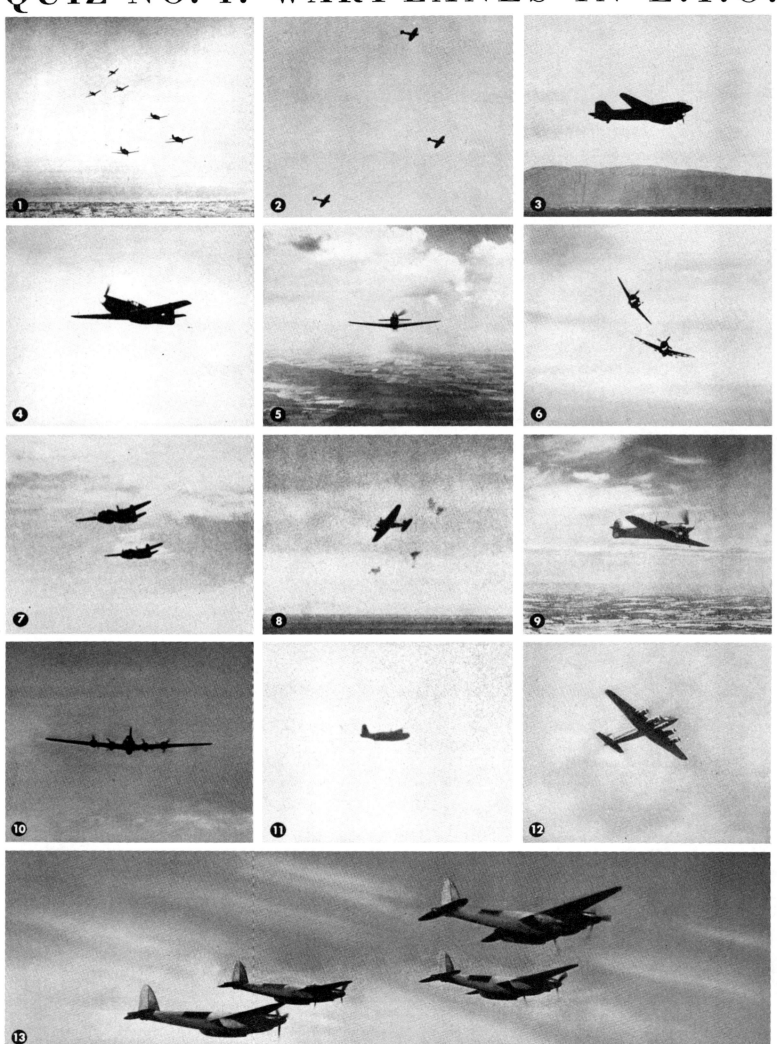

(For key to numbers, see p. 50)

EXHAUST PATTERNS

Shown here are results of an RAF study of exhaust flame patterns from 10° below astern. Trickiest of these six views is the owlish-looking Mosquito (No. 2) whose engines cast a bright flame on both sides. Odd pattern cast by He-177 (No. 4) shows four long light streaks formed by each engine, while the Me-110 (1) reveals engine exhaust only on the inside of each engine. B-25 (3) does the exact reverse and like the B-24 (6) throws its flame pattern only to the outside. The B-17 (5) is alone in this group in having exhaust position directly behind engines. Intended as an aid to recognition, it is important to note that these patterns reveal only the position of exhaust flames, not their intensity.

NEWS & MISCELLANY

NEW SILHOUETTE

A provisional silhouette of Japanese single-engine Tojo is given below. Tojo is a single radial-engine, low-wing monoplane. Wings resemble those of P-47 in plan view, have moder-

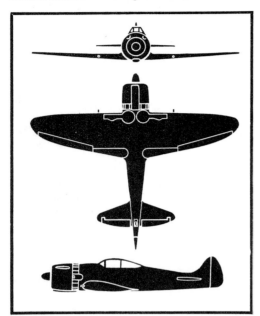

ate dihedral. Broad wing, heavy engine, and short fuselage, give Tojo a stubby, compact appearance. The landing gear retracts inward. Tail plane is set unusually far forward of fin and rudder, providing an excellent recognition feature.

The smallest Jap fighter thus far encountered, Tojo mounts the most powerful engine yet found in any Jap SSF. Not quite so maneuverable as Zeke, it is faster, climbs and dives better. No protection is provided for pilot, fuel, or engine, and, when hit, Tojo explodes as spectacularly as did his predecessors. Armament consists of two synchronized 7.7-mm. MG in the fuselage and 1x12.7-mm. MG in each wing. Tojo is unique among Jap fighters in that it has a four-piece wing. This is a heavier construction than the usual Jap one-piece wing but should make Tojo easier to maintain.

NEWS

The Ju-188 is a new type, fast medium bomber that was developed from the Ju-88B, which apparently was an intermediary model between the standard Ju-88A and Ju-188. The redesigned wings with increased span and completely new tail unit, compared with the Ju-88A, suggest an attempt to produce an aircraft with improved flying qualities, take-off and ceiling, particularly with heavy loads carried externally. This bomber is a twin-engine, low-wing monoplane. The tail unit is of a new design, the fin and rudder being both higher and wider than that of the Ju-88A and very square in general shape. Nose is redesigned for greater visibility and to accommodate increased armament.

•

Italian aircraft are in use at present by both the Germans and the Allies. Following is a list of Italian planes (for abbreviations see p. 6):

Mc-200	1E-SSF
Mc-202	1E-SSF
Mc-205	1E-SSF
Re-2001	1E-SSF
Re-2005	1E-SSF
Cant-Z 1007 bis	3E-HB, (T/B)
SM-79	3E-T/B,(HB)
SM-82	3E-HB,(C)
SM-84	3E-HB,(T/B)
Cant-Z 506 B	3E-F/B,(LB,R)
Cr-42	1E-SSF
G-50	1E-SSF
G-55	1E-SSF
Re-2000	1E-SSF
Ro-37 bis	1E-LB,R
Ca-311 & Ca-312 bis	2E-LB,R(T/B)
Rs-14	2E-F/B
P-108	4E-HB(T/B,C)
Br-20M	2E-MB,(T/B)
Cant-Z 501B	1E-F/B,(LB,R)

•

Notice: The bottom of page 7 in the January issue of the *Journal* was removed by the U. S. Navy prior to distribution for security reasons.

TRAINING AIDS

War Department Training Circular 131, Dec. 14, 1943 has been published outlining all the War Department training aids available for aircraft, naval vessel and armored vehicle, recognition training. Consult it for information on how to obtain these aids and the basis of issue to the Ground and Service Forces.

CORRECTION

Slide number 883 bears the title "U. S. Army Transport, C-46—Lodestar 6/30/43." The title should be corrected to read "U. S. Army Transport Glider Tug, C-46—Commando 6/30/43."

RECOGNITION COVERAGE IN NAVAL TRAINING COMMANDS

Primary Training

FLIGHT PREPARATORY SCHOOLS:

U.S. NAVY PLANES	CLASS A
U.S. ARMY PLANES	CLASS A
BRITISH RAF PLANES	CLASS A
BRITISH FLEET AIR ARM	CLASS A
U.S. WARSHIPS	CLASSES A&B

PRE-FLIGHT SCHOOLS:

JAPANESE PLANES	CLASS A
BRITISH WARSHIPS	CLASSES A&B
FRENCH WARSHIPS	CLASSES A&B
MERCHANT VESSEL TYPES	

PRIMARY TRAINING STATIONS

GERMAN PLANES	CLASS A
JAPANESE WARSHIPS	CLASSES A&B
GERMAN WARSHIPS	CLASS A
LANDING CRAFT—U.S., JAPANESE & GERMAN	

Intermediate Training

Review of units introduced in Primary Training utilizing distant views of planes and warships. Introduction of planes and warships added to training lists while cadets are in Intermediate Training.

Operational Training

OPERATIONAL TRAINING UNITS:
Selected review of units introduced in Primary and Intermediate Training; review of enemy planes to include performance and characteristics data.

NAVAL AIR GUNNERS SCHOOL:
Japanese, German and British fighter and attack bomber planes, and U. S. and Japanese warships as listed in Aviation Free Gunnery Central Standardization Committee Syllabus for Naval Air Gunners Schools and Aviation Free Gunnery Units.

Technical Training

U.S. NAVY PLANES:	CLASS A
U.S. ARMY PLANES:	CLASS A

(Transports Excluded)
NOTE: Selected review in Operating Squadron covers planes and ships according to geographical areas and missions of personnel.

QUIZ ANSWERS

QUIZ No. 1
1. Beaufighter	9. B-17
2. Mosquito	10. C-47
3. Betty	11. Lily
4. Me-210	12. Ju-52
5. FW-190	13. Ju-88
6. Halifax	14. Ju-87D
7. Typhoon	15. Me-109F
8. He-111	

Quiz No. 2
1. Soviet T-34
2. German six-wheeled armored car
3. German PzKw VI, Tiger
4. Jap Medium Tank, 2597
5. Jap Light Armored Car, 2597
6. German PzKw III
7. German PzKw III (short "75")
8. British Bishop
9. German one-ton Armored Half Track
10. U. S. 105 mm. Howitzer Motor Carriage M-7
11. U. S. Medium Tank M-4
12. Soviet T-70 Light Tank

QUIZ No. 3
1. Br. BB King George V Class
2. Jap CA Tone Class
3. Br. BB King George V Class
4. Br. CV Illustrious Class
5. Jap BB Kongo Class
6. U. S. Pass.-Cargo, LST, LCI
7. U. S. CA New Orleans Class
8. U. S. Modern Combination Passenger-Cargo
9. Br. BB Nelson Class (Rodney)
10. World War I—2 Freighters & Oiler
11. U. S. CVE Sangamon Class
12. U. S. 110-ft. SC
13. U. S. DD Livermore Class
14. U. S. CV Ranger—U. S. DD Livermore Class
15. U. S. DD Fletcher Class

QUIZ No. 4
1. Warhawk P-40	8. He-111
2. Spitfire	9. Typhoon
3. Skytrain C-47	10. Fortress
4. Mustang P-51	11. Sunderland
5. Airacobra P-39	12. FW-200 C
6. Thunderbolt P-47	"Kurier"
7. Boston A-20	13. Mosquito

CREDITS

"HELEN," T-100 M/B

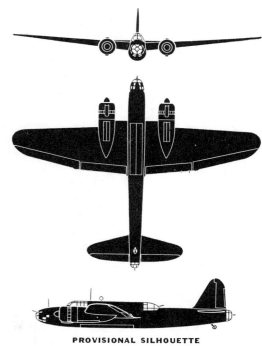

PROVISIONAL SILHOUETTE

PROVISIONAL SKETCH

DISTINGUISHING FEATURES: Twin-engine mid-wing monoplane. Leading edge inboard of the engines is farther forward than outer section, like the Mosquito. Trailing edge of the wing has a broken taper ending in a broad rounded tip. Radial engines are underslung. Fuselage decreases in size only slightly toward tail section, terminating in gun position. Span is about 68 ft.

INTEREST: Though this plane has been known to be in production for some time, it is now appearing in operation over India, Australia, and Southwest Pacific areas. The remains of a few crashed Helen's have been examined, and recently this plane has been photographed from the air. Results to date have been insufficient for a satisfactory calculation of its performance.

SPAN: approx. 68 ft.
LENGTH: approx. 54 ft.
APPROX. MAX. SPEED: 270—80 m.p.h.
SERVICE CEILING: 35,000 ft. (Max.) estimated, 30,000 ft. (Normal)

JAN. 1, 1944
FROM DATA CURRENTLY AVAILABLE

WAR DEPARTMENT FM 30-30
NAVY DEPARTMENT BUAER 3

RESTRICTED

NOTE: This page is to be cut along dotted lines (*above* and *below*), added to the proper nation's section in the Recognition Pictorial Manual. The dots indicate perforations.

"NICK," Type 2

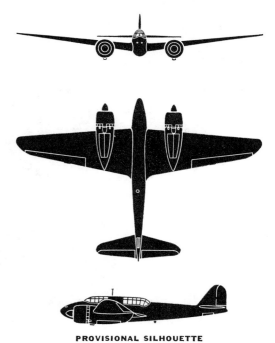

PROVISIONAL SILHOUETTE

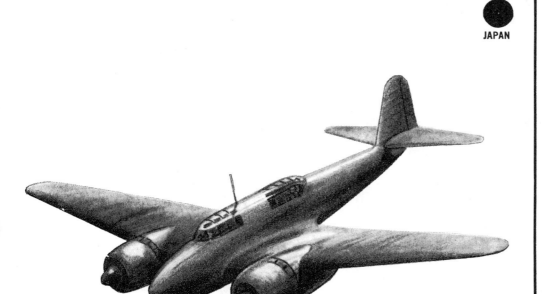

PROVISIONAL SKETCH

DISTINGUISHING FEATURES: Twin-engine low mid-wing monoplane. Engines are underslung with a deep nacelle continuing back under the wing to the trailing edge. The fuselage is unusually slender and streamlined from pointed nose to tail. The wing, engines, greenhouse, and tail closely resemble those of Lily.

INTEREST: This airplane has been reported operating in the Southwest Pacific area for the last few months. Very little was known about it until some recent photographic data was secured by our attacking aircraft. Nick is now recognized as an operational plane and will probably be seen in increasing numbers.

SPAN: 50 ft. approx.
LENGTH: 34 ft. approx.
APPROX. MAX. SPEED: 350 m.p.h. at 17,600 ft.
SERVICE CEILING: 35,400 ft. (Normal wt.)

JAN. 1, 1944
FROM DATA CURRENTLY AVAILABLE

WAR DEPARTMENT FM 30-30
NAVY DEPARTMENT BUAER 3

RESTRICTED

A

HELEN, one of latest operational Japanese twin-engine airplanes, has wingspan and armament of a medium bomber, but performance details are undetermined. Helen is distinguished by broken line of wing's trailing edge; leading edge projection between nacelles.

NICK was recently photographed in an Army Air Forces raid on Wewak (see *Journal*, Nov. issue). While a fighter version of Dinah has been reported for some time, Nick is the only Japanese twin-engine fighter so far definitely established as being operational.

A

B

C